Forever on the Road

D1548637

MEMOIRS AND OCCASIONAL PAPERS
Association for Diplomatic Studies and Training

In 2003, the Association for Diplomatic Studies and Training (ADST) created the Memoirs and Occasional Papers Series to preserve firsthand accounts and other informed observations on foreign affairs for scholars, journalists, and the general public. Sponsoring publication of the series is one of numerous ways in which ADST, a nonprofit organization founded in 1986, seeks to promote understanding of American diplomacy and those who conduct it. Together with the Foreign Affairs Oral History program and ADST's support for the training of foreign affairs personnel at the State Department's Foreign Service Institute, these efforts constitute the Association's fundamental purposes.

Forever on the Road

A Franco-American Family's Thirty Years in the Foreign Service

NICOLE PRÉVOST LOGAN

Memoirs and Occasional Papers
Association for Diplomatic Studies and Training

Washington, DC

New Academia Publishing/SCARITH Books, 2011

Printed in the United States of America

Library of Congress Control Number: 2011921074
ISBN 978-0-9832451-0-0 paperback (alk. paper)

 An imprint of New Academia Publishing
P.O. Box 27420, Washington, DC 20038-7420

 www.newacademia.com
info@newacademia.com

To Alan and our children

Philip, Sylvia, Diane, and Karen

Contents

Foreword

Roger Kirk, U.S. Ambassador (ret.)

Nicole Prévost Logan's book gives us fascinating insights into the varied countries in which she lived. It shows how an energetic, adventurous individual who happens to be a diplomat's wife, and who often holds an outside job as well, can benefit by her experiences. The book's fascination comes not only from where she lived—Taiwan, Turkey, Lebanon, the Soviet Union, and several African countries. It is also *when* she and her husband were there. They were in Taiwan and Turkey when neither one was the modern, sophisticated place it is today. They were in Beirut during the civil war of 1958, in Moscow at the close of the Khrushchev era, and at times of tension or strife in most of their African assignments.

The author skillfully relates the varied, often frightening situations she and her husband encountered, such as being under house arrest for a week in Guinea, with dubious government "guards" protecting them. Even in describing such situations, she adds humor to a sense of the drama and tension involved. Readers will feel as if they were right there with the Logans, especially as Nicole gives a frank sense of her own reactions at the time. Hers is not a dry tale; it is an adventure story. And it covers a broad span of cultures, geography, and history.

Nicole was determined to dig into the places where she lived. She wanted to make contact with the local people and to learn about, and enjoy, their culture. Already bilingual in French and English, she studied the language wherever she was—whether Chinese, Turkish, Russian, or Arabic. She often held a job, working for the U.S. government, a private enterprise, or a nonprofit organization. This brought her into intimate, working contact with the local population. Where this was not possible, she cultivated interests that would build friendly bonds with interesting people. She tells us about these people, giving us a personal insight into the societies in which she lived.

In many cases, she and her husband, Alan, built these relationships in countries where the authorities tried to minimize such contacts. As one who was in the U.S. embassy in Moscow at the same time as the Logans, I know how hard this was and, in many cases, how daring. It was risky to be attacked by name in the communist party newspaper, as her husband was. Expulsion or U.S. government displeasure could follow. That the Logans were the embassy couple whose four car tires were "mysteriously" slashed at a time of tension testifies to the concern their contacts were giving the Soviet authorities.

This book is not all about personal experiences, however. Nicole also gives us insights into the political situation in many of the countries in which she lived. She is particularly effective in describing some of the social crosscurrents underlying political developments, something we see all too rarely in analyses of world events. It makes the book doubly interesting.

The Logans were a devoted couple and a real team. Alan was a skillful diplomat. He could turn an acrimonious discussion between adversaries into a productive exchange. At the same time, he was careful to make those he dealt with, whether in Washington or in the field, face the facts of a situation, even if those facts were unpleasant. His wife writes mainly about her own experiences, but she gives us enough hints of her husband's activities to see how much she admired and depended on him, as he did on her.

The book ends with the Logans' last diplomatic post. Since that time, Nicole has lived an active, adventurous, and varied life that could provide material for another book. It has been a pleasure for my wife and me to know the Logans, and I am sure the readers of this book will understand why.

Preamble

We spent thirty years traveling from post to post in the heroic days of the U.S. diplomatic service. It was a pre-terrorism era, when our embassies had not yet become fortresses and their occupants forced into a siege mentality. These were years of wonder and adventure when American diplomats were respected and felt embarked on a mission.

We were a Franco-American couple. Alan, my husband, born in France to a French father and an American mother, was raised in Arizona and California. My own father came from Normandy, my mother from Brittany. I grew up in Paris and discovered America after receiving a scholarship to study at Stanford University in California.

Over the years, the wide-eyed woman I was at first became a more mature person, interested in major developments such as apartheid in South Africa.

Those were the days when a wife was proud to team up with her husband and support his career without financial compensation. But the price was high for the roving Foreign Service wives; they had to abandon the idea of their own career. With an enormous amount of determination and adaptability, they could find a job only to have it cut short by the next move.

The study of the culture, politics, history, and other facets of each given country led me to discover what made that country unique. We, the Foreign Services wives, had become experts at zeroing in on those gems.

Alan plays an essential part in my story. His outgoing and opinionated personality as well as his fighting spirit may contrast with the arrogant and bureaucratic image one often has of a diplomat. Although I was far from being privy to all his activities, I was well aware of his convictions and also a witness to his battles and to what he accomplished as a Foreign Service officer.

Four children were born along the way—in Taiwan, Turkey, and Lebanon. Their education, pursued in various boarding schools and universities in Switzerland, Italy, England, France, and the USA, added to their multicultural outlook and linguistic abilities.

Boxes full of letters, documents, diaries, slides, pictures, and home movies lay forgotten for a long time, until interest expressed by friends about our exotic life prompted me one day to write my memoirs.

It is a very personal account, intended to bring back to life experiences of a distant past taking place in distant countries.

Acknowledgments

I would like to thank the persons who have supported me in the writing of this book and who helped make the process more stimulating.

Butsy Lovelace, magazine publisher and historian of the island of Nantucket island, provided forceful remarks at the early stage of my draft. Claude Moisy, the former president of Agence France Presse, and his wife, also named Claude Moisy, a teacher, shared their professional recommendations over a delicious Parisian lunch. Heidi Shinn, part of the publishing side of the Center for Strategic and International Studies (CSIS) in Washington, D.C., was always available with friendly and constructive advice.

A very special thanks to Margery Thompson, ADST publishing director, for her invaluable guidance, support, and unflinching patience throughout. Nancy and Tom Buchanan, former U.S. consul general in Leningrad, introduced me to ADST and had the kindness to provide me with precious logistical support every time I visited Washington.

All my gratitude to Ambassador Roger Kirk, who helped me from the start in many different ways and generously agreed to write the foreword.

Finally my four children contributed to the choice of a title through brainstorming sessions. They supported and advised me continuously while waiting with curiosity for the finished product.

1

Taiwan 1951–1956

Taiwan in the early 1950s was the center of the world. In those days, the world still knew it by its Portuguese name, Formosa. Two and a half million Chinese had moved to the island in 1949, chased from the mainland by Mao Tse-tung, president of the Peoples Republic of China. Taipei became the seat of the Kuomintang, or National Government of China, led by Chiang Kai-shek. Between China and Taiwan, the situation was unstable. The Nationalists did not unpack their suitcases, vowing to go *ta hui ta lou*, back to the mainland. The offshore islands, Quemoy and Matsu, were under frequent fire from the Communists. Taiwan was swarming with the military.

I did not fully realize this at the time, but two other military conflicts were making this region the most dangerous in the world: the Korean War (1950–1953) and the conflict between France and Indochina (1946–1954).

American foreign policy was focused on the Far East in those days. The U.S. government showed an intense interest in the small piece of land that was Taiwan. Economic aid poured in, implemented successively by agencies called ECA, MSA, FOA, and ICA. The results of this policy were phenomenal and immediate—Taiwan became a model for projects in other developing countries.

Alan, my future husband, after graduating from Stanford University with a master's degree in economics, went east to Washington, D.C. He found a job immediately and was appointed industry officer with ECA in Taipei, Taiwan. The budget he was going to handle during this first job turned out to be the largest of his diplomatic career.

Alan arrived in Taiwan late in 1951. His job consisted of helping build schools, roads, factories, dams, and other such projects. For several months, along with four U.S. aid officers his age—Norman Wycoff, Chester Pavlovski, Phil Emerson, and Dick Dasch—Alan led the life of an adventurous bachelor. Pictures show him on frequent field trips with Dr. Hubert G. Schenck, the ECA mission head, riding trucks, visiting work sites, and talking to workers and farmers. At the end of the day, the visiting officials were entertained at banquets in Japanese-style guesthouses, in the company of young ladies, the Taiwanese version of geishas I assume.

I came into the picture in February 1952 and joined Alan in Taiwan. But before proceeding with my diplomatic story, I need to rewind my tape a little.

I grew up in Paris, the youngest of three children. My beautiful, artistic mother died when I was eleven. My father was an officer and a graduate of Saint Cyr military academy (the equivalent of West Point). He believed in a strong education for his children, so our household became a degree-making factory. After producing an engineer and an Air Force academy graduate, my father decided that his daughter should study law and political science. I entered the Institut d'Etudes Politiques, known as Sciences-Po, a very competitive *grande école*, and at the same time started studying toward a law degree. Because there was no room in the Sorbonne amphitheater, not uncommon for France, I used transcripts of the courses and obtained my *licence en droit* without having attended a single lecture.

My life took a sudden turn when I successfully competed for the single AAUW (American Association of University Women) graduate scholarship awarded to a Frenchwoman in the field of political science. The international travel was financed under the Fulbright program. I crossed the Atlantic on the SS *Ile de France,* awed at the prospect of the unknown.

I met Alan on the second day after my arrival at Stanford, during an orientation party for foreign students. I overheard two young men using the crudest French language to describe the new female students, assuming no one could understand them. One of them was to become my husband. He lived with his mother, Harriet Wood, and his brother, Frank, in Menlo Park. The family "adopted" me. Their hefty meat-and-potato Sunday dinners were most appreciated by a starving young student.

After graduation, I was spending Christmas in New York in the elegant upper-eastside townhouse of a cousin of Harriet's. During dinner, the phone rings. It is Alan calling from Taipei. He suggests that we get married by proxy on the phone. This way, he explains, the U.S. government will pay for my trip to the Far East as a spouse. I am stunned. I think about this proposal for a minute and tell him I really do not find it romantic enough and decline the offer. Endowed with a practical mind, Alan suggests a plan B: "Why don't you come to Bangkok, I will join you there. After we get married, the rest of the trip to Taiwan will be reimbursed." This idea was more appealing than the first, although many problems remained to be solved.

First, how was I to pay for my trip from France to Thailand? Fortunately, I had saved enough of the food money provided by my scholarship to pay for the trip. But the main emotional hurdle was to return to Paris and announce to my father that I was leaving again, and, even worse, getting married. In retrospect, I feel this was a cruel thing to do. *Le colonel* was sad, but he did not try to stop me. He gave me some extra money in case I changed my mind. Two years later, when my father met Alan, he declared, "For an American he really is not bad!"

Traveling economy class, I was allowed just one bag. Unable to carry all my clothes, I had to wear them. When I landed at the Bangkok airport, I must have looked like a butterball turkey. The damp heat of Thailand was suffocating, and I proceeded to strip off layer after layer of sweaters, jacket, raincoat, and overcoat.

Bangkok had definitely more charm in the 1950s than it does today. The Oriental Hotel had the old elegance of a bygone era, with enormous rooms cooled by powerful overhead fans. The rooms opened onto louvered porches. The traffic downtown was light. We drove through the city in pedicabs. The boat ride on the canals (called *khlongs*) was the best way to see the colorful scenes of a population living on water surrounded by many temples.

We were married at the *Amphur Bangrak,* or town clerk's office, on February 25, 1952. The procedure took place in the local dialect and our marriage certificate was written in Thai. We never ascertained whether the document represented a marriage certificate or a dog registration. (This is typical of Alan's kind of humor, to which the reader may grow accustomed while reading this story.) Our witness was the U.S. vice consul, who sent us on our way after a glass of champagne and a hearty handshake. The Americans registered the marriage, and Alan was legally married in the eyes of U.S. law. But the French refused to recognize our marriage, because we had not "published the bans" for three weeks. As a result, and unbeknownst to me, I was to "live in sin" for many years. Under French law, my children were considered bastards until I rectified the situation twenty years later.

We had dinner in one of the best restaurants of the capital. I was wearing an embroidered white linen dress, which felt like it weighed a ton and was very hot. At the time I thought it was most glamorous to be married in such an exotic place. Looking back though, Alan and I realized that a traditional marriage, surrounded by relatives of all generations and friends and with children running around, would have been better. To create more memories, we decided to get married again two years later in a church service in the Stanford University nondenominational chapel. We had prepared a liturgy text in the past tense. So, the minister asked, "Did you, Nicole and Alan, accept … ?" We answered, "Yes, we did."

From Bangkok, we made a stop in Saigon. The visit was short but important for me, since my family's history is tied to the fate of Indochina. My father was twenty when, as a young officer straight out of Saint Cyr, he was assigned in 1900 to the northwest border between Tonkin and China. His mission was to monitor the raids of the "Black Pavilions," or roaming gangs of bandits coming from the north. My father remained in Indochina for more than twenty years. My brother Jean, who made his career in the French Air Force and retired as a general, also served in Indochina. In 1949 and 1950, he took part in 148 air missions conducted from Gia Nam, one of the two military airports of Hanoi. As a fighter pilot, he was then flying the American "King Cobra."

As Alan and I walked on the streets of Hanoi, we could see Vietnamese squatting on the sidewalks. They looked poor and were dressed in black, with dirty cloths tied around their heads. I was struck by their hostile gaze. Their attitude was not surprising since, by 1952, the war between Ho Chi Minh and France was dragging on. The conflict ended with the Geneva Agreements in 1954, after the bloody battle of Dien Bien Phu, where the defeated French lost 15,000 troops.

To Alan's great surprise, Bob Dupeyre, his French father and an oil company executive, happened to be in Hanoi at the time. He joined us for dinner at a rooftop restaurant. Alan's parents had divorced when he was seven years old, and his mother had moved to Arizona with her two sons. It was only at the age of eighteen that Alan renewed ties with his father. Alan's mother, Harriet, knew about this, but never met Bob's new French family. This young American who visited them every year mystified Alan's four half-brothers. They were not told the truth until years later. I found it ironic that the only family member who saw us at the time of our marriage was a father that no one except Alan officially recognized.

Our next stop was Hong Kong, where Alan took the time to place an overnight order for a white sharkskin suit. The crossing of the Taiwan straits in a small passenger ship was rough, but I do not recall minding it. The names on our cabin door—Alan Logan and Nicole Prévost—must have appeared shocking at the time. We were on our way to our first overseas assignment, which was to last until the beginning of 1956.

The ECA families lived in houses scattered around Taipei. Ours was located in a residential area inhabited by Chinese and Taiwanese. There were no other foreigners around. The architecture of our house was Japanese. Our roof was made of heavy tiles to protect us against typhoons. The walls were thin to limit the damage during earthquakes. The whole thing made no sense to me: I had a vision of our home flattened under the massive roof like a house of cards at times of natural disasters. During the typhoon season from May to September, the thunderstorms were violent and so were the winds. I am glad to report that our house never did collapse.

Tatamis (straw matting) covered the living room floor. No one entered our house without removing his or her shoes. This was a ritual accepted by our visitors even during dinner or cocktail parties. In the sunken vestibule, provided with benches, our guests would don grass slippers. In order to adjust to the style of a Japanese house, Alan cut off the legs of the living room furniture. When our son Philip started walking, at barely ten months, the coffee table's corners were just at the right height for him to hit his head. There was a raised alcove in the living room, perfect for flower arrangements. This is where, at Christmas time, we placed a tree decorated with popcorn attached to strands taken from my ponytail. The sliding doors, made of paper, opened onto a tiny garden surrounded by a wall and fragrant with gardenia bushes.

Alan spent hours drawing the plan of the house and was very involved in its decoration. After we painted our bathroom forest green, he decided to perk up the scenery by adding snowflakes. We called this work of art "Snow in the Jungle." During the first of our many jaunts to Hong Kong, we bought curtain material. He did most of the sewing, using a tiny hand-held sewing machine. Unlike a regular machine, the stitches were made with only one thread, so if one pulled on that thread, the whole thing would come undone.

There was absolutely nothing to buy in Taiwan. Several times a week, Alan sent calls for help to his mother. She became our lifeline and sent us supplies, ranging from records and films to vitamins for our puppy "Jelly" or swimming flippers. She practically saved Alan's life by sending him a nose-clip for diving.

In Taiwan, as at every other diplomatic post, the servants occupied an important place in our lives. Alan had made arrangements to hire a house staff before my arrival. After lengthy negotiations, he had set a salary for the cook and topped it by a sum that was supposed to compensate for the money the latter agreed not to steal from us when shopping. Our cook, Li-Sung, was from Shanghai. He was skinny, ageless, and had a beautiful young wife and a cute daughter, who spent hours memorizing her lessons by rote. I never set foot in the kitchen because it was the cook's domain, and also because it was rather unappetizing. After Philip was born, the kitchen became totally off limits. The foreigners' cooks knew each other and everything about their masters' private lives. Li Sung would hear through the grapevine where we were going for dinner, and we would find him helping our host's cook.

Every morning a stream of street vendors sang out their distinctive calls to advertise their wares. One of the most picturesque, the trader in human manure, stopped at our house with buckets and poured out the unmentionable slush in his "honey wagon." The vegetable gardens do superbly with this stuff. Little children gathered near our front door when Li Sung bought vegetables, fruits, and meat for the *Mei Kuo Jen* (Americans). He would buy the meat and then keep it until it was almost spoiled in order to make it deliciously tender.

Alan and I loved going to the movies. We would order an office car, usually a rundown station wagon. The traffic was quite light, made up of pedicabs and bicycles rather than cars. We would leave our residential district by the wide avenue Chung Chang Pei Lu and reach the busy downtown. There were no tall modern buildings like today but mostly rows of shacks with shops and eating places patronized by squatting customers. Like other foreigners, we would sit in the balcony at the movie theater. I always chose the seat at the end of the row near the exit in case of an earthquake. Although earthquakes are very frequent in Taiwan, we did not have a single bad experience. The only time we got nervous was during a concert in Taipei. The chandeliers started swinging ominously, but the orchestra continued playing and the audience seemed undisturbed. I pretended to remain calm.

Life for "expats" was easy and pleasant. Foreigners would mix at dinners and cocktail parties with Taiwanese and Chinese. The latter had brought with them a cross section of the food from every region of China, and the variety of dishes was incredible. I was introduced to shark's fins, egg nests, and monkey brain, which was served still warm and quivering. We sat at round tables, and the host would pick the food for us with his chopsticks. A round of rice-wine toasts greeted the arrival of each new dish. At the end of the meal, washed down by a clear broth, the guests would get up. After a few burps to show their appreciation for a delicious banquet, they would make a quick stop at the spittoons placed strategically by the doors and then leave immediately.

One of Alan's closest associates at work was a Taiwanese with an aristocratic bearing. We got to know him and his family quite well. Thanks to this relationship we understood better how the Taiwanese felt toward the mainland Chinese. The Taiwanese had come to the island in the seventeenth century from the Fukien province in China. Fifty years of Japanese occupation, from 1895 to 1945, left a highly educated class. When the Nationalists moved in, Taiwanese pride was hurt at the loss of control of their island and at being forced to yield most of the political power to the new immigrants. A mainland Chinese became the president of the Taiwanese provincial government.

Our Taiwanese friend devoted his spare time to growing orchids. A few years later under tragic circumstances, we saw this Taiwanese family again in Ankara, Turkey. A pot of boiling water had seriously burnt their young daughter. We visited her at the hospital many times and did all we could to help them. Their gratitude was most touching.

Another striking figure among Alan's friends was a tall handsome man from Manchuria in Northern China. He was half Chinese and half Russian and gave Alan private lessons in Russian.

Alan was a ham actor. Spurred on by the enthusiasm and professional talent of our friends Marge and Ed Martin, working for the engineering company J. G. White, a group of theater amateurs was created. We produced a play each month. Only two rehearsals were allowed. Amazingly, the audience did not even notice that the actors held their scripts. Alan starred in several productions. In *Bus Stop*, he was perfect as the cowboy from Elkhart, Indiana, who befriended the Marilyn Monroe character. He also played in *The Iceman Cometh*. I was unsurprisingly cast as a French character in *The Women*, written in 1936 by Clare Boothe Luce. One of the most exciting plays our group performed was *A Murder Has Been Arranged*, which, for once, was shown in a real theater. During an elegant dinner party, an actor collapsed on the stage, and the suspense built up into a mystery and the final *coup de théâtre*.

One of my first tennis partners was the Chinese minister of defense, who had a round belly like many upper-class Chinese. He held his racket as if he were playing ping-pong. He was quick and with a snap of the wrist would fire deadly shots. Throughout our diplomatic life I have found tennis a wonderful way to mix with a cross-section of the population. Sipping lemonade at the tennis club's bar, we were able to exchange conversations with the most important personalities of the country.

Soon after my arrival in Taipei, I started Chinese lessons. At first we were a small group of students, and the classes took place at the office. Then the rest of the students dropped out one by one, and I was the only one left. In the end, I received private lessons twice a week at my house. Donald Pao, my teacher, taught me *kuo yu*, "national language" based on the Mandarin dialect spoken in the Peiching region. By the time we left Taiwan I could read about 1,200 characters, which allowed me to make some sense out of the newspapers. Jim Crane, the Information officer, and I became the model students in a language course broadcast on the Taipei radio for several months. All this knowledge faded away as soon as I stopped doing my daily calligraphy exercises to help me memorize the Chinese characters.

My recollection of Taiwan was of an island hanging on the edge of the deepest ocean abyss in the world. It is an unstable land shaken by daily earthquakes. Violent storms erode the soil of crumbling cliffs. The interior of the island is a rough mountain range, with deep gorges, torrents, and vertiginous slopes. The tropical forests are almost always shrouded in low clouds. The Japanese had built roads, tunnels, railroads, suspension bridges, dams, and power lines. Guesthouses and temples could be found in the most remote places. When the Japanese left in 1945, nature rapidly reclaimed its rights. The roads disappeared, the tunnels collapsed, and the wooden boards of the bridges rotted away. The Chinese were afraid to venture in this rough region, inhabited by aborigines who had been headhunters and cannibals until the mid-1930s.

We prepared our expeditions into the interior of the island carefully. We had to plan our route, where to stop, and what equipment to bring. But the most arduous negotiations concerned hiring and paying the Taiwanese or aboriginal bearers. They would bargain over the prices and complain that the itinerary was too difficult. A higher pay usually took care of the deadlock. All this haggling, in which I enjoyed taking part, was conducted in the Chinese language.

While trekking, our food consisted of bowls of rice spiced up by tins of meat or fish we had brought. Boiling water for tea or instant coffee was always available but not cold drinking water. Sometimes I had to brush my teeth in Scotch. On one trip, Alan brought a small tent that we had bought at the *Vieux Campeur* shop in the Latin Quarter of Paris. But most of the time we slept on the *tatami* floors of the government's guest houses. Our Taiwanese bearers carried all our equipment, including a stove and sometimes a toilet.

We were wearing clothes from head to toe to be protected from mosquitoes. But nothing could protect us from bugs and leeches covering our legs when we forded streams. At times the trail wound through twenty-foot-high tooth grass. The bearers cut the main stalks to create a passage; however, we were attacked by hundreds of small saws on the back of the remaining leaves while pushing our way through.

Some of the trips still remain in my memory as thrilling adventures. We walked several times through the island over the rugged divide. To cross the island and end up in Lotung on the North East coast, Alan and I had to walk for ten hours straight. In one of our pictures I see the cheap tennis shoes I was wearing. They would not have assured any protection had the pile of snakes we encountered on the trail attacked me. Hundreds of species of snakes can be found on the island. One of the most dreaded, the "hundred-steps snake," allows its victim to walk only a hundred steps before he or she drops dead. It is hard to imagine, but I have never been colder than I was on this tropical island. As we reached the ridge at 2,150 meters altitude, our face was whipped by hail and sleet. The pass was covered with snow and the streams were ice cold. We were shivering in our plastic raincoats.

Many of the Tayal aborigines, of Malayan origin, had never seen a foreigner, and we were treated like royalty in each village. The members of these most primitive tribes were tiny and frail. The women carried the heavy loads of firewood, and the men carried the baby. They seemed to be clinging to the face of the mountain with their prehensile feet. Their shoes consisted of straw soles tied to their ankles. They wore handwoven striped ramie cloth. Men and women often held a small pipe in their mouth, apparently reflecting constant use of drugs. The houses nestled among vegetable gardens spotted with the bright colors of pea and melon flowers.

One of the most pleasant excursions we took was a four-hour-long drive on a push-car from Ulai to Remogan, a village south of Taipei. The push-cars had been used for logging in the past. Driven with no apparent effort by Taiwanese, we rode along cliffs, over streams, under wet and mossy rocks, close to waterfalls, and down gorges with spectacular drops. The piercing and monotonous cries of birds and cicadas followed us. Giant ferns showed their hairy black trunks with dead lower branches. Between the tall trees covered with ivy, vines looped in intricate designs. The atmosphere created by such dense vegetation made the traveler feel dizzy. We were overwhelmed by the scent of warm, damp earth mixed with the strong perfumes of flowers.

The highest peak on the island is Mount Morrison, which is well traveled and made accessible by logging trails and even a train for most of the way. The second-highest mountain, named Tsu Kao Shan, or Mount Sylvia (12,750 feet), had never been climbed by Westerners. The aborigines were reluctant, almost frightened, at the idea of coming with us, and the chief of police of a nearby village said we should not go, particularly since the weather was threatening.

We went anyway. We rode for a while in our Ford, followed by the bearers in a jeep. The road rose up the steep slope 2,000 feet above the riverbed. The slow clearance of the car crashed against rocks hidden in the grass. We had to squeeze into half-collapsed tunnels. The rotten planks remaining on the suspension bridges made the crossings perilous. Our guide would motion us "a little to the right, now to the left." As we progressed toward the halfway point, Alan looked puzzled, as the guide was indicating right and left at the same time. His sign language meant that the passage was impossible. The ascent on foot of the mountain was extremely slow. There was no trail and the bearers had to chop the dense grass with their machete. The exhaustion was such that our British friend Anthony Snellgrove collapsed: the effort had been too great. It turned out later that he had contracted polio during that trip. Three years later I named my first daughter Sylvia after the mountain we had conquered.

Our longest trek took us across the island from Taichung to Hualien, a distance of sixty-four kilometers. The road that followed the East-West Tie Line had vanished soon after the departure of the Japanese because of earthquakes and typhoons. It was beautiful to go from valleys to high ridges, to balance on suspension bridges hanging several hundred feet over the rushing torrent, and to walk across huge dams. For me, however, there was a terrifying part: a stretch across a sheer cliff that had been sliced away by a massive landslide. The trail was so narrow that we had to walk sideways. Fortunately I was young and only moderately afraid of heights in those days.

Looking back I realize how courageous —even reckless—it was for a young married couple to have agreed to live for several years in such a remote country, where letters and newspapers took weeks to reach their destination, a country with a lack of amenities, poor medical facilities, and unstable political conditions as a backdrop. Even the U.S. military hospital, part of the Military Assistance Advisory Group, or MAAG, where Philip was born, was reminiscent of the *MASH* field hospital, but without the humorous part.

In the absence of a good radio, or television, and with only a scant choice of movies, letter writing was central to our lives. I have reread the numerous exchanges of letters from California with Harriet and from Paris with Papa and Susu, my stepmother. The comfort the letters gave us still seems vivid. They brought us the news from the rest of the world. Besides supplying us with all the things lacking in Taiwan, our families became my literary agents and helped me publish some of my articles in the American and French press.

Taiwan felt like an army camp, constantly under threat from the outside and policed from the inside. Police passes were required when traveling in the interior, as many parts of the coastline were closed to civilians. As foreigners, even as Americans generously aiding the economy, we had the feeling of being under constant surveillance. (I guess this prepared us for future assignments in countries such as the Soviet Union and Guinea).

The military situation in the region was volatile, and the region was on alert. In a letter to his mother on May 26, 1952, Alan described the air raid he heard while watering the garden. It appeared that a new U.S. aircraft carrier was in the Taiwan straits with forty planes standing by for action. The Nationalist radar had picked up the activity and thought the Communists were coming. The Communists had thought the Nationalists were attacking. A tense and dangerous confusion on both sides of the straits resulted from this incident.

The Taipei community was cosmopolitan. Besides the Taiwanese and Chinese, the Americans constituted the largest group, including members of the embassy, the AID mission, the U.S. military forces (MAAG), and engineering companies such as J. G. White. Many nationalities were represented on the island, including the British, Germans, Dutch, French, Siamese, and Brazilians.

We had close friends among the British diplomats. Given that the United Kingdom had not recognized Taiwan as a nation, its representative was accredited to the provincial governor of the island and not to the central government. The British head of mission, Alec Hermann, and Dossia, his wife, lived in an elegant residence in the seaside town of Tamsui. It was a Dutch colonial building with verandas all around. The Hermanns entertained beautifully, and friends often made the short drive from Taipei. Dossia was a White Russian born in Manchuria and had many colorful stories to tell. Their Scottish dance evenings were famous. Taking part in them when six months pregnant kept me in shape.

I had a special connection with the French embassy, given that I was one of the handful of French nationals on the island. I believed they had adopted me. Alan and I were often included in their social events. I remember Jacques Loquen, Agence France Press chief, who was quite a character, of massive build with curly hair. Another was Commandant Daubas, military attaché, who always had a wife far away in France. I remember Roger Duzer, a young third secretary; later, as an authority on the Far East, he pursued a brilliant diplomatic career as ambassador to Pakistan, Laos, and Australia. We often hiked together through the interior.

Among the people we knew, some extraordinary characters stand out. One was the daring, literally suicidal Russian-born wife of the French ambassador, Georges Cattand. She did not spend much time on the island, but when she did she made a splash in our community. One day she and Alan were swimming in the strong surf of our ("our" meaning open to foreigners) beach in the north. A riptide current took both of them away from the shore. As we watched nervously from the beach, we made preparations to rescue them using a heavy wooden fishing boat. Eventually Alan and the ambassadress swam back by themselves. Apparently they had not panicked and had conversed about the problems of the world as if they were at a cocktail party.

Another even more terrifying incident occurred near one of Taiwan's many dams. Our Russian friend decided to climb down the deep silo of the intake. The ladder was increasingly slippery with moss as it disappeared into the abyss-like bottom. We watched Madame Cattand freeze, unable to move and ready to be swallowed by the furious maelstrom of the rushing current. Eventually she struggled her way back up.

I recall the first Bastille Day of my diplomatic life with some shame. The French *chargé d'affaires*, Joseph Seguret, and his harp-playing spouse were planning a glittering event at the government guesthouse. They had ordered forty-five cases of champagne from France. Only forty-one reached the embassy. The French officials immediately suspected that the four missing cases had been diverted at the customs office. M. Seguret threatened to cancel the ceremony if the crates were not cleared on time. The ultimatum worked, and the party took place smoothly. Alan and I were among the official guests; and, unaccustomed to drinking champagne, I gulped down two glasses effortlessly. Then I went up to an upstairs bedroom to "powder my nose." Coats were piled on the large bed, and I thought I would sit down a minute. After that everything went black, and I missed the wonderful reception!

In letters to his mother Alan often threw himself into diatribes about U.S. policies. Anyone wishing to learn firsthand about Alan's forceful opinions should dig into the dozens of letters he wrote. I have always known Alan and Harriet to have an incredible interest in politics. Their discussions often turned into a duel between a very liberal Republican and a fierce Democrat.

It is not uncommon for the United States to be torn by partisan politics. Reading the 1952–53 family correspondence, I realized the vehemence of political feelings going on in those days. Alan, being a staunch Democrat, thought Ike would be a total disaster if elected. China, Korea, and Taiwan were at the core of U.S. foreign policy, the way Iraq, Palestine, Afghanistan, and Pakistan are today.

Alan expressed what some people might have deemed subversive ideas about Chiang Kai-shek and U.S. policy toward China. He described with irony the "simple life" led by "the Gimo" (nickname given to Chiang Kai-shek on the island) and by "the Madame," his wife. In a letter from December 29, 1952, Alan wrote: "In 1949, there were very few 'China Hands' who did not detest the Nationalists."

In his letters Alan presented somewhat of an indictment of the U.S. economic assistance to Taiwan. He wrote:

Millions of our good US taxpayers' dollars are being freely disbursed on Taiwan. Given our foreign policy, these expenditures are probably justified in a general sense; but the justification of specific projects is not as clear. All you need is the ability to make general statements in beautiful phrases, and you could get five million dollars to spend on a fertilizer plant. Quite sizeable amounts of money have been spent on worthless projects. We send glowing reports to the Congress.

Alan always wrote with a dry sense of humor. One of his typical tongue-in-cheek stories described our meeting with Adlai Stevenson in March 1953:

Me: "Mr. Stevenson, I am Alan Logan and this is my wife Nicole. We are with MSA and JCRR."
He (Stevenson): "Howdy-doody," [or something].
Me: "My mother told me that she almost married a close relative of yours, but I can't remember which one."
He turned to Nicole and said, "It's too bad she didn't. We would be cousins."

Stevenson was friendly, witty, highly intelligent, and observant. He was brilliant in getting around embarrassing questions during press conferences. During huge gatherings, attended by several hundred people, he would treat each one as an individual and never said the same thing twice.

Six months after my arrival in Taipei, I started working in the information office of the Joint Commission on Rural Reconstruction, located in the Union Building. JCRR's objectives were to protect the rights of the people, promote land reform, and improve the farmers' working conditions. The office was made up of four Americans and a jolly group of Chinese. Busy typewriters, visitors' conversations, and laughter across the room created a lively atmosphere. The open windows of the Union Building let the noise from the central square pour in. Elegant in their native dresses, with high collars and a slit on the sides, the Chinese women acted free and emancipated. Many of them smoked. They were well educated and constituted the upper level of the society. Many of them were wives of professionals, officers, or ministers.

As a photo editorial assistant I was responsible for sorting and filing the many pictures of official events on the island, such as the visit of the Seventh Fleet, the inauguration of a dam, or the opening of a housing project. The role of the information office was to present Taiwan as a showpiece of the U.S. government economic aid to developing countries. Photographs of a steady stream of visitors such as Nixon, Adlai Stevenson, Clare Boothe Luce, and numerous members of Congress piled up on my desk. I enjoyed being the first to have the scoop on the latest news. Eventually my job grew more complex as I learned how to use these pictures to design feature stories, posters, and exhibits.

In September 1952, we spent one week in Hong Kong. For me, this and several other visits we made there epitomized the glamorous and exotic life we led as diplomats in the Far East. Every sight, every encounter was an adventure. Those are the bygone days when we felt like special people.

Landing at Kaitak, Hong Kong's old airport, was an acrobatic feat, since there was barely enough room between mountain and water. One immediately became engulfed in the very British atmosphere of well-kept lawns, double-decker buses, and Chinese traffic police as stiff as their London colleagues. In contrast, the Chinese districts showed decrepit buildings and the poverty of the crowds. On the construction sites, the workers—mostly women—were balancing cement, stone, or dirt on bamboo poles. In the smothering heat, totally covered in black shiny cloth, their faces drawn by exhaustion under their coolie hats, they went up and down in a doleful, mechanical way.

Driving around the British colony on winding roads we would discover a scenic point more spectacular than the previous one. Clinging to the slopes were the beautiful residences of wealthy Chinese or the British. It was hard to believe that, less than ten years earlier, the British colony had suffered the harsh and brutal military occupation by the Japanese.

At cocktail time we stopped in the lobby of the impressive Peninsula Hotel and met with acquaintances who, like us, had come to Hong Kong for a shopping spree. The Parisian Grill was the restaurant *à la mode*. This is where I had my first taste of garlicky snails. A violent windstorm interrupted the fish dinner we were going to have on one of the floating barges in Aberdeen. A short visit to the gambling casinos of Macao was also a must. We took every opportunity to cross the bay by ferry. Around us were junks, loaded with whole families and their bundles. Ocean liners, like the *President Wilson*, penetrated deep into the bay. The activity of these vessels and people was incredible.

During another trip to Hong Kong, Robert W. Rinden, a friend from the U.S. consulate, invited us on his small sailboat, to which he had brought along a cocktail basket. He turned the skippering over to a deckhand, and the three of us had a perfectly decadent sail by moonlight in this beautiful setting, while sipping martinis. (In 1959 Bob was to open the American embassy to Guinea as chargé d'affaires *ad interim*.)

Alan was outraged by Ike's victory in November 1952. In his letters, he went on page after page trying to convince his mother of his point of view. I do not have her replies, but apparently she stuck to her guns. Alan was particularly harsh on Nixon.

For the first Christmas of our married life, we went skiing in the resort of Shiga Heights in Japan. A beautiful lodge with an immense fire greeted the guests, who were mostly non-Japanese: Danish doctors who had spent four years on a hospital boat off the coast of Taiwan; U.S. Air Force pilots; five huge Texans from the navy, red, noisy, and cheerful; and a Swiss working for a chemical company. On the ski slopes, Alan slid easily on parallel skis and was noticed for his graceful style. The Japanese used other methods. They went straight down at breakneck speed. Their skis were crude boards without safety bindings. They were unable to turn or stop. The ski patrol would crash into the chairlift queue, and they even hit me once. But somehow there were more broken skis than broken legs. In a timely manner, Alan sprained his ankle in the slush on the last day of our two-week stay.

We became perfect tourists after that and visited Nagano, Kyoto, Nara, Osaka, and, of course, Tokyo. With my new Japanese camera,

I took black and white pictures of Alan walking on crutches in the immaculate gardens of temples and the Imperial Palace. The sight of Japanese people taking pictures of people taking pictures was new to me.

In March 1953, Alan was promoted from "junior program analyst" to "industrial economist," heading his own department. Although he had a junior rank, we felt rather important in our official functions. As executives of the International House, we met the highest members of the Chinese government. I remember being the only woman at a banquet and sitting at the right of the premier, conversing with him in Chinese and even making a short speech.

Life went on easily in Taiwan, interrupted by a home leave to France and California. Flying in the 1950s was always an adventure. Unlike today, planes were unable to avoid most of the storms. It was scary to fly straight into thunderhead clouds. I cannot begin to count the number of dinner trays that spilled over me. Traveling in first class was small compensation for the roughness of flying.

Propeller planes did not have much fuel autonomy, and planes had to make frequent stops. Flying around the world from Taiwan to California via France, then returning over the Pacific took many days. For first class passengers, the land accommodations provided by the airlines were sumptuous. Starting from Taipei, we spent one night in Singapore in the palatial Raffles Hotel. One of our most romantic ports of call was in an oceanside hotel in Ceylon (Sri Lanka). The road from the airport went through lush cultivated fields. Elephants slowed down the traffic. In the sweltering heat, a swim would have been welcome, but the water was so hot that it burned my toes. The brief stay at the Karachi airport and another at Basra airport in southern Iraq were both forgettable memories. However, a stopover in Beirut gave us a chance to explore the whole country as a preview of our future posting to Lebanon.

The period of our lives as "married bachelors" was coming to an end. In 1955, Philip was making his approach. I started feeling nauseous and faint at the daily cocktails and dinners. With time, things got better, and I resumed a normal life. I was able to swim or play tennis at the Friends of China Club almost until the end of my pregnancy.

The date of the expected delivery came and passed. Days, even weeks went by and still, nothing. A close friend from the U.S. embassy, Jacque Ewing, was just as late as I was, although it was her fourth child. Alan, practical-minded as usual, decided to take advantage of the situation and make the race profitable by designing a sweepstake. The Taipei community placed their bets on who— Jacque or me—would win the race. The stakes grew higher. We asked an intrepid and dashing bachelor friend, Jack Fitch, to take both of us on a jeep ride in the mountains. The rougher the road the better, we told him. It still did not help. Finally, I reached the finish line first, when Philip decided to make his grand entrance a whole month overdue.

The MAAG military doctor who had treated me during the pregnancy was absent and a complete stranger took over. The ordeal was pretty ghastly. The breech position caused violent pains for seventeen hours, in spite of a couple of Demerol shots. Alan provided his moral support from the tennis court. The needle of the epidural broke and the spilled liquid did not help me much. And then, bliss. Little Philip was perfect. I was in a common room at the hospital, and friends came with flowers. I felt like a queen, but was quite vulnerable after the delivery. When I tried to watch a science fiction movie in the hospital, my nerves could not stand it and I had to leave.

When I returned to the house, I was pampered by all. The cook's wife had been promoted to "baby amah," and a "wash amah" was hired. I brought Philip up in a complete antiseptic surrounding. Everything he touched was sterilized. I was totally ignorant of how to raise children; and away from elder relatives, my only source of knowledge was Dr. Spock's book. Philip paid a high price for my lack of experience.

For eight months Philip enjoyed an active social life, as he was carried around first in his basket, then in his Taiwanese stroller. He spent his afternoons with us at the Friends of China Club. Installed on a colorful pad with his toys, he loved being in the middle of the action. The baby amah would watch him and at the same time create adorable little slippers and pinafores for him. Our best friends and regular tennis partners, among them Dick and Jacque Ewing, or Walt and Laura Jenkins, both couples from the U.S. embassy, were always nearby. On weekends Alan would strap Philip on his back the way Taiwanese children were, using long strips of hand-woven blue checker material.

During our trip to Japan for Christmas, Philip enjoyed crawling in the plane and "licking ashtrays," to use Alan's crude words. The contrast from the sterilized world to the world of germs must have been too violent for him. We settled in our suite at the Frank Lloyd Wright Hotel in Tokyo (the hotel has shamefully been razed to the ground since then). Harriet had flown from the United States to join us. We went to the PX and then to a Kabuki theater at night. The following day Philip became violently ill with diarrhea and vomiting. He was rushed by ambulance to the Catholic Saybo Hospital, where they immediately proceeded to fight his life-threatening dehydration. As I left the hospital, a nurse was about to give him glucose with a syringe fit more for a horse than for a baby. This was the saddest day of my life. In the taxi, I fell into uncontrollable sobbing.

Alan and Harriet forced me to go sightseeing. We spent most of our time in Nara, visiting temples and pagodas, and acquired some beautiful old Japanese prints. Philip struggled to get better for about two weeks. And then, one night, Harriet called us from her hotel room: "Philip will be OK." Being a Christian Science practitioner, Harriet had the power to see deep into the minds of people and to be part of their recovery in times of crisis.

We left Taiwan in January 1956 and joined our friends Dossia and Alec Hermann and Laura and Walt Jenkins in the quaint little Austrian village of Ehrwald. Philip, who had returned to his birth weight at ten months, started his recovery, cuddling up in a sleigh and attended by a healthy young Austrian maiden.

2

Turkey 1956–1957

Turkey was the briefest of our assignments since we were to stay in Ankara only fifteen months. Alan had passed the written part of the Foreign Service examination in Taiwan; and after we'd heard the positive results of the oral exam, we transferred from Turkey to Lebanon, our first State Department post. I was particularly proud of Alan when I learned that only 7 percent of the applicants were successful.

In 1956, after leaving Taiwan and spending home leave with our respective families, Alan started his new job in Turkey. He was working with the U.S. Aid Mission again, now called ICA (International Cooperation Agency). Just a few years earlier, in 1947–48, Turkey had signed an economic assistance agreement with the United States as part of the Marshall Plan. A program of military cooperation was also initiated and several American bases were built, as well as medical facilities for the troops. In 1952, Turkey became part of NATO.

Our house in Ankara was located high on a hill on the edge of town. Beyond our orchard we could see the limitless expanse of the barren hills of the Anatolian plateau. It felt like being on a green island surrounded by arid land.

I remember Turkey as a rugged country. The populations living near the Aegean and the Mediterranean have had a great deal of contact with the outside world over recent years. But in the Ankara region in the 1950s, things were different. Even today, if you look at guidebooks, most of the information concerns Istanbul and the coastal areas. Ankara has yet to rank high as a tourist destination.

But since we were not tourists, this was not a problem. We did not mind the harshness, because we relished the rich history, the stark landscape, and the interesting human contacts.

Turkey did not want to repeat the error made by the Ottoman Empire when it allied itself with Germany and suffered the fate of the defeated countries after World War I. In 1941, Turkey had signed a nonaggression pact with Berlin, but in February 1945, it declared war on Germany just in time to meet the conditions required to participate in the San Francisco Conference and the newly created United Nations. To the great disappointment of the Soviet Union, Turkey received the rights to oversee the traffic in the straits of the Bosporus and of the Dardanelles.

Ankara, the capital created in 1923 by Kemal Atatürk, the first president of the Republic, had, in some areas, the clean and well-designed look of an artificial city and thus offered a mixture of architectural styles. Old districts had an oriental flavor, with bazaars or *souks*, where one could buy glazed ceramics with dominant green and blue motifs, copper objects, leather, beautiful lamb's wool, and also angora wool from goats. Elsewhere the city had wide, shady avenues lined with elegant shops and restaurants. Atatürk Boulevard, or *Bulvari*, was the main thoroughfare, cutting the city from north to south. Group taxis, called *dolmushs* (meaning stuffed in Turkish), would shuttle along the main axes, picking up or dropping passengers at full speed. Ministries and administrative buildings stood out in their neoclassical architecture. The mausoleum of Kemal Atatürk, a grand and severe block of geometric form with a massive colonnade, overlooked an esplanade that dominated the lower part of town. Soldiers, marching like automatons, guarded the monument, which had been completed only three years before we arrived in Turkey.

Located at an altitude of 2,400 feet, Ankara has a continental climate with frigid winters and hot, dusty summers. The town spreads over hills, the best residential areas having majestic views over their surroundings. The district where we lived was called Kavaklidere, which gave its name to a famous wine. Several embassies could be found in these areas. At the other end of town, the Citadel, a rock jutting from the valley, consisted of several ramparts built by the Galatians and the Romans in the early centuries of the Christian era.

Philip was barely a year old when we arrived in Turkey, and Sylvia was already on the way. We needed lots of help. Our household consisted of Fatma, a kind country woman, and her perky daughter Misherref, a girl of about thirteen whom we hired just to play with Philip. Johnny, very proud of his Anglo-Saxon nickname, was the gardener, guardian, and handyman. Zara, the maid who pretty much ran the show, was a sophisticated young woman in her late twenties.

This was my first Muslim country. Although Atatürk had founded a secularized, Western-oriented nation, attitudes were deeply anchored in Islam. Women were considered inferior and many were still illiterate; such was our maid Fatma, who could not read nor even count money. She always held her headscarf with her teeth to hide part of her face. In the countryside, farmwomen remained veiled in spite of the government's edicts. Quite often, our emancipated Zara encountered difficulties while using public transport, perhaps because her way of dressing was too Western. Ankara was definitely a man's world! I was almost scared by the Turkish men hanging out at cafés, with their fierce looks and heavy mustaches.

A frightening incident happened to me not far from Ankara. Alan and I loved to hike. At age one year and a half, Philip would tag along and run like a little goat to keep up with us. But one day, the two of us were alone. As usual, Alan was racing ahead and I lost sight of him. I was climbing up a steep and rocky slope. I was about to reach the top when a head popped up over the ridge. A man extended his hand as if to help. He pulled me up but not all the way. I realized then that his intention was not to help but to force my gold bracelets off my arm and let me drop down the cliff. I was too petrified to utter a sound and call for help. By a miracle, Alan came back and scared the man away.

I found the Turkish people at times hostile. I still remember a Sunday outing with the children, when we were driving through an isolated village in the Anatolian countryside and suddenly found our car showered with stones. Perhaps they had never seen foreigners before and were frightened by the sight of our turquoise Chevrolet.

As is always the case in the diplomatic life, especially in a country with forty-three embassies, the busy schedule of dinners, cocktails, official visits, teas, bridge parties, tennis tournaments, and weekend outings was essential for meeting the influential population and better understanding the issues involving the country and the region. Encounters acted as memory pegs into the general history of the period. For instance, I recall attending a reception at the Iraqi Embassy on May 2, 1957, one year before the assassination of King Faisal II, following the coup led by General Kassem that ended the Iraqi monarchy. Kassem was himself overthrown by Saddam Hussein and shot in 1963. Another evening, Alan and I had dinner in a downtown restaurant and had a chance to eat the best caviar I ever tasted. Our Iranian hosts had arranged to fly the caviar from the Caspian Sea region.

Under the umbrella of the United States of America Operations Mission to Turkey, the United States maintained an important presence in Turkey. In addition to the embassy, the military, and the aid-administering ICA, there were business interests mainly related to civil engineering, petroleum exploration, and drilling activities. Alan was part of the Economic Policy and Programs section of ICA. Over the years we remained in touch with several embassy members such as economic officer Malcolm Thompson and our friend and tennis partner Leonardo Neher, who had joined the Foreign Service in 1954 as consular officer and ended brilliantly as ambassador to Upper Volta (now Burkina Faso) thirty years later.

Although Alan was not part of the American embassy yet, we were frequent visitors to the building. Unlike the present days when the compound would be protected from possible terrorist attacks with concrete barriers, it was wide open and easily accessible from the avenue.

Among the people we knew at the Embassy, I particularly remember U.S. Economic Counselor Robert Moore and his wife, Joanne, who welcomed us warmly to Ankara. They probably remain in the memory of American Foreign Service officers (FSOs) as one of the kindest and most professional couples of all. Bob had an impressive career including several ambassadorships. He came from a family of Robert College academics in Istanbul. This educational institution produced generations of Middle East professionals who played a crucial role in the transformation of the region after the collapse of the Ottoman Empire. The college opened in 1863 and is the oldest American school outside of the United States still in existence.

I found the women of the well-to-do classes highly educated. They held important positions in the professional world as lawyers, doctors, and members of the parliament. At the same time, they always looked as if they had just returned from a trip to a Paris grand couturier. As I scan through my Turkey engagement calendar, names of friends come back to life: Leila Sambel, Fisek, Yalsin, and Isik.

In 1957, the Turkish-American Women's Cultural Society published a book of Turkish recipes. I still enjoy leafing through the yellowing pages of this small book. The basic ingredients of Turkish cooking are lamb, yogurt, eggplant, *pilav,* meaning rice, and goat cheese. With the paper-thin dough, or *börek,* one can make a variety of dishes. Turkish food is highly flavored and nutritionally well balanced.

I took Turkish lessons for several months. The Latin alphabet, established in 1928, facilitates the study of the language, but the overall linguistic remoteness from the familiar Greek and Latin heritages creates problems for a student from the West. I still recall a few greetings like *gule gule* (good-bye), *nazilsiniz?* (how are you?), or *teshukkur ederim* (thank you). But I am best at saying "no" like a real Turk, snapping my tongue against my front teeth and throwing my head back.

In Antiquity this land was at the crossroads between Mesopotamian civilizations and the states bordering the Eastern Mediterranean and the Black Sea. Successive waves of migration brought Hattis, Hittites, Phrygians, Urartus, Persians, Galatians, Greeks, and Seljuk Turks, sometimes from the west, sometimes from the east. In 1453, Mehmet II, a sultan of the Ottoman Empire founded in 1299, conquered Constantinople, bringing an end to the Byzantine Empire. The Ottoman Empire was to last until 1922. In the 1950s, the wealth of ancient vestiges existing in Turkey was well known but mostly unexcavated except for a few German sites.

Ankara is located at the center of what used to be the Hittite country in the second millennium BC. Soon after arriving in

Ankara I became fascinated by the mysteriousness and might of that empire. Ankara was the ideal jumping off place to explore the Hittite culture. Unlike Greek or Roman remains that have survived in so many countries, the Hittite ruins are specific to the Anatolian plateau and cannot be seen anywhere else in the world.

My first acquaintance with the Hittites occurred when I visited the collections displayed in the Museum of Anatolian Civilizations, located at the foot of the Ankara citadel. I still treasure today a book written by Seton Lloyd, the grand old man of ancient Near East history. Seton Lloyd had been appointed director of antiquities of the Baghdad Museum in 1939, and in 1948 became director of the British Institute of Archaeology in Ankara.

One weekend, Alan and I drove 150 kilometers east of Ankara to the modern village of Boğazköy—the site of Hattuşaş, the capital of the Hittite Empire. The setting of huge boulders and rocky hills was rugged, almost threatening. I was struck by the massive remains of Cyclopean walls of rough stones assembled without mortar that surrounded the town. A gate, flanked by two seated lions, was one of the several openings in the wall. A short drive away, reliefs of marching soldiers were carved into the face of an escarpment.

The Hittite empire was at its peak in the thirteenth century BC. It was one of the key players of the Near East and the equal of Egypt. The two countries competed for control of the commercial corridor running along the Mediterranean coast from Syria and Palestine. This confrontation ended with the victory of Pharaoh Ramses II at the battle of Kadesh in 1274 BC. This battle is probably the most important military event in Near Eastern history. It was followed by a certain equilibrium in the region.

My mother-in-law, Harriet, accompanied us on many of our trips in Turkey. Widely read, she loved French culture and besides knew much about the history of early Christianity. Before joining us in Ankara, she had read a biography of Eleanor of Aquitaine by Amy Ruth Kelly. (Published in 1950, the book is still the definitive biography of the queen). Thanks to this background, Harriet was bringing with her a fresh perspective on the ferment resulting from the Crusades between the medieval world of Western Europe and the Arab world. Eleanor of Aquitaine was only 25 in 1147 when she accompanied King Louis VII of France, her first husband, during the arduous trek of the second Crusade through the Anatolian plateau.

Places and scenes we saw while traveling in the Turkish countryside included herds of sheep being sheared in the spring, menacing shepherd dogs as big as Saint Bernards preventing us from crossing fields, and narrow valleys bristling with tender green poplars leading to cool springs.

Cappadocia in eastern Anatolia is a forest of oddly eroded mounds. Early Christians took refuge in the caves they dug into the rock. We caught on film a gathering of women around a fountain that looked like a biblical scene. The hotel accommodations in which we stayed were more than Spartan: only a curtain separated our room from the common sleeping quarters!

Driving along the southern coast of Turkey felt like a relief from the harshness of the interior. The Apostle Paul had a predilection for Cilicia, the coastal region in southern Turkey where he spread the Gospel. Ancient vestiges appeared untouched: the Greek temple of Soli-Pompeipoli and amphitheater of Diokayseria and the Roman town and harbor of Korikos. Crusader castles and fortifications still stand on the water's edge, Silifke among them. One of my photographs caught a totally naked eighteen-month-old Philip surrounded by a group of mesmerized young village girls near a Crusader rampart.

Another trip took us from Ankara to Istanbul through hilly and picturesque scenery. The moderate climate had a European feel. It was the month of Ramadan, and I sympathized with the plight of the workers on a construction site for not being allowed to drink. We enjoyed visiting the Bursa area with its beautiful tiled baths and mosques, particularly the Muradiye mausoleum. The following winter we returned to this area to ski.

We visited Istanbul often. We loved the bristling and cosmopolitan city, its beautiful mosques, the elegance of the residences built along the Dardanelles, and of course Topkapi Palace, or *Sarayi*. But in Istanbul, somehow, we did not feel as truly in Turkey as we did in Ankara.

Sylvia was born in the U.S. military hospital on July 6, 1956. She was a happy baby and made me laugh all the time. The beginnings were auspicious, since she had let me enjoy the 4th of July festivities and appeared only after I'd spent a day at the races. At six months, she was sleeping twelve hours straight and gained weight regularly. What a difference it was from Philip's various ailments and rough nights! At nine months, she could stand and had one tooth.

In March Alan and I went skiing in Zurs. We left baby Sylvia with our friends and colleagues, the Spielmans, and took Philip with us. He was on his skis at 20 months! Zurs is above the timberline and has magnificent slopes. Harriet and her other son, Frank, were there also. My progress in the B+ ski group (Alan, of course, was in the A group) came to a brutal stop after my spectacular fall.

The ski instructor had taken our class on a walk away from the paths, with skins attached to our skis. The weather was beautiful and even so hot that I had to roll up my sleeves. But the slope remained icy and crusty. My fellow students started practicing slalom. My turn came. I was nervous and afraid of being unable to anchor the edges of my skis. And that is exactly what happened. Halfway through the turn my skis ran uncontrollably straight down the hill. I slid perhaps 50, perhaps 100 feet, I do not know. My bare arms left bloody shreds of skin on the snow. The fall had produced a second-degree burn. I returned to Ankara with huge bandages around my arms.

Early in 1957 Alan, Philip, Sylvia, and I started our long and magnificent drive from Ankara to Beirut. The Taurus mountain range is geologically young, with jagged peaks, similar to the Rockies. As we went over the pass, we saw an encampment of ragged, wild gypsies. When Alan attacked the winding road in its brutal descent with too much vigor, I can still hear one-year-old Sylvia saying "Careful, Daddy."

The scenic road, bordered with oleanders, brought us down to Syria. We reached Iskenderun (also called Alexandretta), then went through the towns of Hamas, with its huge water wheel, and Aleppo, with its formidable citadel, and made a stop at the Krack des Chevaliers fortress on the Mediterranean coast. The handsome city of Damascus was next, with its fertile surroundings, busy *souks*, and elegant mosques.

We arrived in Beirut late in June 1957.

3

Lebanon 1956–1960

We spent almost four years in Beirut and loved every minute of it as we immersed ourselves in the trilingual dynamic life of this city called the Paris of the Near East. Diane and Karen were born there. We were caught in the middle of a minor civil war and were snow-bound a whole week in the ski resort of Les Cèdres. We crisscrossed every part of this beautiful country, full of history.

To mark our independence from the rest of the Americans we settled in an oriental house away from the Ras Hamra district, where most of the foreigners lived. The house was located on Patrakie Street, marking the boundary between the Christian district and the Muslim Basta. This location became crucial in 1958, when a civil war erupted and we found ourselves in no man's land during the battle.

Being totally bilingual in French and English, Alan split his tour of duty in Lebanon between economic and political work at the Embassy. At first he was involved with the English-speaking government officials dealing with such matters as trade relations, investment, and industrial projects, and also with the private business community. Many of these people had been educated in England, in the United States, or at the American University of Beirut (AUB). The most popular meeting place was the downtown Alumni Club, where everybody spoke English. After about one year Alan's work switched to political affairs and required him to establish relations with the francophone government circles.

The political system of the country was structured to give Christians and Muslims an equal representation in the government. The president of the republic was a Maronite, the president of the parliament a Shi'ite Muslim. The other religious groups—Greek Orthodox, Greek Catholic, Armenian Orthodox, Armenian Catholic, Protestant, Syrian Catholic, Roman Catholic, Sunni Muslim, and Druze—were also represented. This delicate balance of power had been designed after Lebanon acquired its independence in 1943, ending the French protectorate, and was still in existence.

The list of government officials the embassy gave us showed both the religion and the hometown of each member of the government. It was important to know, given that each political family had a "fief," or domain, located in the mountainous landscape of Lebanon. For instance Suleiman Frangie, a Maronite who lived in a modern apartment building at the end of our street, had his political base in Zghortha, high in the mountains on the way to the Cedars. To meet the awe-inspiring Kamal Jumblatt, the Druze warlord, and his armed entourage, we had to penetrate deep into the narrow valleys of his Chouf stronghold near Mount Hermon.

Another particularity of Lebanese politics was that the political power was in the hands of family dynasties and passed from generation to generation. Even today one can recognize the same family names in charge of the political scene, such as Edde, Gemayel, Chamoun, or Jumblatt.

Our contacts with this elegant, sophisticated, and widely traveled francophone community were stimulating. We met them on the beach, at bridge gatherings, and playing tennis at the DTL club, where everybody spoke French. Many of this community's members had been educated in France or were graduates of Saint Joseph, the Jesuit university. As a rule they spoke French and Arabic, often starting their stories in one language and reaching the punch line in the other. They had absorbed the French culture. The works of their best writers can still be seen in French bookstores, as they are in the Lebanese ones.

The women were buying their clothes in the French capital. The fashionable Ras Hamra district reminded me of the Avenue Victor Hugo in the 16th arrondissement of Paris, with its fashion boutiques and stores displaying Western food. Another choice location for foreigners and wealthy Lebanese society was the Grotte aux Pigeons district, where modern apartment buildings standing high on the edge of a cliff overlooked the Mediterranean, with the

Saint Simon beach in the distance. Downtown, the Bristol Hotel and the nearby restaurants and park attracted elegant crowds. Hotel Saint Georges, which received its name from the legend of St George killing the dragon, was built on a bay, right on the water. My hairdresser was conveniently located in that hotel.

The commercial center of Beirut and the older neighborhoods were in the east of the city. A large square called Place des Martyrs was the heart of the town. My driving memories in those busy streets were of a dangerous game. Nobody respected the lights, which were usually not functioning and often covered with spider webs. The rules of the road consisted in bluffing the other driver and assuming he would give in. The Lebanese driver lets his shoulder hang out of the car window, allowing the free arm and hand to do all sorts of expressive gestures.

Beirut suffered much during the years of civil war (1975–1990). Many of the historic districts were bombed out. Before reconstructing them, a major effort was made to excavate the remains of the old Phoenician city called Berytus, buried for many centuries.

In the 1950s it was unconceivable for a well-off family to live year-round in Beirut. Most families had their weekend and summer retreats up in the hills. Among these we often visited the Babikians, a rich Armenian family, and other friends in Shemlan, Aley, Yarze, Zahrle, and elsewhere.

When some Lebanese acquaintances asked if we would like to come to their younger brother's wedding, we said we would be delighted but of course we did not want to intrude on a strictly family affair. Our scruples were swept away as we approached the brightly lit open-air restaurant in Bhamdoun. Cars were parked all around and several hundreds guests were already there. As we were led between tables lit by multicolored lanterns, a mixture of fashions could be noticed, from the severe black clothes worn by village women to the latest Yves St Laurent line in cocktail dresses. The popular Sabbah started singing in a storm of applause. Several black-clad Bedouins from La'lou' went through a strange dance on and around a clay water jug. By the time Samya Gamal started belly dancing among the guests everyone became wild with excitement.

It was my first diplomatic post, and I had to follow the rules of protocol. This was a bit easier for Alan, since he was learning the ropes of his new job at the office. Within one day of my arrival I had to pay a courtesy call on the wife of our ambassador; no matter that I had two young children, did not know any one, and had no help yet. I dressed formally (hat and gloves were required at luncheons and other formal functions). I still see myself waiting in the entrance of the residence, nervously holding the right number of calling cards, one from me, two from Alan, carefully folded at the upper right corner to show that I had paid my call in person. Things got easier later, but at the beginning I felt very sorry for myself.

Looking back at the guidelines given by the American embassy to newcomers regarding expected behavior, what to say, what not to say, how to dress, I am amazed at how I was able to put up with some of these constraints through a large part of my diplomatic life. The fate of junior wives depended on the attitude of the ambassadress and of the superiors in the embassy hierarchy. I remember having tea at the home of Mrs. Barnie Ramsauer, the political counselor's wife. I was holding my cup delicately, sitting at the right end of the sofa. My hostess remarked that I had better enjoy that seat since, as a rule, it was reserved for the ambassador's wife. This remark was nothing personal, just a reminder of the rules. While in Washington, a few years later, we saw Barnie often and were happy when she agreed to become the godmother of our daughter Diane.

Eventually a number of other U.S. diplomats' spouses and I rebelled. In 1973 we climbed on the barricades, and our taskforce produced recommendations that undid the ridiculous parts of the system. Looking back at my whole "career" as a U.S. diplomat's wife, I must say that I followed personal rules of politeness, common sense, and above all, respect for the local culture. For the rest, I tried to be myself and not to lose my spontaneity.

The new American ambassador, Robert McClintock, appointed to Lebanon in January 1958, had a colorful personality. Not tall but elegant and dynamic, he would drive around town with panache. Always accompanied by his *chaouch*, or aide, who dressed like a Turkish official with a fez on his head and wearing baggy pants. His perfectly groomed black *caniche*, or poodle, had an assigned seat in the front of his official limousine.

Someone had given us the judicious advice to find a nanny among the young women educated in a Catholic convent. We found Andree in the institution run by the Soeurs de Saint Vincent de Paul. She stayed with us until our departure from Lebanon. Maids came and left, but Andree was the stalwart anchor of our family. Behind our house was a courtyard with a small house, and this is where Andree lived. She was wonderful with the children and spoke perfect French. The sisters had taught her to do beautiful embroidery. A particularity of Andree is that she ate lots of garlic. The overpowering smell of garlic would make us cry when we entered her room. We did not object to this because the delicious Lebanon cooking is rich in garlic and furthermore, garlic is supposed to provide protection from all sorts of ailments (which, by the way, is not entirely true, since the people, in this part of the world, are often ill).

On January 24, 1958, Diane was born in a French maternity clinic on rue de Damas. I was admitted in the morning. Things progressed normally in a most civilized way. I was keeping myself occupied with some knitting and reluctantly stopped to be wheeled off to the delivery room. French Professor Malinas had a severe look with a generous pitch-black mustache. The pains finally got bad, and I asked doctor and nurse to give me something to alleviate the pain. "Just keep out of this, we are busy" was their answer! On the whole, though, it was a fairly easy experience.

Things had not been as easy for Alan. During his first visit to the hospital to see us, he looked very excited but also a little sheepish. Only later did I learn the reason. He had been so anxious to see Diane and me that he had raced through a one-way street the wrong way and had totaled the car!

Our little family was growing. The kids looked adorable (of course). They did not have the huge amount of toys and stuff children have today. Next to our bedroom the children's room had, for main furniture, a metal footlocker covered with a red plaid blanket. Philip and Sylvia would watch their little sister lest she fall on the marble floor. The children were so close in age that the youngest one was always entertained by her older siblings.

We spent most mornings at the St. Simon beach, where we had a two-room wooden cabin. The children played in the white sand by the calm Mediterranean waters. It is while swimming on this beach that, a few months later, we were to see a contingent of U.S. Marines jumping off landing craft.

Some steps in the courtyard behind our house led to the small garden in front. Two accidents took place on those steps. A few days before Diane was born, Philip fell and his forehead needed six stitches. Diane's accident several months later was more dramatic. She fell off the steps while attempting to drive down in her tricycle. She bit her tongue so badly that it was almost severed. Alan had the courage to hold her when the doctor operated on her. The first night after surgery I did not leave her bedside fearing that the swelling of the tongue would cause her to choke.

I have always found the Middle East one of the most fascinating regions of the world. I was interested to learn how new nations were carved after the breakup of the Ottoman Empire. During our time in Lebanon general unrest was spreading through the Middle East while the Pan-Arabist movement was strengthening. The shah of Iran had returned to the throne after the execution of Prime Minister Mosaddeq in 1953, but his power was shaky.

The crucial problem, however, that was to last unresolved into the twenty-first century, was the Israeli-Palestinian conflict and the never-ending civil conflict leading to several *intifadas,* or uprisings, as well as military conflicts in south Lebanon and the Gaza Strip. The two main *intifadas* lasted from 1987 to 1993 and from 2000 to 2005. The 1950s only marked the beginnings of the troubled era doomed to tear this region apart. At that time the UN peacekeeping forces were quite visible in Beirut. I remember our children shouting with excitement *"les Jeeps de l'ONU"* every time they saw the white vehicles dashing around town. Several friends and I liked to meet on the beach to discuss these problems, which seemed as impossible to solve then as they do today.

During our stay in Beirut we drove twice to Israel, once following the Mediterranean coast and directly into Israel, the other time driving through Jordan and going over the Allenby Bridge. This was the only access into Israel when coming from an Arab country. With the help of our embassy we had replaced the license plates for American diplomats residing in Lebanon by innocuous New York plates.

There was something exhilarating about Israel in those days. The population was hard working and full of hope for the future. We stayed in two kibbutzes, each belonging to different political parties. One was collectivist, where the children lived separately from the parents and adults ate in a common dining hall and received no salary. The other kibbutz tolerated nuclear families, which were allowed to live in individual homes. But in both types we found the same climate of idealism and acceptance of harsh living conditions as a necessary step toward a stronger country.

I have gone to Israel many, many times since, having excavated in the ancient Philistine city state of Ashkelon with a Harvard-led archaeological expedition from 1985 to 1993. Israel has changed a great deal during those years! The kibbutz mentality has been replaced to a great extent by the traits of a consumer society. Massive construction, in Jerusalem or on the West Bank, seemed to have become a priority. Ashkelon, less than twenty miles north of Gaza, has become a booming town, with comfortable villas and apartment buildings to house the influx of 800,000 Russian refugees (many of them non-Jews) in 1993.

In 1958 Alan and I saw the grim refugee camp of Palestinians near Jericho. The houses, looking like cement cubes, without water or electricity, climbed up the hill. This was but one of the sixty refugee camps created by UNWRA (United Nations Relief and Work Agency) after the 1948 Arab-Israeli war. When we returned thirty years later, the Jericho camp was a ghost town. The refugees had moved to permanent refugee camps, which look today like crowded towns. The Shatila camp in the Beirut suburbs remained well known after what has been called the "Sabra and Shatila massacre" in September 1982.

A long flight of stairs ran alongside our house in Beirut. One of the neighbors who lived above us appeared to be a journalist. In fact, his position as Middle East correspondent for *The Economist* was his cover, and he was actually an intelligence agent, Kim Philby, the most famous English spy of the twentieth century. Son of a British diplomat, he attended the best schools in England. He worked as a senior officer in British Intelligence for ten years while being in fact an agent for the KGB. We met him occasionally at official functions, but of course I had no idea then of the hidden world he belonged to. He mysteriously disappeared from Beirut in 1963 to resurface later in the Soviet Union, where he defected.

 The festival of Baalbeck, in the Bekaa Valley, is probably the oldest international festival in the world. Created in 1955, it became a governmental institution by decision of Lebanese president Camille Chamoun in 1956. For me it was a new experience and the first theater festival I ever attended. A series of cultural events took place in the glorious setting of Hellenistic ruins. Jean Louis Barrault, one of the great figures of the Comédie Française and of the French stage, was magnificent in *Amphitryon*, a comedy by seventeenth century French playwright Molière.

It may sound surprising but there is quite a lot of snow in Lebanon. The Baidar pass, halfway on the road to Damascus, is a scenic spot overlooking the descent into the Bekaa Valley and offered easy slopes for the children to ride their sleds on. But we got more snow than we wanted during a trip to the Cedars ski resort, half a day's drive from Beirut up a winding mountain road.

The morning after our arrival we could not open the windows of our chalet, because the snow almost reached the roof. Everything was beautiful, quiet and covered with several feet of snow. An avalanche had broken the single ski lift that stood in the middle of a wide-open area. For a whole week we remained snowbound. The children thought it was great and spent the days running their sled among the cedar trees.

Alan and I took two longer trips. One was to Petra, the pink Nabatean city in Jordan, best know for the beautiful Roman and Hellenistic facades of tombs and temples built into the face of the rocks. A group of French friends living in Beirut had chartered a plane. As is often the case, the heat of the desert caused turbulence in spite of the cloudless sky. I had brought pills to help against nausea during my pregnancy. (As far as I can recall, this was the only time I ever used them). As I was about to take the pill, a friend of ours, a tall athletic man, saw me and asked if he could have one. Everybody got sick on the plane except the two of us. As we were making our approach onto the tiny airport, our plane bounced back up at the very last minute. Our pilot had decided that there was not enough room for both a cow and our plane on the runway. We landed safely the next time around.

The second trip, this time by car, took us to Palmyra, in northern Syria. Already known in the second millennium BC, the city developed under the Romans as a trade route linking Persia, India, and China. It became most prosperous under Queen Zenobia in the third century AD. Her power became a threat to Rome, which took her prisoner. We drove a long time through desolate country. Once in a while one could see the carcass of a dead animal or the remains of a mausoleum. We slept among the ruins of Queen Zenobia's palace. I still remember my fear of encountering a scorpion that night. On the way back I really did let Alan down. He had trusted me with the navigation and I lost the road. We would have been totally disoriented had we not had a compass.

I have to mention a group of American friends whose families played a vital role in the history of the American University of Beirut (AUB). I am alluding to the group of Arabists who left their mark on the map of the Middle East. Our friends David Dodge and Malcolm Kerr belonged to that group. We often saw them and their families and joined them on weekends at their country houses in the hills. David was acting president of AUB in 1982 when he was kidnapped by terrorists and held captive for one year in the Bekaa Valley region. AUB president Malcolm Kerr met an even more tragic fate: he was gunned down outside his office in 1984.

In 1866 the Syrian Protestant College opened with sixteen students. It became the American University of Beirut, or AUB, and in the 1950s had 8,000 students. Daniel Bliss, David Dodge's great grandfather, who was educated at Amherst, was the first president of the university. The Revered Stuart Dodge became the first president of the board. The school created an atmosphere of free thought, which contributed to the birth of Arab nationalism.

Foreign Service officers such as Ambassador Talcott Seelye were also part of this Arabist elite. Most of them had been educated in institutions of higher learning like Williams College, Amherst, or Princeton. The FSOs who specialized in the Middle East continued their studies of Arabic at the Shemlan Language School, located near Beirut.

I undertook the study of Arabic. The classes were held in the American Embassy, handsomely located on the beautiful corniche, or waterfront, lined with palm trees. Of the several students who showed up the first day of the Arabic class very few remained by the end of the week, the others apparently discouraged by the tongue-twisting sounds imposed by the instructor right from the start.

I found the study of this language difficult for several reasons. For many months we only learned spoken Arabic, and I missed the support of the written language. When I started to read, I discovered that the spoken and written languages were remote from each other. Furthermore, as the Arabic script is based on a nonpictorial alphabet without vowels, one can only read if one understands the meaning of the sentence. I decided it was a catch-22 situation.

Besides writing regular columns for the embassy newsletter and learning Arabic, my main intellectual endeavor was to study archaeology. I was fortunate to have as professor the head of AUB's Department of Archaeology, the renowned scholar Dr. Dimitri Baramke. He was a Palestinian refugee from the town of Nablus in what is today the occupied West Bank. He introduced us, firsthand, to the Phoenician civilization. His lectures were followed by field trips to historical sites.

Called Canaan in the Bronze Age of the Bible, Phoenicia stretched along the Mediterranean coast roughly where Lebanon and southern Syria are today. Phoenicia was a seafaring country, whose ships spread out across the Mediterranean to Cyprus, Malta, Sardinia, and all the way to Spain. In Tunisia the Phoenicians were called Punic by the Romans. One can still find in Lebanon the remains of Greek temples, of Roman towns, and of medieval constructions such as Crusader forts, continuously inhabited throughout the ages.

The millenia of human occupation of the ancient city of Byblos has long attracted archaeologists from many countries. The most important find was the evidence of a Phoenician alphabetic script of twenty-two characters, the ancestor of our alphabet. Our family often visited the small port, a short drive north of Beirut. The waves crashing over huge blocks remaining from the pier made the place look alive. I hovered over the children, ready to catch them, when we climbed on the tower of a crusader fort without any railing.

In the summer Dr. Baramke led an Early Bronze excavation site in the Bekaa Valley where I had a chance to do my first digging. One day, at the end of a class, he announced to his students that he had just opened an ancient tomb and asked us if we wanted to buy some of the burial goods, including a Middle Iron mug, a Late Bronze dipper, and a Byzantine lacrimatory (tear bottle). How much times have changed! Today, were we to be caught taking ancient artifacts out of a country, our next stop would be a prison.

At age three Philip had difficulty reading his letters, and I was disappointed with his slow progress. I was trying too hard because he was the first child. Karen, the fourth child, grew up like a weed, and the results were just as good. Sometime toward mid-May I had a morning of panic when I frantically tried several kindergartens in town for Philip, age four. The British Community School gave priority to English and Commonwealth children. Philip was too young for the American Community School. The French College Protestant closed its registration in May. Fortunately the Germans accepted registrations until the end of June. As a result of the saga of hunting for schools, poor Philip had to go to a German kindergarten, then an English one, then a French one. When we returned to the United States, Philip finally had a chance to attend a regular American school.

One day, in late morning, I was returning with the children from the beach. The streets were unusually quiet. A woman popped her head out of a window and cautioned, "Quick, go inside, there is a civil war going on." It was mid July 1958. The buildings were shuttered and our neighborhood was deserted. We rushed to the house. Soon Alan joined us.

We happened to be on the front line separating the Arab quarter, or Basta, from the Christian Patrakie district. Our house was soon engulfed in rounds of bullet fire. I remember feeling more excitement than fear in the midst of this noisy shelling. I quickly told the children to hide under the dining room table. My priority was to stop them from looking out the windows.

Our study was a beautiful room with many windows curved in a Moorish style. Alan had a very heavy metal desk, which followed us around the world. During the shooting, Alan crept under that desk and remained on the phone with the American embassy. He started giving a live report of the action, just as a CNN reporter would do from any war frontline. Accounts of Alan's exploits were related in several books. Beatrice Russell, the author of one of those books wrote: "When the economic officer (Alan) called, we could hear someone firing just outside. Alan said, "Hear that? That guy has been firing steadily since eleven o'clock. He does not seem to be aiming at anything—just keeps firing in the air. We've had two bullets in our living room, however. I dug them out of the woodwork for souvenirs."

In Beirut, street fighting started between rebels and the government forces. A prison was stormed. Sporadic explosions could be heard around town. Being in the middle of a civil war is most confusing, and it took me some time to understand what was happening and why. The Middle East situation was particularly tense following the Iraq coup that toppled King Faisal II on July 14, 1958. Syria and Egypt had just formed the United Arab Republic. In Lebanon, Rachid Karame, the Sunni Muslim prime minister, wanted a "rapprochement" with the UAR and supported Nasser and Arab nationalism. Lebanon's president, Camille Chamoun, a Maronite Christian, felt threatened and called the United States for help, since the Lebanese army seemed unable to cope. The American response was swift. President Eisenhower authorized the dispatch of two aircraft carriers, the USS *Essex* and USS *Saratoga*, which sailed from Greece. Overall, about 14,000 U.S. Marines took part in the operation.

All the official American families had to be evacuated from Beirut in July 1958. This order happened to coincide with our scheduled home leave. When we returned from the United States in late summer, there was another outburst of violence, resulting in a new curfew. Would we be evacuated? we wondered. One morning we saw several tanks approaching on our street—the no man's land between the Christian and Moslem districts. This was the only time I felt really scared. I imagined the fierce gun battle to ensue if the tanks were to be attacked. Fortunately the tanks kept on going and disappeared down Patrakie Street without firing.

During periods of lull we went on with our normal life. We even spent time at our beach, about eight kilometers south of

Beirut. The children and I were there one day when we saw a small group of U.S. Marines, looking rather relaxed, disembarking from a landing craft. Whenever the situation seemed calm, I took the car to go shopping. I continued playing tennis at the Alumni Club. My regular partner, Bea Russell, and her husband, Earl, also with the American embassy, were close friends. A few years later we heard the terrible news of Earl's death. Bea and Earl had been walking in the Mauritanian desert with other people. Earl somehow left the group and became totally disoriented from sunstroke. He never recovered.

The situation grew quieter, and a new government was formed. The "troubles," though, lasted for several weeks.

I enjoyed my life, which allowed me to spend a lot of time with the children while also being involved in a number of activities. Although Alan worked long hours, he still found time to skin-dive along the rocky shore near Beirut or in deep waters. He enjoyed telling the story of his encounter with an apparently quite friendly shark.

But most of our weekends were dedicated to the family. Every Sunday we would drive along the coast or into the mountains. Lebanon is a small country, but one can discover a new place every time one sets out in the car. We drove east over the Lebanese mountain range and into the fertile Bekaa Valley, where we knew a restaurant offering delicious frogs' legs; we had picnics among the ruins of Greek temples; and we visited Tyre and Sidon, the two most important Phoenician port cities in Antiquity.

One summer, the children and I moved our quarters to Ainab, while Alan commuted to work, sixteen miles away. The accommodations in Ainab were simple, but it was wonderful to be on the slopes of Mount Lebanon overlooking Beirut. The hotel was in a forest, and the temperatures were cool.

We regularly attended the Cine Club of Ras Beirut. Afterwards we would drop by Angelo's to enjoy their famous cannellonis. One evening a Charlie Chaplin movie was showing. In my advanced stage of pregnancy I found the wooden seat rather uncomfortable and was unable to join the general laughter surrounding me. At one point I told Alan I should be going to the hospital. Reluctantly he got up and drove me to the AUB medical complex. Dr. Williamson was called, and she barely had time to put on her medical scrubs.

Karen was born on November 18, 1959. She looked like a typical Logan. The first time Harriet saw her in her crib she said, "All I could see were her huge eyes." Our life in Beirut was really a family time, since we had four children aged four and under. I seemed to be always pregnant then. My big bed was the main square of the household in those days. I keep an adorable picture of Diane holding Karen on her lap. During the "quiet time" of the afternoon, the children were playing noiselessly in their bedroom, and I was nursing Karen while studying Arabic.

One weekend we went on a very long hike with embassy friends, Richard and Ann Murphy. (Dick later became ambassador to Syria and assistant secretary of state for Near East and South Asian affairs under President Reagan.) Our destination was a remote region near Tripoli in northern Lebanon. The nature was wild and deserted. We met children in rags tending their flocks. We had heard that the area was dangerous and that we were taking the risk of being attacked by bandits. Nothing of the sort happened, and the walk was great.

On October 15, 1960, we left Beirut for Washington, D.C., and our first home assignment.

Photo Gallery I

Aborigines on a mountain trail, Taiwan, 1954.

Alan and Nicole in an aborig-
ine village in Taiwan, before
trekking across the island.

On the top of Tsu Kao Shang, or Mount Sylvia (l. to r.) Nicole, Taiwanese guide, Alan, Anthony Snellgrove, 1954.

JCRR Information Office, Taipei, 1955. Credit: cartoon drawn by a Chinese member of the JCRR staff.

Village women and their donkey in Cappadocia, Turkey, 1957.

Harriet and Alan in the Cappadocia wilderness, 1957.

In our Ankara garden, the maid Fatma with
Philip and Sylvia, 1956.

A group of Turkish peasants during the sheep-shearing season on the
Anatolian plateau, 1957.

Philip and our turquoise Chevrolet in a Kavaklidere street, Ankara, 1956.

Nicole, holding Philip, and Harriet, in front of the Atatürk mausoleum, Ankara, 1956.

Snowboound at the Cedars, 1958 (l. tor.) Diane, Philip, Sylvia.

Nicole, Philip, and Sylvia, St Simon beach, Beirut, 1957. This is where the U.S. Marines landed in July 1958.

Our house on Patrakie Street, near the Moslem *Basta*, Beirut. The stairs at left led to the house of the famous British spy Kim Philby. During the civil war, Alan was on the hot line with the American embassy from the room with the Moorish windows at right in 1958.

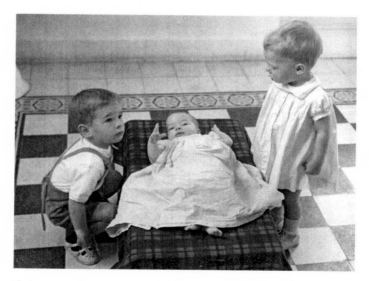

Philip and Sylvia watching Diane. The footlocker was the only piece of furniture in the marble floored bedroom, 1958.

The Logans on the SS *America* in New York before sailing for Europe and the Soviet Union.

Soviet citizens intrigued by the four Logan children in front of the Bolshoi Theater, Moscow, 1964.

53

Karen, Philip, Sylvia, and Diane standing near the Moskva River. In the distance, the nineteenth-century Great Kremlin Palace and the Kremlin cathedrals dating from the fifteenth through seventeenth centuries, 1965.

The sixteenth-century cathedral of our Lady of Smolensk, Novodevichi monastery, Moscow, 1966.

4

Soviet Union 1964–1966

Russia – or rather the Soviet Union – was for me the most interesting of our overseas assignments. During the two and a half years we stayed in Moscow, my life was on a high. There were not enough minutes in the day to accomplish everything I wanted to accomplish. Alan would despair at being tied down in his office at the Embassy, reading the daily *Pravda* (official voice of the government), while I was having the time of my life.

Our assignment in the Soviet Union coincided with the removal of Nikita Khrushchev from power and his replacement by Leonid Brezhnev. We were in the midst of the Cold War era, marked by a fast pace of events. In 1960, the Soviets had arrested the pilot of the U-2 spy plane, Francis Gary Powers, releasing him in 1962 in exchange for a Soviet spy. In 1961, the East Germans had constructed the Berlin Wall, followed in 1962 by the Cuban missile crisis. When we arrived in Moscow in 1964, the atmosphere of the "thaw" brought on by Khrushchev was still lingering in the intellectual and cultural world. A slim ray of hope was the underlying thread during our stay in the Soviet capital.

The publication in 1956 of Aleksandr Solzhenitsyn's *One Day in the Life of Ivan Denisovich,* which described life in a Soviet Gulag, seemed a breakthrough toward a limited freedom of expression. Needless to say, this book was required reading for all newcomers to Moscow. We found other timid signs of liberalization in the theaters, literature, and the arts. But it would be a long time until real progress was to take place, as the accession to power by Brezhnev would be marked by cultural stagnation and even repression for another eighteen years until his death in 1982.

It was the third year of our home assignment in Washington. We liked our life in North Arlington. Our farmlike little house had a well, a sandbox, and a miniature log cabin. We added a breakfast nook and two studies to the existing small rooms. The children and I would get scared watching the TV series *Outer Limits* in the basement family room. Our marvelous live-in maid Barbara took care of the children and the house beautifully. Conveniently, the Nottingham Elementary School was just across the street.

In the fall of 1963, I achieved my qualification to teach in the Arlington public schools. I began working as a suffering high school French teacher of "active" kids who hated French. So when I heard the news that Alan had been selected to go to Moscow, I was elated. We had to start intensive training in Russian at the Foreign Service Institute (FSI), the State Department language school. I was luckier than Alan as I could study at FSI longer than he could. The West Africa Desk, where he was working at the time, was reluctant to let him go. In addition, the Moscow embassy wanted him earlier than planned, thus further curtailing the normal language training usually offered to "Russia Hands." Fortunately, Alan was an extrovert and had such great linguistic ability that he never had a problem connecting with Russians or any non-English speakers.

The FSI method of total immersion is an interesting one. It consists of memorizing and mimicking whole sentences with the right inflection of voice. The drills are intended to create fast automatisms. The dialogues contained in each lesson dealt with concrete situations of daily life. We memorized them to such an extent that they are still engraved in our brains today. Our instructors were native Russian speakers supplemented by an American linguist. Part of the day was spent in the language lab. I was in front of the tape recorder with my headphones on when the news reached me that President Kennedy had been shot in Dallas. Like the rest of the world, I remember exactly every minute of that tragic day. The FSI was immediately closed, and I drove home in tears listening to the radio.

The move to Moscow required an unpleasant battery of immunization shots for the family: typhus, typhoid, tetanus, polio, and more. One day Karen, my youngest daughter, got so terrified of one more needle that she ran away from the doctor's office. We had to chase her through the Falls Church parking lot.

In mid-March 1964, we sailed from New York to Le Havre on the ocean liner SS *America*. Traveling in first class was always a lavish adventure. We had to dress up formally for dinner, and the food was superb. We particularly enjoyed the generous servings of caviar. The children, aged from five to nine, loved exploring the ship as Alan and I took turns at the exhausting task of supervising them. During the crossing we discovered that Sylvia might have the measles. We kept her in the cabin, but soon our room steward found out and the poor girl was quarantined. The "hospital" was a ghastly and scary place down in the entrails of the ship, right behind the propeller. One could feel the boat crashing into the waves. Alan spent the nights there to comfort her.

The children and I remained for a while with my family in Paris before joining Alan in Moscow on May 7. There was no apartment available for us, so we spent a few wonderful days at the American Embassy *dacha*, or country house. Alan commuted to work. The dacha was a large, rundown building surrounded by pine trees. The crows made a deafening noise. A small stream ran by the property and marked the limit beyond which we were not allowed to go. We could walk to the village, though. One Sunday we entered the church. The place was full of people, and it was only when we bumped into an open coffin with a body lying in it that we realized it was a funeral.

Our first apartment in Moscow was located in the Donskoi district in a small building facing a wall. Only foreigners lived there. The construction was recent and still smelled of wet cement. The floors were sloping, which made it hard to close doors and windows.

After a short while we moved to Leninsky Prospect number 45. The address was easily recognizable with the many windows of Agentsvo Transportnovo, or Transport Agency. The building was an impressive quadrangle enclosing a huge area planted with scrawny trees (by the end of the 1990s, it had become a real forest). Foreigners lived in one of the four sides. The Americans, who all happened to have large families of three or more children, had their own staircase. We were particularly close to Roger and Betty Kirk and their four children, but I remember also other families, including the Akalovskys, the Katzes, and the Brements. Our apartment was on the sixth floor, with tiny balconies overlooking the courtyard. Soviet families lived in two other sides of the complex. A preschool occupied the fourth side. The exciting thing was that, unlike any other Moscow housing for foreigners, such as the Kutusovsky complex, we lived together with the Soviets. Children of all nationalities played together, exchanged marbles and pins, skated in the winter, or played soccer in warmer weather.

Our apartment consisted of two small ones joined together. The four children slept together in one room. Another bedroom had been transformed into a playroom with our piano. Every spare inch of the apartment was used to store supplies and food ordered from Denmark or bought at the Embassy Commissary. Rolls of toilet paper and paper towels climbed all the way to the ceiling. We would order *foie gras* and other delicacies from Lamonzie, a fancy shop in Perigord, France.

We stayed in Moscow for two and half years, six months longer than the normal two-year tour of duty. This is pretty amazing, given that Alan had the honor of being blasted by the Soviet authorities on a whole page of *Pravda* he shared with Malcolm Toon, the political counselor. In spite of virulent accusations, the two of them were not declared PNG, meaning *persona non grata*.

Alan was one of three diplomats in the embassy's political external section, which covered the relations between the Kremlin and the rest of the world. Roger Kirk was responsible for Asia, William Luers for South America, and Alan monitored the relations between the Kremlin and Africa, the first to occupy that position.

The imaginative *Pravda* journalist described Alan as "looming in the dark chapels of the Kremlin cathedrals" in cloak-and-dagger fashion. He was accused of being in contact with African students attending Lumumba University, which was obviously a large part of his job. The Patrice Lumumba People's Friendship University had been created in 1960 to help the peoples of the Third World, according to the Soviet government.

We attended several farewell parties for colleagues who had been declared PNG and forced to leave the Soviet Union in retaliation for the eviction of Soviet diplomats from the United States. These events were heart-wrenching, because the victims had dedicated their professional lives to becoming Kremlinologists. Their careers were thus destroyed.

Retaliation from the Soviets could take other forms. One day, returning from a trip, we found the four tires of our red Ford station wagon, which we had parked near the railroad station of Bielo Russia, slashed with a razor. Apparently, a Soviet diplomat in Washington, D.C., had encountered some problems, and we were the ones to pay for it.

Members of the American embassy were well prepared to survive a daily life of suspicion and the stifling feeling of being considered spies. When we first arrived, we were briefed in a "safe room" about what to expect, what not to talk about, and what not to do. Unlike the Americans, the diplomats of small African embassies had not been told what to expect prior to arriving in Moscow and, as a consequence, had to overcome all sorts of difficulties.

The "bugs," in other words the tape recorders and cameras, were aimed at us the whole time, even in the car. Someone joked that we diplomats were providing employment for the local population, since it took about fourteen people to process the audio and visual tapes generated by each diplomat. The best way to scramble our conversations was to turn up the volume of the music or turn on the shower. The din of cocktail party conversations was also pretty good at protecting us from prying ears. Once in a while though, we would relax our caution. At the end of dinner parties, for example, we would bring our guests to the door and linger there. It was a mistake since "they" had probably installed a few extra "bugs" in our brick-walled entrance hall as well.

This spying game could create amusing situations. Once, at an official cocktail party, I was talking to a foreign diplomat when I suddenly realized that three Russians were around me, holding their drink, obviously eavesdropping on our conversation while appearing to be oblivious to the whole thing. Another time, Alan and I were walking through the old town of Baku, the capital of Azerbaijan, when we noticed a little man stealthily following us. He would quickly hide behind the corner of a building each time we turned around. It was like a Pink Panther movie with Peter

Sellers. I started laughing, but Alan remarked, "Do not make fun of that poor guy; he has to earn his living!"

Sometimes it was useful to be spied on. A team of American-supervised Soviet plumbers, electricians, and others handled the maintenance of our apartments. If something did not work, all we had to do was aim our voice at one of the microphones and complain very loudly. Like magic, when we later returned to the apartment, the repair would be done.

A soldier in a sentry box guarded the entrance of our stairways day and night. The minute we left, he would immediately pick up the phone and call the next military official taking the relay on our route to announce our departure. At every instant they knew where we were and guided us in case we had made a wrong turn. Whenever driving outside of the city, we would occasionally leave the areas open to foreigners, sometimes intentionally and sometimes not. Immediately a militiaman would appear out of nowhere and whistle us back onto the allowed path.

One might think that we were totally cut off from the people, given that we were under constant surveillance, but in fact we never felt that way. We persistently sought to meet the people by grasping or creating any opportunity to do so. The secret was that we had learned the rules of the game and were always pushing the limits of the possible, being careful not to endanger ourselves nor our friends or acquaintances.

However, living in Moscow was not for everyone. Even among the embassy members, only two or three couples like the Kirks or ourselves were able to bear the restrictions of a police state and to enjoy the challenge of playing by difficult rules the way we did.

Being with my four children made it easy to break the ice (no pun intended) and engage in conversation with Soviet citizens. If it was cold, the women would admonish me, saying my children should be more warmly dressed. Riding in a bus or walking in a park, I always met with friendly stares from people. "You are so rich," they were telling me, meaning that I was so fortunate to have such a large family in a society where one child was the norm.

Before a theater performance we always read the program notes. If there was a word we did not understand, we would simply ask the person sitting next to us. When we traveled by night in Russian trains, it was hard not to start chatting with passengers occupying the next berths. Occasions for accidental exchanges were multiple while shopping in *kolkhoz* markets, department stores, bakeries, and bookstores, eating in *stolovaya* (cafeterias), and visiting art galleries. I rapidly acquired the Muscovite habit of joining a queue even before finding out what was offered. The waiting was part of the fun, since it allowed us to chat in the line.

We found out that a good way to meet Russians was to cook mushrooms together. This was our experience during a camping trip we took from Moscow to Finland. We piled the whole family into our Ford and stopped every night in a camping ground. Conversations flowed easily as we shared the common kitchen. We were scared of eating the mushrooms we had collected ourselves and ended up giving them to the Russians for whom mushroom-picking is an art and a cherished pastime.

Another of my favorite activities, which also gave me a chance to talk with the *narod*, or people, was to visit museums, particularly the small ones, such as the Tolstoy or Pushkin "house museums." The women guarding the exhibits, usually elderly, were happy to share a wealth of information with us. Friendly, generous with their time, and very knowledgeable, they would tell us endless stories.

But the best example by far to illustrate how rich our chance encounters were is what happened to us on October 15, 1965. Alan and I were having dinner in the excellent Aragve restaurant off Gorki Street. We sampled the *zakuskis*, or appetizers, then attacked the main course. Two young men sat down at our table without asking for permission, as is the custom in Russia. After a vodka aperitif we had switched to wine. Alan offered some to our table companions. They accepted, and we started talking. We talked for several hours. We knew that many topics of conversation were absolutely taboo, so there was no allusion made to the fact that Nikita Khrushchev had been overthrown from his position as secretary general of the Communist Party that very day by Brezhnev upon his return from vacation in Pitsunda, Abkhazia.

It was well after midnight when our table companions suddenly got up. No good-byes, no exchange of names. They were making sure that no one would see them leaving the restaurant in the company of foreigners. This encounter was only safe for them as long as it remained anonymous.

Alan and I were most fortunate to serve under Foy Kohler, a highly professional and, at the same time, kind and supportive ambassador. He and his wife extended their welcome to both of us in the warmest manner during a small lunch at Spaso House, the American ambassador's residence. They explained what they expected from us and stressed that we were to play an important role within the embassy team. At receptions and cocktails each embassy staff member had a specific task. We were to arrive at least twenty minutes early at official functions in order to study the guest list beforehand and receive our marching orders.

Culture, treated as a safe neutral ground, was a way for the United States to make inroads toward better relations with the Soviet Union. Receptions held at Spaso House had a specific cultural theme. The controversial and very visible Mme. Yekaterina Furtseva, the Soviet minister of culture, reigned over these events. As an example, more than a hundred Moscow State Philharmonic musicians were invited to meet the members of the Cleveland Orchestra. The Fourth Moscow Film Festival in July 1965 was the occasion for the worlds of cinema, theater, art, and literature to meet.

Frequent film showings were organized at Spaso House for large audiences. These were serious events organized with a purpose. As an example, the guest list for a reception following the showing of *Around the World in Eighty Days* included the Union of Writers, the main personalities of the Bolshoi Theater, and officials from the Ministry of Foreign Affairs.

Exhibits, such as "Architecture USA," were held on fairgrounds and attracted huge crowds. Young American guides with a perfect knowledge of the Russian language would offer comments on their displays, but the Soviet visitors were mostly interested in finding out about life in America, how large the houses were, and what were the prices of cars or the salaries of workers. The American guides would oblige gladly.

The American embassy was not the only one waging this "cultural war." The French Embassy hosted a number of luminaries such as the cosmonauts Yuri Gagarin, who flew into space in 1961, and Valentina Terechkova in 1963. Valentina was quite a pretty woman. The popular French singer Gilbert Becaud was a hit at the Estradny Theater.

Each country had its own retinue of poets or musicians. The most famous poet, Yevgeny Yevtuchenko, was a familiar face within American circles. He had become an icon among the Russians ever since the publication of his poem "Babi Yar," written in memory of the Jews killed by the Nazis near Kiev. I still remember my heroic efforts to discuss abstract art with him in the Russian language during a dinner party given by the American cultural affairs officer in his apartment at the Chancery. The French Embassy also lured Yevtuchenko, as well as Andrei Voznesensky.

With a voracious appetite Alan and I attacked all aspects of Russian culture—music, opera, ballet, theater, architecture, and the beautiful literature and language. Opera, ballet, theater, and music played an essential part in the life of Muscovites. In a society where living space was limited to a few square feet per person in communal apartments, the performing arts represented an escape from their dreary life and satisfied the craving of a well-educated urban populace. Besides, tickets were cheap, sometimes only a few *kopecks.*

The brilliant colors of the operas contrasted with the grayness of everyday life. Operas were massive productions, taking place sometimes in the Bolshoi Theater, sometimes in the Palace of Congresses inside the Kremlin. The show would start at 6 pm and last close to five hours. I would pick Alan up at the Embassy. Cars were so few that we were able to park our station wagon right in front of the Bolshoi.

We always chose Russian operas rather than Italian or French, especially the ones steeped in the history or folklore of old Russia. We enjoyed Mussorgsky's *Khovanshchina* about the rivalry between *Streltsy* (archers), *Boyars* (noblemen) and Old Believers. Glinka's *Ivan Suzanin* tells the story of the peasant hero who defended Russia from the Poles in 1612, during the "Times of Troubles." But it was *Boris Godunov* that we loved best. In this opera, Mussorgsky retraced the last anguished days of Tsar Boris, who believed that the false Dmitri coming from Lithuania was indeed the slain *tsarevitch.* The incredibly rich settings took the spectator from the Novodevichi Monastery to the Kremlin, to St. Basil's on Red Square—an experience quite unlike the minimalist opera productions of today in the West. The colors were vibrant with a dominant red. The chorus was enormous and produced rich sounds. The voices of the main singers were incredible, especially the basses. The extent of their waistlines sometimes made it hard for the two supposedly young lovers to embrace.

At the intermissions the audience would rush to the buffet. Alan and I loved that pit stop. We would order a *butterbrod,* a thick slice of crunchy bread with an unspread chunk of butter, and a soup-spoon full of caviar. The delicious combination was accompanied by a glass of champagne.

The theater is an important part of the Russian culture. The Russian audience adored the traditional nineteenth century plays by Chekhov or Ostrovsky, staged in theaters like MXAT or Moscow Art Theater. They knew every word of the dialogue by heart.

Theaters also acted as a way to express a subliminal commentary on the communist regime in a country lacking freedom of expression. When playwrights went too far in their attacks on the government, the play was swiftly taken off the billboard. This is what happened to the plays of Tvardovsky and Bulgakov.

Among the many theaters, we particularly enjoyed the Sovremennik, which featured the popular actor Oleg Tabakov, and the Vakhtangov, located in a classical building on Arbat Street. The Vakhtangov was founded by one of the greatest Russian directors and continued the tradition of Vsevolod Meyerhold and Constantin Stanislavsky.

Contemporary productions attracted eager crowds at Lyubimov's *Taganka* Theater, which opened in 1964, the year we arrived in Moscow. Its first play was Bertold Brecht's *The Good Woman of Szechwan.* It was an electric evening in 1965 when we saw *Ten Days That Shook the World,* after a story by John Reed, the American journalist who took part in the 1917 Soviet revolution. (Warren Beatty was awarded an Oscar for playing Reed in the film *Reds* in 1982). Lyubimov's staging was surprisingly modernistic and obviously delighted the Russian Intelligentsia

It was also in 1964 that the poet Vissotsky became the lead actor at the Taganka Theater. He was a bard who sang in a raucous voice about the lives of the simple people, with their joys and their sorrows; but he was also a harsh critic of the system. He married Marina Vlady, a beautiful French actress of Russian origin, but did not spend much time in France. He was adulated by generations of Russians; and after his death in 1980, at age 42, his grave in central Moscow became a place of pilgrimage.

One day we received a special invitation to the Kremlin Theater. On the intimate stage of this private theater, Laurence Olivier gave an incredible performance of *Othello*. The great British actor was portraying his character as a man from the Caribbean islands, his face made up a dark brown, speaking in a sing-song voice.

The Russians also had a passion for ballet. They knew each work and the main dancers so well that they would start applauding even before they performed their solo pieces. When we booked our seats, we made sure that the best dancers were performing. Many times we were fortunate to see Maya Plisetskaya, one of the greatest ballerinas of the twentieth century. Born in 1925, she was still dancing in 1996. She performed Tchaikovsky's *Swan Lake* about 200 times. In the *Dying Swan* ballet with the music by Saint-Saëns, her incredible arms fluttered like wings or ripples on the water. The public would enter into a trance when she appeared on stage. If she was the biggest name on the Moscow stage in the 1960s, she was also the nicest person. Alan tells the story about his chance encounter with her in the Brussels U.S. consulate in the 1970s. Both of them had come to apply for a visa. While waiting, they struck up a conversation and started talking like old friends.

On Sunday mornings at the Bolshoi the children had their own ballet performances, where they loved sitting on the first row overlooking the orchestra pit. These were not kiddie productions, but the highest quality ballets like the *Hunchback Horse* or *Sleeping Beauty*.

The several halls of the Conservatory of Music on Guertsena Street were always packed. It was interesting to stroll among the Intelligentsia crowd in the courtyard before a performance. The concerts would be of superlative quality. I remember a concert when father and son David and Igor Oistrakh were playing a concerto for two violins by Johann Sebastian Bach. I never heard anything like it: the two violins were simply talking to each other. I often attended international competitions there and enjoyed listening to young virtuosos from many countries.

The Russians craved a window onto the West. Radio programs from the west were scrambled, and, of course, there were no foreign

TV programs. The common people usually read the Soviet newspapers posted on street billboards. Only a few privileged readers had access to the foreign press in the main public libraries of the capital.

This is why the Russians were so eager to see American movies, which we showed at our apartment twice a week. A close friend, Federico di Roberto, third secretary from the Italian embassy (in the 1990s, he returned to Moscow as ambassador), would provide a running translation of the dialogue. Our guests also enjoyed these showings because they gave them an opportunity to see our home and discover how we lived. One evening, a full delegation of the African section of the Ministry of Foreign Affairs descended upon us. Alan had left to pick up one of the guests, and I was alone to receive the Soviet officials. The six men rushed in and, like locusts, spread throughout the apartment looking at all the rooms. They were particularly interested in checking what type of books we had on our shelves.

A very special Soviet guest, Vladimir Dudintsev, appeared at one of our movie showings. His 1956 novel *Not by Bread Alone* had made quite a splash. The story of an inventor struggling against Soviet bureaucracy, it infuriated the officials but pleased Western readers. A frequent guest at our apartment was Mark Bernes, the well-known movie actor and singer. He would stand in our living room reciting his lines and generate a contagious emotion. Some years later, in Volgograd (the former Stalingrad), as we walked along the paths of the military cemetery, we were accompanied by a moving voice mourning the deaths of 1.5 million Soviet soldiers during the battle against the Germans in 1942-43. It was Mark Bernes's voice.

Poetry readings were most popular in Moscow. The crowds seemed mesmerized by authors reading their works employing the rich, deep sounds of the beautiful Russian language to expose their souls. The readings sometimes took place in cramped apartments, with guests sitting wherever they could find room. If someone wanted to smoke, he or she would go out on the landing, since smoking in a public place was *nekulturny*, or not civilized.

Poets were considered valued members of the intelligentsia. Anna Akhmatova, born in 1889, was a revered poet in Russia. She started publishing during the 1910s. The Bolsheviks executed her former husband, poet Gumiliov, in 1921 and imprisoned her son, Lev, a few years later. Her masterpiece *Requiem*, composed between 1935 and 1940, concerns the people's suffering, most particularly women's, under the Stalin era. She was partially rehabilitated in the early 1960s and for the first time was allowed to travel abroad, where she received international prizes. When we lived in Moscow, her name circulated among the intellectual circles, both Russian and foreign. She died in Leningrad in 1966, the year we left the Soviet Union.

One weekend we were invited to the dacha of Bella Akhmadulina, the most famous woman poet since Akhmatova. Friends and guests gathered in Akhmadulina's secluded rustic dacha to listen to her reading. On the bridge leading to her house we met young girls and a group of people dancing to the sound of an accordion. This privileged group did not seem to have a care in the world.

My memories of Moscow are usually associated with winter scenes, Siberian temperatures, and permanent snow on the ground. After the last summer days, when we were still able to play tennis outdoors in the sports complex of Luzhniki, the winter started with a bang. The central heating systems in all the capital's buildings were turned on simultaneously like clockwork in early November, whatever the outside temperature. Small Russian children looked snug all bundled up in their fur coats and hats. Their *valenkis* boots, made of black felt and rubber slip-on shoes, protected them completely from the cold. *Babushkas*, or old women, were hard at work clearing the road.

At the end of the winter, mountains of snow were left on the sidewalks. We had to leave our car in the courtyard, since there were no garages. Many occupants of our building would run an electric cord from their floor of the building to their car, thus avoiding problems caused by a frozen battery. We could not do that since we lived on the sixth floor. Our Italian friend Federico started his Mercedes by remote control and let it warm up before he came downstairs. The Russians were full of admiration for this high technology.

Cars had to be clean at all times, and the police strictly enforced this rule. It was a hard rule to comply with, since the streets quickly turned to mush. For the Russian drivers coping with the winter was a real *tour de force*. Cars had no defoggers, and windows had to be kept open whatever the temperature. Windshield wipers were often stolen, so they often had to drive without them.

A short drive from Leninsky Prospect # 45 would take us to the gothic skyscraper of Moscow University and a beautiful esplanade overlooking the whole city from the Lenin Hills, now returned to its former name of Sparrow Hills. Skiers would slide down the embankment toward the Moskva River. Another popular slope for sleighing, below the fortified walls of Novodevichi Monastery, ended on a frozen pond.

The paths in the parks were frozen over, and we would spend our Sundays skating around Gorki Park, stopping occasionally to eat a steaming *pirozhki*, or small meat pie. Loud speakers would pour out joyful music. The courtyard inside the Embassy was turned into a skating rink. We liked to go cross-country skiing near Moscow. Across the fields we could see the hardy Russians enjoying their favorite pastime, tumbling into the snow and rolling over in it. A special treat for the children was a ride in a troika through the frozen forest.

As Alan's job consisted of monitoring the relations between the Kremlin and Africa, many of his colleagues among the African embassies formed a jolly group, which met regularly. They liked to call themselves the group *"des sans chemise et sans pantalon"* (without shirt and pants). The group also included diplomats from the Middle East, Asia, and Europe. All could speak French and English equally well. The ambassador from Senegal and his wife, the Loums, were the aristocratic leaders of the group. The Egyptian ambassador was a poet. Nejib Bouziri, the Tunisian ambassador, and Ferida, his wife, a pharmacist by profession, lived in an elegant residence of the nineteenth century nobility on Katchalova Street. The previous occupant of that house had been Lavrenty Beria, the chief of secret police under Stalin. The rumor was that secret tunnels linked the residence with the Kremlin underground.

Gatherings among foreign diplomats provided a relief from the repressive existence we led in Moscow. I can still see *Le Monde* bureau chief Henri Pierre clowning between couples on the dance floor with a red rose hanging over his ear. *Newsweek's* Moscow chief, Bud Korengold, and his wife Christine, organized a "Roman Orgy." Picking at grapes from reclining couches felt like utmost decadence.

We had ambitious plans for Philip's schooling and hoped to enter him in a Russian school. During the summer of 1964, he started private lessons in Russian so that he could—or so we thought— join a local school. Soon we realized how hard it was for him and how heartless on our part to put so much pressure on him. So we changed our plans: Philip, age 9, and Diane, age 6, were registered at the American-International School situated downtown near the Ministry of Foreign Affairs. Sylvia, age 8, and Karen, age 5, were to go to the French school located in the French Embassy, a fairytale-like pseudo-gothic brick residence built by Igumnov, a nineteenth-century textile magnate. I do not recall the rationale for splitting the children in this fashion. But they all seemed to thrive in the very different education systems. Both schools had students from many countries, speaking English in one and French in the other.

We registered Diane in the neighborhood music school. Practically every city block had one. From an early age Russian children start music theory and play an instrument in a severe and strict environment. When I brought Diane to her class, I could hear what sounded like prodigies playing in every room.

Two wonderful French *au pair* spent one year each with us and were our lifesavers. Maryse was a postdoctoral student in Russian linguistics, a rare opportunity for her to be in Moscow, since no foreign students were accepted to Moscow University in those days. Being free during the day allowed her to practice the language a great deal. Marie Louise, who was with us the second year, did not speak Russian but was an accomplished pianist. Both were attentive with the children while taking advantage of their Russian experience.

We did not have as much luck with Soviet maids. We tried several ones unsuccessfully and became worried that we would be blacklisted by the UPDK, the governmental administration for the diplomatic corps. So, when this organization sent us a not particularly pleasant solid-looking middle-aged woman, we made an effort to keep her. She worked a few hours per week. It was more than obvious that her main job was to report on us. We assumed she was at least a lieutenant in the Secret Service. Every Thursday she would tell us openly that she had to go to a "meeting."

Harriet, Alan's mother, came to visit us. She stayed in the National Hotel overlooking Manege Square and the Kremlin, where the adventures of Kay Thompson's *Eloise in Moscow* also take place. Unfortunately, Harriet did not relish her stay as much as Eloise did. She received weird phone calls in her room every night, and the stress became too great, so she left the country after a few days.

It might seem like a paradox but during the frequent visits I made to the Soviet Union in the years following our Moscow assignment in the mid-sixties, I found that the American embassy was closing itself off more and more from the Russian people. Especially after the new U.S. Chancery was built, the compound turned into a fortress protected by high-security devices. The embassy personnel lived within the walls, existing in a self-sustaining world, with greenhouse, bowling alley, entertainment, shopping, and medical facilities.

On June 12, 1964, a reception was given at Spaso House "in honor of the Inter-University Committee on Travel Grants Representatives." It turned out that the Soviet couple assigned to us there became our closest friends. In fact, our acquaintance was to impact that family permanently. Yevgeny Sokolov's official title was chief of the Foreign Department of the Academy of Pedagogical Sciences. Rita, his wife, was a tall and vivacious woman working for the Russian Academy of Sciences. We struck an immediate friendship and began seeing each other frequently. I remember visiting them in their one-room apartment, where they lived with his mother and a baby girl. The grandmother slept in the kitchen with the child. They owned practically nothing. Once, I complimented the single painting hanging on the wall and felt terrible when she offered it to me. Having a private apartment made them part of the privileged class, though. In the 1960s, the great majority of Muscovites lived in communal apartments.

We became even closer over the years, especially after Rita married her new husband Nikolai Philippov, an engineer at Moscow University. Whenever we met them, it was essential that we follow the unspoken rules. To be able to see us on a regular basis, they were probably recruited to report on us. On our end, we had to keep the American embassy informed about our meetings and conversations. This was the price we had to pay on both sides. They passed the scrutiny of the police guard at our apartment without any apparent problems whenever they visited us for dinner or to watch movies or to share Thanksgiving with us. We never stopped exchanging letters. Every time they traveled outside the Soviet Union (within the Iron Curtain countries), she would send me postcards.

Rita was my best friend. She was a brilliant scientist working on the fairly secret field of plasma research at the Russian Academy of Science. She talked profusely, had an effusive and warm personality, and laughed a lot. Her English was much better than it appeared at first. Like most educated Russians, she was widely read, including in English literature, and could recite by heart entire pages of prose or poetry. She had a passion for the theater. Through a cousin of hers, who was a stage director, we were able to attend rehearsals and go backstage.

In the late 1980s, Rita introduced me to the archaeology circles of Moscow and to members of the Academy of Sciences. Thanks to her, I was able to join the Russian team excavating the remains of a seventeenth-century estate situated on the grounds of the Pushkin Museum.

We spent many evenings with Rita, Nikolai, and their friends around the proverbial Russian kitchen table. There was food to munch on, washed down by vodka, wine, cognac, or whatever they could find. We talked about everything under the sun except politics late into the night. Strangely enough, every time we visited Rita and Nikolai in their apartment or in their country dacha, they were accompanied by a couple of friends. I realize now that the "friends" had been drafted to carry on their surveillance assignment.

Years later, Alan arranged for their younger daughter Olga to be accepted at Hotchkiss Prep School in Connecticut. Olga was the first Russian student ever to study independently in the United States without being part of a chaperoned group. With a strong mathematics and physics background acquired at Moscow State University, she had no trouble being accepted to Dickenson College. After college, she moved to New York City and joined the ranks of successful young people in the financial world during the boom years.

We heard the terrible news of Rita's illness and death on July 4, 1990. We were in Odessa at the time after completing the circumnavigation of the Black Sea on *Katy II*, our 44-foot French ketch sailboat. The end of her life was very sad. As long as she had been useful to the Soviet system, she enjoyed the privileged status of the *Nomenklatura*. But when she became too ill to deliver, she was treated as a reject. Ravaged by cancer, she was kept on a stretcher, given the lack of a proper bed in a ward. Her other daughter, Julia, who was a pediatrician, was the one to give her morphine shots to alleviate the pain. Later in the 1990s, I stayed with Nikolai year after year while I worked on excavation projects in central Moscow.

Although the communist regime had tried to suppress religion, churches were overflowing at the main feasts of Easter and Christmas. On those days, the police would surround the churches to stop the "hooligans" from creating trouble at the doors. Easter at the Novodevichi Monastery was a joyful occasion to eat *paskha*, or cream cheese cake. Sitting on long benches by the church doors, old women were selling painted eggs and other handmade handicrafts. The liturgy in an Orthodox service is very lengthy and may last all night. The faithful stand. Dramatically, priests emerge from and disappear behind the gilded iconostasis. Multiple candles, icons, beautiful music, and an overwhelming scent of incense create an atmosphere of intense religious emotion.

We celebrated one Christmas in the Patriarch's Cathedral of the Epiphany built in North East Moscow. It was the largest church in Moscow at the time. The service lasted until early morning, but somehow the Russian church music was so beautiful that we did not mind standing for hours. The Russian congregation, which consisted mostly of old women, stood in the back of the church. The diplomatic corps and foreign guests had their own area near the apse. I noticed the German-Austrian actor Curt Jurgens standing beside me.

Missing during these religious celebrations were the bells. For seventy years the Soviet government forbade the tolling of bells. When they were heard again, after *Perestroika* in 1985, their beautiful sound took our breath away. We still treasure an LP recording of the bells of monasteries and churches from various provinces that Russian friends gave us.

Communism created its own school of painting. "Socialist Realism" was an idealized form of art that was supposed to inspire the population to be productive within the framework of the communist society. Some of these works are quite good, and I enjoy looking at the permanent exhibit of them shown at the New Tretiakov Gallery every time I visit Moscow. The sculpture of a youthful factory worker and a healthy woman farmer seen at the Park of Economic Achievements near Moscow is one of the best-known examples of this art. Ironically, this monumental statue had been placed on the Soviet pavilion erected for the Exposition Universelle held in Paris in 1937, facing the building representing Nazi Germany.

From 1932 until 1956, not a single exhibit of contemporary art from abroad was allowed in the Soviet Union. During the Khrushchev era, signs of liberalization in the arts appeared with the first exhibits of artists like Picasso in 1957. For Russian artists, however, all doors remained closed, although some of them were able to show their work in galleries in London and other cities. At the Manege show in 1962, Khrushchev ridiculed Russian contemporary abstract painters, comparing their work with what a donkey could paint with his tail. When we lived in the Soviet Union, it was only in the secrecy of their apartments that Russian artists could show their work. Nonofficial painters were accused of "formalism" and considered parasites by the Soviet government. Some of the artists were declared mentally ill and locked up in insane asylums. Others were reduced to alcohol. A few survived by doing illustrations or menial work. We had a chance to meet several of these artists and to purchase their work. Personally, I think the 1964–66 period produced the most talented modern painters Russia has known. They worked under incredibly harsh conditions. Their studios were cramped, they had no painting supplies, and they relied on some of us to buy those supplies abroad. They used wrapping paper because they lacked canvasses. One of the paintings we bought was done on an oven baking dish.

Some of the prominent artists we knew included Oscar Rabin,

his wife Valentina Kropivnitskaya, Plavinsky, Nemukhin, Sitnikov, and Zverov. Oscar Rabin was considered the leader of the "dissident painters" in 1965. The open air exhibit he organized in September 1974 was bulldozed. We visited his studio near Preobrajenskaya (Transfiguration) Square, located in a dilapidated district far from the center of Moscow. We bought two of his gloomy paintings, dominated by gray and heavy black outlines and stressing the difficult life. In the larger painting, representing Moscow, a light touch of pink indicates a sunset and the faint hope for a brighter future. Rabin's "nationality" was Jewish. He later immigrated to France and now lives in Paris. Ironically Oscar Rabin was the guest of honor at a lavish event hosted by the Russian embassy in Paris in the spring of 2009. For me, who had first known Oscar during terrible times, this rehabilitation was most moving. His wife, Valentina died in Paris that same year.

Sitnikov, an extremely talented artist, lived across the street from Derjinsky Square, where the Lubyanka prison and KGB headquarters once stood. A long canoe hung from the ceiling of his incredibly crowded apartment. He was a former inmate of an insane asylum and showed us his asylum ID card with pride. He died miserably in New York.

Georges Costakis, a Greek national working for the Canadian embassy, was an anomaly. The several rooms of his Moscow downtown apartment were filled with major paintings, from Impressionists to Constructivists (Tatlin), Primitivists (Goncharova) to Rayonnists (Larionov), and the great names of abstract art like Kandinsky and Malevich. When he left the Soviet Union, he made a deal with the Soviet government whereby he would leave half of his paintings in Moscow and be allowed to donate the other half to a museum in Athens.

In contrast to the struggling artists I just described, one painter was much luckier and was accepted by the Soviet authorities. His name was Ilya Glazunov. We met him and his wife quite often and enjoyed their company. He painted mythical characters from Russian medieval history and folklore. He also illustrated the novels of Dostoevsky and Gogol. His figurative style appealed to Western taste by presenting the "Russian soul" in its most romantic and tragic manner. In July 1964, his one-man show in the Manege nineteenth-century building attracted a large public, but it was somewhat controversial given his ambivalent attitude toward the authorities. He became well known abroad by doing commission portraits of celebrities such as Gina Lollobrigida and public figures such as Indira Gandhi or the King of Sweden. His triplex apartment on top of a modern building overlooking New Kalinin Avenue was always full of both Russian and foreign potential clients. A giant mural in progress occupied a whole room. On the upper level of his apartment, which one reached by steep stairs, an exceptional collection of priceless icons was displayed.

His beautiful wife, Nina, was the daughter of Alexander Benois, an early twentieth-century painter associated with Symbolism, the Ballets Russes, and part of the "World of Art" movement. Benois was particularly known for his theater settings and costume designs. For mysterious reasons, Nina fell to her death from the top floor of their building in the late 1990s.

For most people St. Petersburg is the jewel of Russian architecture. It is true that the northern city, created by Peter the Great in 1703, is probably the most elegant example of eighteenth- and nineteenth-century baroque and classical styles in the world. On the banks of the majestic and misty Neva River, surrounded by magnificent palaces, St. Petersburg appears like a museum to the visitor. In Pushkin's poem, written in 1833, "The Bronze Horseman" becomes the symbol of this beautiful city. At the same time, the equestrian statue impersonates the tsar and the cruelty of authoritarian power. The "little man"–a recurrent theme in Russian literature—desperately looks for his beloved throughout the city, to be finally crushed by the frozen storm of the Neva River.

Personally, I have always found Moscow more interesting in spite of its chaotic architecture, or maybe because of it. One never knows what one will find around the corner, since styles of different periods coexist. This was even truer in the 1960s than it is today. One would come upon a wooden *isba* next to a modern building, a baroque palace of the nobility next to a Stalinist skyscraper, or a fifteenth-century church near an Art Nouveau apartment.

The earlier settlements of Moscow go back to the eleventh century, as the 1990s excavations near the Kremlin and the old city

Kitai Gorod have established. (Kitai was improperly named "Chinatown," since Kitai means China but also "fortress" in the Tatar language.) From the oldest stone buildings dating back to the fifteenth century still standing to the Eclectic and neo-Russian style, the capital's architecture is long and rich.

It was to discover the little-known treasures of Moscow's architectural history that five of us–American, French, Swiss, and Norwegian—created the GEW, the Group of Enthusiastic Women. Twice a week, we would visit a district, stop by buildings of interest, discover hidden courtyards, and explore churches.

The first area we studied was Lefortovo, a neighborhood built in the severe classical architecture of North East Moscow, where foreigners settled in the seventeenth century. Peter the Great spent a great deal of time there visiting his Dutch and German friends. This tour was led by one of our friends.

We soon realized that we would learn more if we had a professional guide specialized in architecture. I was responsible for the organization of the excursions and decided to turn to a local tourism bureau. Foreigners had never approached them before, and they were as thrilled as I was. Our jovial U.S. naval attaché, Bob Bathurst, fluent in Russian, became the interpreter. His enthusiasm well suited the mood of the GEW. Our guide, used to a Russian audience, made lengthy commentaries. For instance, the study of the fifteenth-to-seventeenth century architecture took several days.

The GEW rapidly became popular and grew in scope to include a cosmopolitan group of several dozens participants. The International School lent us their school bus to transport our ever-growing numbers. The group's excursions included visits to churches, monasteries, a chocolate factory, a perfume factory (my daughter Sylvia still remembers the powerful essence of rose that was extracted from the flowers), a horse farm, the museums' reserves, the Mosfilm studio, a Pushkin literary tour in Moscow, the archaeology of the Kremlin, and more. One of the most fascinating visits was to the school and backstage area of the Bolshoi Theater. We saw a class of young girls and boys, their bodies taut with effort, under the strict supervision of demanding teachers. We even saw prima ballerina Maya Plissetskaya and other main dancers of the Bolshoi

Company doing their warm-up before the performance. Their legs were wrapped in rags and coarsely knitted ankle warmers.

The GEW was institutionalized, if I may use that expression, in the 1980s. The eager volunteers who followed in our footsteps and organized excursions and other activities from scratch were eventually replaced by full-time paid "family liaison" specialists, assisted by Russian personnel. The difficulty and the novelty of what we accomplished were gone. By then, most of the American spouses were employed by the embassy (replacing Soviet personnel from 1987 on). In my opinion, they had lost the luxury of the time we had to create and do the unusual.

In Soviet days, we foreigners could only travel freely within a radius of twenty miles from Moscow, except for certain closed areas. Any longer trip required special permission from the UPDK, the section of the Foreign Ministry that handled services to foreign diplomats. Even with these restrictions there was a plethora of interesting places to visit: estates of the aristocracy, churches, and monasteries such as Zvenigorod, Zagorsk, Istra, Kolomenskoye, and others. Among our most frequent fellow travelers in the 1960s and through the following decades were the Mussers. Mac worked with the American embassy. Evelyn is an outstanding photographer and was always eager to explore the country and meet the people of the Soviet Union. For me, the most beautiful churches belong to the early period of Russian history from the twelfth to the fourteenth centuries. I love the severe lines of the fortress-like Pskov churches, the reliefs on facades and portals of the twelfth-century Cathedral of Dmitri in Vladimir showing the syncretism between Christian and pagan motives, and the perfect harmony of the Church on the Nerl, built in 1165 near Suzdal.

It was during one of our many trips to Suzdal that Alan and I came upon an unexpected scene of people dressed in medieval costumes. The crowd was crossing a makeshift wooden bridge over the Kamenka River and climbing the steep bank toward one of the fortified monasteries. It was a scene being shot for a film directed by Tarkovsky about Andrei Roublev, the fifteenth-century icon painter. A few days later, we saw another part of the story being filmed in the town of Pechore near Pskov.

Our visit to Uglich was an example of how we used a crack in the system to push the limits of what was allowed. Uglich is believed to be where the tsarevitch Dmitri, last son of Ivan IV, was assassinated by order of Tsar Boris Godunov. A small Kremlin stands on the bank of the Volga there and includes the palace of Dmitri and several churches. The palace, built in 1482, is one of the rare secular buildings of that century still standing in Russia. It is built of fine bricks and decorated with colorful tiles.

In the 1960s, Uglich was closed to foreigners. By some odd regulation one was forbidden to reach it by private car or by train. Only a taxi ride was allowed. Somehow we found this out. So, we took the train from Moscow, then hired a taxi. Our taxi drove through the checkpoint. The barrier closed behind us. For years afterwards no one from the embassy was allowed to go through that gate.

Within the areas open to foreigners was Peredelkino, a very special retreat where members of the *Nomenklatura*, the top echelons of the Communist Party, had their secluded dachas. But the village was better known as the place where the poet Boris Pasternak had lived and was buried. His tomb, in a small cemetery on the edge of a field, became a shrine and was always covered with flowers. Several times a year, the readings of his poetry took place on his grave.

Alan made frequent official trips throughout the Soviet Union, including Siberia and the Caucasus, quite often in order to accompany members of the U.S. Congress. One of the official visitors Alan enjoyed most was New York Representative Barber Conable. After being elected several times, the congressman was appointed head the World Bank in 1985 by President Reagan.

Sometimes Alan and I had the pleasure of traveling just the two of us, making casual acquaintances on the way. We went to all but one of the republics of Central Asia—Kazakhstan, Tajikistan, Turkmenistan, Azerbaijan, and Kyrgyzstan. We were unable to visit Tashkent in Uzbekistan, however, because of a recent earthquake. Since natural disasters did not exist in the Soviet Union (!), no foreign eyes were supposed to see the damage. Incidentally, after he retired, Alan spent three months in Bishkek, capital of Kyrgyzstan, under the auspices of a Washington-based nonprofit organization as an advisor to the foreign minister, Roza Otunbayeva. Ms Otunbayeva made the top of the news in the spring of 2010 when she was appointed head of the transitional government following the clashes between Uzbek and Kyrgyz ethnic groups.

We found the local markets of Central Asia particularly picturesque, enjoyed the appetizing smell of shish kebab, and observed the women in their colorful costumes and the men relaxing in the shade while drinking tea. I remember being in a small plane flying lower than the Hindu Kush range of the Himalayas. Our fellow passengers were a farmer and his family taking their goat to market.

On another trip, this time to the northern regions of Russia, a small ferry took us to the early eighteenth-century wooden churches of Kizhi, located on an island in the middle of lake Onega. After retirement, Alan made it his cause to open up the inland waterways of the Province of Karelia to international boating, and he succeeded. Thanks to his efforts, Karelia was the first Russian province to allow free access to foreign yachtsmen.

In the exceptionally cold winter of 1966, with the temperature dipping lower than twenty-eight degrees Celsius below zero, we visited St. Petersburg (Leningrad in Soviet times). Alan, his eye behind the camera as always, asked me to pose for pictures. I was standing stoically in the middle of Palace Square when an old woman approached Alan and warned him to go inside immediately, "Your wife's nose is getting white and she is going to lose it," she warned. Fortunately, the elegant Astoria Hotel where we were staying was nearby. We rushed to the hotel and ran the hot water in the bathtub: this was the only way we could survive in our enormous, freezing bedroom.

Since the mid 1960s, I have returned to Russia more than fifteen times, led tours from Siberia to Ukraine and from Central Asia to Karelia. Involved in Moscow archaeology, as mentioned above, I published articles about the Russian archaeological expeditions in Moscow and in Panticapeum, or modern Kerch, a Hellenistic site in eastern Crimea.

Today, the Volga River cruises take throngs of passengers through regions that have been inaccessible because of the lack of roads. On my last visit to Russia in 1998, I found it exciting to spend ten days on the 30-foot sailboat of Dutch friends, traveling down the Volga from Yaroslavl to Nizhny Novgorod, called Gorki until 1990. Gorki was the place of exile for nuclear physicist Andrei Sakharov in the early 1980s. We were caught in a sudden storm and managed to save two Russian fishermen about to drown in the strong current.

I feel that my stay in the Soviet Union marked me more than any other assignment had. Fascinated by this country, its culture, and its language, I decided to resume my courses toward a graduate degree in Russian Studies at American University in Washington, D.C.

5

Guinea 1966–1968

In October 1958 Sekou Touré, president of French Guinea, said *"Non"* to General De Gaulle and chose to leave the *communauté* of former French colonies. Instead, he became the president of the newly independent Republic of Guinea. When Alan and I and our children arrived in Guinea's capital of Conakry in 1966, we found a country impoverished, living under a police-state system more oppressive than the Soviet Union we had just left. In contrast, we found the Guinean people to be the proudest and handsomest people we were to see in Africa.

Another Logan misadventure occurred during the crossing of the Atlantic on the SS *United States*. Seven-year old Karen was racing along the gangway where a shelf, used by the stewards to rest their trays, had been lowered and left in that position. Karen ran into it with an impact so strong that it knocked her down, leaving her with an enormous bump and a giant black eye.

We flew from Paris towards Guinea on the French airline UTA, with a stop in Port St Etienne, Mauritania, lost among immense sand dunes near an ocean whose turquoise color gave a misleading impression of coolness.

Alighting from the plane in Conakry, we felt as if we had plunged into a hot, steaming bath. The airport was cheerful, surrounded by abundant flowers and swaying palm trees. A few kilometers to the capital took us through an exuberant vegetation that hid sordid tin- or thatch-roof houses. The red laterite soil was baking in the sun. As we neared the city, the buildings became taller. Their unfinished floors seemed to be held together by rusty metal rods.

The capital is situated on a peninsula. One could see the remnants of a well-laid-out downtown area. Huge old mango and frangipane trees lined the wide avenues. Residences with louvered verandas and balconies stood in overgrown gardens by the sea. But one could also notice black mildew and decay spreading on the constructions.

In spite of the obvious poverty of the people, the Conakry pedestrians seemed unhurried, exuding a sort of contented lethargy. Since one lives mostly outside in that part of the world, we witnessed private scenes of total *dolce far niente*, the men lying in lounge chairs or hammocks, discussing the events of the day. The tall and beautiful women with aristocratic bearing, wearing flamboyant *boubous* and turbans wrapped high on their heads, moved slowly in a regal manner. I still remember one of my Guinean neighbors splitting logs with an axe, elegantly dressed in a pale blue muslin dress.

I had received a friendly letter from Molly Whitehouse, the wife of the deputy chief of mission (DCM), Charles Whitehouse, telling me all about the "superior" house which had been assigned to us. What we found was a large structure without any character but lots of rooms, closets, terraces, and an unfinished pool complete with a snake settled at the bottom. The flat, spacious, treeless yard would be great for games, Molly had suggested. This was not the only time in our wandering life that well-intentioned ranking officers' wives had presupposed our taste. But each time, over the resistance from above, we opted not for the practical but for the spectacular. Before describing the small paradise where we eventually moved, I must pause briefly at the big, uninteresting house where exciting events soon took place.

Two weeks after our arrival in Guinea, on October 30, we heard confounding news: the Guinean delegation en route to the OAU (Organization of African Unity) meeting to be held in Addis Ababa, Ethiopia, had been arrested in Accra, Ghana. Since February 1966, President Kwame Nkrumah of Ghana had lived in exile in Guinea as a personal guest of Sekou Touré. The relations between Ghana and Guinea were tense. Since the Guinean delegation was on a Pan-American Airways plane, the Guinean government immediately accused the United States of having fomented a plot against Guinea and made our country responsible for Ghana's action. In retaliation, U.S. embassy personnel and their families were put under house arrest.

It was a Sunday and the dumbfounded Americans returning from the beach, still drowsy with sand, sun, and salt water, rushed to their cars to go home. Radio Conakry blasted the news every half hour. The children and I went to spend the night at the house of the embassy doctor, Dr. Wilde, and his wife. Alan, as chief of the Political Section, went straight to the office since he was the duty officer. He finally made it home at two in the morning after crossing several road blocks. Reluctantly, we left our friends' house and moved back to ours. We were notified that we were then under house arrest.

Monday morning, Alan left for the office. At 10 am, as I was helping the children do their homework, I noticed a group of Guineans approaching our gate. With a shock I noticed that they were carrying guns. They were wearing ragged civilian clothes. The whole situation began to worry me: my husband had the car, and there was no telephone in the house. The closest Americans lived more than one mile away. Alan returned in the afternoon, escorted by a *gendarme*, and reported that the other American embassy families were also under house arrest. Hurriedly, he said that in case of trouble we should climb over the wall to our immediate neighbors, the United Arab Republic (UAR) Chancery and the Yugoslav Embassy Residence.

Then he left. The children and I went on a reconnaissance expedition to study the escape routes over the walls. Hardly had we walked a few steps from the house when a threatening voice yelled, *"Rentrez tout de suite à la maison!"* ("Get back inside immediately!"). We noticed two guards in a tree over our fence, waving their guns at us. The group by the gate was getting bigger. Philip tried to open the shutters of his room and was yelled at again.

In the evening we heard the news that Robinson McIlvaine, the American ambassador, had found his house broken into and his wife Alice cornered into a room with their two children. The McIlvaine family remained under house arrest for a couple of days.

The atmosphere in the streets of Conakry was volatile. The eighth anniversary of Guinea's independence was being marked by demonstrations and huge gatherings at the stadium to hear speeches given by the president.

On the third day of being prisoners in our home, the civilian guards were replaced by men in khaki or faded blue uniforms. They belonged to the Militia, but not to the Gendarmes, who were a regular government police force.

Our fear went up a notch when our regular night watchman opened the gates to let the Militia enter. Now, they were practically in our house. One of the soldiers had brought his sheepskin. He took off his shoes, and there, in the shade of the mango tree, accomplished his afternoon prayers.

Colleagues from our embassy stopped by our house several times to offer their help and ask if we needed food. They were met with hostility by our guards. *"Tu ne peux pas parler aux Logans.* (You can't talk to the Logans). Bring them food if you want and then get out!"* A *gendarme*, politely and in good French, tried to intercede. Alan explained that he was a diplomat and that we had an agreement with the Ministry of Foreign Affairs. A sullen-faced young guard holding a bare bayonet answered, *"Je m'en fous, tu es en prison."* ("I don't give a damn, you are in prison.")

Later, a Peugeot pulled up in front of the house. A man in a Mao Tse-tung tunic came out. In perfect French he explained to us that he was responsible for the district and had orders to protect the Americans. However, nothing could be done yet to free us, since the armed guards had received orders from the local committee, which in turn was answerable to the section. But the section was now in session so nothing could be done. This meant more waiting. We remained prisoners in our own house for a whole week, much longer than the other embassy members.

This was our first introduction to Africa. Was it a preview of our life for the next two years? By then we had established friendly relations with our neighbors, the Egyptians and the Yugoslavs. They asked if we needed anything, cigarettes, bread? The Yugoslavs were handing toys over the fence. We were living in a bare house since our household effects, including books and toys, had not yet arrived. Surrounded by threatening guns, the children commented that it was the worst Halloween they'd ever had.

The first year, our four children attended the American-International school, but I also wanted them to follow the French school programs. I enrolled them in a French government correspondence course. I must say that our efforts to bring them up in two languages over the years have paid off, since they are bilingual today and are in turn bringing up their own children in the two languages.

Eventually, we moved into the house we really wanted. It was built as a circular *paillote*, or hut, with a thatched roof. A French architect had designed it and, for practical reasons, had built a cement roof under the thatch. A vast living room, a dining area, and a bar opened onto the terraces. The furniture was made of bamboo. It was impossible to keep books, clothes, or records in this non-air-conditioned part of the house, given the risk of mildew sprouting overnight from the humidity. The light streamed from windows all around. A series of terraces, shaded by palm trees, gradually descended toward the ocean. The swimming pool was a jump away from the house. In spite of the limited space, living in the *paillote* was utterly exotic.

Guinea is famous for its African ballets. The orchestra that accompanies them consists of various types of drums originally tied to magic and a *balafon,* an interesting instrument comparable to a xylophone. Several calabash gourds attached underneath the keys create the balafon sound. The Ballets Africains are quite famous and never stop touring the world.

Conakry had no theater, no cinema, no art gallery, and no concert hall. But it is amazing how a cultural void will trigger unsuspected talents. As a result, we expatriates came up with various skills we did not know we had. Our small community never felt it was lacking cultural entertainment.

Under the artistic guidance of one of the spouses, Philip, my oldest child, did his first painting, showing an ability he would need later in his profession as an architect. I opened a ballet school in our house for children and adults. With the help of Armand from the embassy administrative section, we tied long bamboo sticks to our living room furniture. My students used this improvised *barre* to do *pliés, relevés,* and *arabesques.* The classes ended with a happy splash into the pool.

We even produced a ballet performance for a sizeable audience. The choreography of the ballet marked the peak of my stage career. The "Tom-Clownery" libretto included three parts, with music by Ravel ("Suite de la Mère l'Oie"), Rossini-Respighi ("Boutique Fantasque"), and Saint-Saens ("Carnaval des Animaux"). My three older children were starring in the performance, which lasted all of three minutes! Since that time I have been full of admiration for choreographers who can produce two-hour-long ballets.

A crocodile story may give a flavor for the carefree life, spiced with practical jokes, that we were leading in Conakry. We were invited to a New Year's party at the pool of the Feldmans (he was head of the Conakry Technical Institute). Alan had bought a young crocodile, not more than four feet long, and put him in our bathtub for a couple of days. The children and I were scared to come near the snapping animal. The night of the party, Alan sneaked in with his "friend" and threw him into the pool. Two guests were swimming at the time. They saw the big jaws approaching full speed. Terrified, they flew over the water and made a frantic dash for the ladder. At the risk of appearing a traitor, I must say I had nothing to do with this joke, which I found cruel.

Guinea's countryside is beautiful because of its varied scenery: small mountains, valleys, lakes, forests, and waterfalls, even caves. Its almost European scale makes it different from the other countries of Africa. In an easy day's drive, one could reach any part of the country. We often took advantage of Alan's official meetings to visit the interior.

Several of these trips were to the mining and industrial complexes related to the production of aluminum. Guinea holds close to half the world's reserves of bauxite. The exploitation of this raw material and the production of aluminum were its main industrial activities. The richest ore deposits are located in the Boke region in the northwest, close to the sea.

One weekend, Alan had to meet the officials of the French company Fria 160 kilometers north of Conakry. The vast industrial complex included a refinery producing alumina and a smelting plant to produce aluminum. The company spread over many acres, and once through the fence, the visitor would be transported into a French landscape. The children and I left Alan in the modern headquarters buildings and went exploring. We found an Olympic-size pool. It even had the type of diving board with three levels that one sees at world competitions. The three older children wanted to play a trick on Karen and hid. Karen arrived, did not see her brother and sisters, and assumed that they had jumped from the highest diving board. She climbed up and jumped from that incredibly high structure. In retrospect, I imagine how scared she must have been, but the desire to emulate her siblings was all that mattered to her.

In the 1960s, the United States, the Soviet Bloc—including Bulgarians, Czech, Poles, and Hungarians—and the Chinese were competing for zones of influence in the freshly independent sub-Saharan African countries. Interesting documents now released show the exchanges between U.S. ambassador William Attwood and Secretary of State Dean Rusk during the Kennedy administration. In one of these documents, a memo to the State Department, Peace Corps director Sargent Shriver wrote: "Now is a favorable time to push out the Soviets." Today, fifty years later, it is sad to note that the Russians hold 85 percent of the shares of Fria, the former French company.

The position of the U.S. government was to promote assistance to the government of Guinea in the form of industrialization and education. About a thousand foreign technicians had been brought to Guinea in those years. At times, this struggle for influence between the different countries took a ridiculous turn. Apparently, a bunch of *bidets,* or footbaths, had been sent from abroad and were now sitting in a field. In their eagerness to outdo the Americans, the Soviets had sent an army of snowplows.

The Chinese came in large groups. They lived in secluded compounds close to their work sites and kept isolated from the rest of the population.

We were well aware of the rivalry between the United States and the Soviet Union, since many of the latter's nationals lived in Conakry. With our recent Moscow experience, Alan and I became the regular representatives of the Western embassies at social gatherings involving the Soviets. Our ability to speak Russian turned out to be quite useful.

Among our Soviet acquaintances were the Konapikhins. He was a journalist from the Tass Press Agency, and his wife was a dermatologist. They hated being in Africa and could not wait to return to their country. Besides, they did not own a boat. Life in Conakry was impossible without a motor boat. The French,

Americans, English, and Dutch all had one. Only the Soviets did not. They came to the beach in large groups by bus and ferry. The Konapikhins much preferred our boat to the transport provided by the Soviet officials.

The McIlvaines and the Whitehouses had powerful motorboats. Ours was a more modest Boston Whaler. Every weekend we would speed up toward "the islands" through a stretch of open sea. We would pass a small island where prisoners were rotting away in an abysmal jail. Then we would reach the island of Roum, probably used by Robert Louis Stevenson as a model for his book *Treasure Island*.

Once, we spent the night on Roum. This is the single time we used the beautiful blue, heavy-duty tent we had bought at the Printemps department store in Paris. It took so long to install and shake the sand off the canvas that we never used the tent again.

Alan liked to live dangerously. It was prudent to stop the weekly escapades to the islands before the rainy season. Although the sight of the violent storms was ominous to watch from our rooftop, Alan would always dare to sail one more time. During a last trip one summer, the sea grew vicious. This is when something funny happened to us and our guests the Konapikhins.

On our way back, a wave broke over the Boston Whaler. It filled up with water, the engine stalled, and the boat appeared to be sinking. The Konapikhins started throwing silverware, cups, and plates overboard. I think they were hoping to lessen some of the ballast. The scene was hilarious, as we were sitting in the water, but not frightening because we were approaching land and the boat was still afloat.

I have some advice for Foreign Service spouses: Do not beat the ambassador's wife at tennis. I did just that in Conakry, and I still suspect that Alan paid a high price later in his professional career because of my victory on the tennis court. (My Tunisia chapter will show that I may have been partially right).

During our stay from 1964 to 1966, the president of Guinea, driven by what might be called paranoia, constantly imagined plots being fomented against him. He would periodically break ties with foreign governments or private groups. The Dutch, KLM, Catholic priests, and nuns were expelled or arrested as we had been.

Sekou Touré came from a poor family from the Madinke tribe, one of the largest ethnic tribes of West Africa. From an early age, he adhered to the Marxist ideology, which he applied to his activities in the postal service's trade unions. He was elected as a deputy to the French National Assembly in 1956.

His presence was charismatic, and the way he brandished the slogan of "the people" electrified the crowds gathered at meetings and mass rallies. Sekou Touré was a handsome man with piercing eyes who dressed in smart outfits that were usually blindingly white or pale blue. He had an entourage of women, who wielded real political power.

Touré ran the country as a dictator from 1958 until his death in 1984. The opposition was ruthlessly eliminated. One of the most tragic cases was that of Ambassador Diallo Telli. We knew him personally in Washington before going to Conakry. A distinguished gentleman, he was one the founders and the driving force of the Organization of African Unity (OAU) from 1964 until 1972. He believed it was his patriotic duty to help his country by going back to Conakry. Upon his return, he was sent to one of the death camps, where he starved to death in 1977. Tens of thousands of dissidents were detained in camps, others were tortured in prison.

Before being appointed to Conakry, Alan served in Washington on the desk covering the five countries of the Entente, that is, Upper Volta, Ivory Coast, Dahomey, Niger, and Togo. While in Washington we had become very close to Dr. Seydou Conte, the ambassador from Guinea, and his family. Ambassador Conte was an exceptional person, a surgeon, poet, metaphysician, and musician. I recall a dinner at the Georgetown residence of G. Mennen "Soapy" Williams, the assistant secretary of state for African affairs. Dr. Conte proposed a toast, and his short intervention was brilliant, articulate, and bristling with wit. He certainly was unmatched by any other person present. Kadiatou Conte, his wife, was a beautiful Peuhl, or Foula, from northern Guinea, one of the dominant tribes of the country. Seydou and Kadiatou made a stunning couple.

However, when we lived in Conakry, we were cautious to keep our contacts with the Contes to a minimum, given the atmosphere of suspicion and the ubiquitous secret police. Being too close to them would have put their life in danger.

I saw Kadiatou a few times, though. In May 1967, she invited me to accompany her to the Donka Hospital, where she was providing her services as midwife, a highly respected profession in Africa. There were about thirty patients in the clinic. It is hard to imagine that there is one doctor per seven hundred persons in the United States, whereas there is one doctor per thirty thousand in Guinean towns and one for seventy thousand in the bush. What I saw was not a happy sight—young girls who did not even know they were pregnant, some already expecting just seven months after their last child, and schoolgirls who had been raped. Widespread venereal diseases were caused by men totally indifferent to the health of their partners and by the lack of education of the women. The women's bodies were wracked by multiple untreated pregnancies, as well as miscarriages. The Contes eventually went into exile to a neighboring African country. They were more fortunate than many of their friends.

In spite of the rupture of diplomatic relations with France, the influence of that country remained strong. Unlike in the British colonial empire, French colonization meant bringing a little corner of France to Africa. This was my personal experience when, in 1972, we made a trip by car from Lagos, Nigeria, to Dahomey (rebaptized the Republic of Benin in 1975). As we drove through Cotonou, the capital, I noticed that the butcher, the baker, the hairdresser, and the mechanic were still French, although the country had become independent from France in 1960. The police and the army behaved and dressed as the French do. The town planning, with wide avenues lined with trees, reminded me of France. At that time, the aspiration of the best-educated Guineans, such as the president, was to study in a French university and eventually reach the benches of the Parliament as deputies.

I found one of the best examples of the impact of French culture on Guinea during a four-day trip that Alan, our two older children, and I took to N'Zerekore, in the midst of the dense forests of southeast Guinea. We were part of an official delegation visiting the region. The flight was short and marked by a bizarre incident: as soon as the Russian-built small plane reached cruising altitude, a blizzard of wet snow started blowing from the air vents onto the passengers.

At N'Zerekore we were received with a great deal of ceremonial speeches and folkloric dances on the esplanade of the Hotel of the Sacred Forest overlooking a lake. The busy program included visits to a sawmill, a raffia- making workshop, and a plantation with a coffee factory and pig farm. We saw an entomological laboratory rich in insects and vipers, where vaccines were created. The scientific station, located on Mount Nimba (altitude 1,752m) was still run by a French researcher. Although the trip was organized by the Guinean tourism bureau, we could detect the traces of French influence everywhere we went.

The trip in this lush region was an adventure into deep Africa. The dense forest was alive with multiple animal noises and giant anthills everywhere. After crossing a suspension bridge and passing a waterfall, we reached a village, where dancing and singing greeted us. The shaman wore a realistic mask made of wood, straw, and beads. In another village we attended an incredible performance of very young acrobats. The tiny girls were thrown in the air by the male dancers, their bodies bent in two, landing precariously on the blade of a knife.

Africa always evokes bugs. Surprisingly, even though we had no screens to the windows of our living room, we never encountered major problems, with the exception of one incident. "Barry!" yelled Diallo, our houseboy (the term used in the former French colonies), to our cook one day. Diallo was standing in the middle of the kitchen, completely panicked. Diane and I rushed in and saw the problem: a huge spider, possibly a tarantula, was caught by surprise in the early morning. He saw us, jumped from one wall to the next, and disappeared.

We always took basic precautions to avoid getting sick. We washed raw vegetables using chlorinated pills. We never kept a wet bathing suit on and always ironed the clothes that had been hanging outside to dry. This was to avoid the risk of insects laying eggs under the skin, with the risk that those eggs would invade the bloodstream. But of course, the major preventive measure was to take medication against malaria. The Sunday morning ritual was an ordeal that lasted forever: Diane and Sylvia could not swallow the incredibly bitter Aralen anti-malaria pill.

However, in spite of Aralen, Alan caught a special strain of malaria while on an official visit to Niger. As he lay in his hospital bed, shivering with fever, through the fog of his delirium he saw vultures lining up on the roof of the next building, patiently waiting for the hospital to deliver a nice meal.

Speaking of diseases, I would like to mention the legacy bequeathed to Africa by a member of my family. In the 1930s my godfather, Lieutenant-Colonel Gaston Muraz, a French army medical doctor, started his research toward the eradication of sleeping sickness, or trypanosomiasis, caused by the tsetse fly. In 1939 he founded a medical center in Bobo Dioulasso, Upper Volta (today's Burkina Faso), which bears his name and still exists today. It is one of the oldest and most active medical centers in West Africa for research and treatment of malaria, HIV, parasites, and many other endemic diseases.

Our stay in Guinea marked the first time that our children went away to camp or school. At thirteen, Philip spent a few weeks in a summer camp in Switzerland. It was his first experience in mountain climbing, and he has relished the high altitude, particularly of the Alps, ever since. The whole family was as nervous as he was when we saw him off at the Conakry airport.

The departure of Sylvia, age 11, to England for a whole year was even more traumatic for all of us. She had been accepted at the Russian Legat ballet boarding school in Kent. We prepared her brown school uniform and dressed her doll in the same outfit. A picture of her ready to fly out with her white name tag around her neck still brings back a lot of emotion. I accompanied her to England. A stuffed hippopotamus I bought for her at Heathrow is still with her today, albeit full of patches, after half a century.

The first term at the school was very hard for Sylvia. Although the buildings were grand and the park was beautiful, the living conditions were harsh. She had to break the ice to wash in the morning. She was so homesick that she kept sending us desperate letters asking us to come and take her out. In one letter she wrote, "I will wait for you next Saturday, and we can leave together." Sadly, the letters took about three weeks to reach us, and Sylvia waited for us in vain.

She flew to Guinea for the Christmas vacations. After swimming in the tropical waters of Treasure Island, the return to foggy

England must have been difficult for her. Fortunately, things improved as the year progressed. Sylvia was in her dream world of ballet, which in fact she has never left.

Guinea was labeled a "hardship post" by the State Department and our stay lasted only two years, with an R & R (rest and recuperation) break to Europe during the summer. It was one of the most colorful and enjoyable of our diplomatic appointments.

6

Nigeria 1971–1973

The British Consulate in Lagos is a corrugated iron
coffin and a plank-like morgue containing a dead
consul every year.

—Richard Burton, explorer, 1861.

Nigeria could have been the lowest point of our overseas life. However, we survived quite well the two years in that country—labeled a "hardship post" by the State Department (as was Guinea)—by owning two sailboats and a pony and belonging to two tennis clubs. During our Nigeria years, first two, then three, of our children went away to boarding schools in Europe. The terrible void they left was compensated by an intense exchange of letters, which provided a vivid day-to-day account of all our lives.

We arrived in Lagos in 1971. The Biafra civil war, highlighted by destruction and unbearable photographs of starving children with bloated bellies, had ended a few months earlier. On January 15, 1966, army officers, mostly Ibos, had overthrown the federal government. The prime minister was assassinated. The Yorubas living in Lagos feared domination by thousands of Ibos. In 1966, General Yakubu Gowon became the head of the Federal Military Government (FMG). In 1967, General Odumegwu Ojukwu proclaimed the independence of the former Eastern Region, Ibo country. Fighting broke out between the FMG and Ojukwu. On January 15, 1970, the secessionist movement surrendered.

At the same time, the recent discovery of offshore oil in the Gulf of Guinea had attracted dozens of exploration and drilling companies. Nigeria became the hub of an oil boom comparable to the one experienced by Texas.

The main companies—British Petroleum, ConocoPhillips, Texaco, Shell, Exxon, Elf, Mobil, Gulf Oil, Agip, and Safrap—rushed to tap the newly discovered reserves. A giant oil-drilling platform named "Ocean Master II," under construction by Mobil, was a structure never before seen off the coast of Africa. Alan's functions in the Economic Section of the U.S. embassy, mainly as Petroleum Officer, propelled us into a world superbly described in the movie *Giants,* starring James Dean and Elizabeth Taylor. The movie is a saga of three generations of Texans dominated by the conflict between cattle barons and newly rich oil tycoons.

Our first impression driving from the Ikeja Airport to the city of Lagos was the sight of car, truck, and bus wrecks abandoned by the side of the road. As we approached the capital, the tropical vegetation gradually made more and more room for crowded clusters of shanty buildings with corrugated roofs.

Greater Lagos spreads over several islands separated by inlets, rivers, canals, and lagoons. The busy downtown of the Lagos Island was a disorganized network of narrow streets, shops, small factories, and outdoor markets. In contrast, a few wide avenues were lined with stately official buildings in typical colonial architecture, decorated with louvered porches and ornate balconies. The museum and the public library were surrounded by manicured lawns and set among flowering bushes.

The residential areas for affluent Nigerians and foreigners in Ikoyi and Victoria Islands followed a bland and regular pattern. There was nothing exotic about Ilado Close (which means "dead end" in Nigerian English), where we lived.

Our residence, like many around us, was an unimaginative boxlike semi-detached house with a screened porch running along the whole facade. The Nigerians must have inherited an aversion for mosquitoes from the British. Unlike Guinea, our Lagos house was equipped with screens and air-conditioners. The rooms were spacious and strictly functional, and the master bedroom was quite large. The color theme I inherited and which I retained in decorating the house happened to be orange and blue. The embassy had generously furnished the residence with two large dining room tables. I turned one of them into my desk when doing research for my Russian paper and preparing my French classes. Daniel, our cook, and Godwin, our steward (a term used in former British colonies), had their own separate quarters in the back of the yard.

Even the garden did not add any redeeming feature to our Nigerian home. It was flat and without trees except for a scrawny palm tree. Two trees had been uprooted early in our stay. They fell over into the deputy chief of mission's yard next to us. An open sewer marked the boundary with our neighbor. Vania, our blond American cocker spaniel, loved to roam through the sewer's grey muck and chase rodents. One day he returned beaming (or so he appeared to me), holding a big lizard in his mouth.

I found life in Nigeria different from the one we led at our other postings. A large colony of expatriates and a strong British influence created an environment that, in many ways, was a replica of the world they left at home. Throughout our diplomatic existence, we rejected the sheltered togetherness of Americans living overseas. We tried choosing houses too unorthodox for the taste of our embassy's administrative officers.

In Lagos our social life had to follow the rules of this homogeneous expatriate community. I was under pressure to belong to an array of women's clubs. It was hard to be original under those conditions. However, I learned to adjust, and in spite of these constraints, I managed to lead an exciting life.

Nigeria is the largest country in Africa, with over 120 million inhabitants (representing an amazing demographic growth from the 55 million figure of 1966!). The Yorubas, who live in the Lagos area, are the third largest ethnic group after the Hausa in the north and the Ibos on the coastal region of the Niger delta in the southeast. The Yorubas have a distinctive personality—self confident, exuding jauntiness. They speak and laugh loudly. A small brochure titled "How to be … a Nigerian?" written by Peter Enahoro, a Yoruba himself, circulated among the foreigners and delighted them. The author writes, with self-deprecating humor, short vignettes describing the customs of the Lagosians. A chapter is devoted to the "dash." A dash is not a tip, it is not a bribe, but a precautionary amount of money to avoid the nonrendering of a service. For example, if a waiter brings you the change for the amount you paid, you give him a dash so that he does not keep that change. Our own experience taught us that it was wise to give money when parking your car. The dash in that case was to prevent something bad from happening.

Looking at the classified ads in the local paper was an enjoyable pastime. The quaint English style and crude handling of the subject matter led to hilarious reading.

Two incidents illustrate my recollection of the Yorubas, who display a mixture of British polish with their own cultural traits. For instance, one would never know when or if our guests would show up. Sometimes they would bring friends and relatives. One evening, we had planned a sit-down dinner with elegant white tablecloth, silverware, and fine glasses, all provided by the embassy. One of our Yoruba guests started playing with his fork. I became worried about the fate of the wine glass in front of him. I was right to be worried; the fork finally smashed the glass to pieces. I am still stunned at the recollection of the scene, especially given that the guest did not even acknowledge what he had done.

Another instance is emblematic of how hard it is to understand people of another culture. During our stay in Moscow we had become quite close to the African diplomats. The African embassies were small, and the life of their members was isolated and hard. So, we had "adopted" some of them, in particular a Nigerian family. We included them in many of our dinner parties and family outings. We were delighted to find the family again several years later in Lagos and hoped to renew our friendly relationship. But the diplomat appeared cold and distant when we met again. It is possible that he felt uncomfortable being unable to match our invitations in his modest house, or maybe because he had no more use for us. I guess I will never know the answer to the question. I want the first explanation to be the real one.

As has often been the case in my multicultural experiences around the world, I was more impressed by the personalities of women than of men. One of my volunteer activities in Lagos was to write for the weekly newspaper *Fancy That*, published by the American Women's Club. I was in charge of the "Profile" column where I conducted interviews with prominent women. I met Bisi Braithwaite, a Yoruba, in her in her downtown office in Lagos. She was thin and wearing a designer outfit from London. She was the mother of six, a graceful hostess helping her husband in his work, and a career woman in her own right. Her great-grandfather— Chief Taiwo—had been a powerful trader in the eighteenth century who owned a large section of Lagos.

Bisi had read law in England. Upon her return to Nigeria she worked for the government in the field of conveyances (property law). In addition to her profession as barrister, she ventured the creation of a boutique. Asked if she felt any discrimination against women in her profession, she smiled and said, "Not from the professional world, but quite often from the clients or the litigants in court. In order to win recognition, women have to prove themselves and have to work twice as hard as men."

Even without much education, women traders in the outdoor markets showed the same determination to take control of their own lives. Most times with a child strapped to their back, they would run their business with an iron hand. They had to be tough in order to succeed in this competitive economic environment.

Throughout our diplomatic career we came to know more than fifteen African countries. I found that each of these countries has its own distinctive and creative form of expression—the innate musical sense and spontaneous harmony skill of Zulu choirs, the superb wooden sculpture of Cameroon, Mali and Ghana, the natural talent of Guineans in creating ballets, just to mention a few. For me, Nigeria stands out in two areas: arts and crafts and a dynamic literary life.

Walking around town one would often find a weaving and dying workshop. Strips of cloth in brilliant colors would be drying in the sun. Artists used the techniques of "tie and dye" and batik to express their creative designs. I own two batiks from Nigeria. On one of them a huge head cracked into two parts can be interpreted as the eerie representation of a split personality.

"Twin 77" was the best-known artist when we lived in Lagos. A twin, or *Ibeji* in Yoruba culture, is a spirit. The death of a twin is surrounded by mysterious rituals. Twin 77 took that name to show that, as a surviving twin, he could make the transition from traditional beliefs to modern society. We visited his gallery in Oshogbo. He was driving a hippy car wearing necklaces, pendants, and rings. One evening, he surprised us by dropping by our house when we were having a dinner party. He had brought his paintings and spread them all over the floor. Our guests were interested, but did not buy anything.

The universities of Ife, Nsukka, and Ibadan constituted centers of Anglo-Saxon culture, enhanced by exchanges of professors and students. The number of student visas to the United States grew from 140 in 1964 to 985 in 1972!

The 1960s produced an exceptional generation of Nigerian writers, among them Chinua Achebe, Cyprian Ekwensi, and the playwright Wole Soyinka. They wrote in English and their readership went well beyond Nigeria's borders. They often describe the traditional life in the village, the rather idealized ancestral values, and the hard transition to the modern style of life brought on by Christianity and Western culture. They write about their country sometimes with a sense of humor and sometimes in a sharp satirical tone about the corruption and the profiteering of city people, particularly politicians and bureaucrats

In January 1973, I attended a symposium at Lagos University to which John Updike had been invited as a prestigious guest speaker. He was forty at the time and a lecturer at Harvard University. He spoke on "the adequacy of the European form of novel to express either African or American forms of reality."

By accident we became the happy owners of quite unusual doors. One morning, a "trader" stopped with his truck in front of our house. He wanted to sell us a heavy mahogany door made of three panels on which I could distinguish carvings of animals, birds, and more. I said "could distinguish" because the wood was a dirty, dark grey color. Apparently, that door came from an African hut and had been exposed to the weather and to cooking smoke. For several weeks I worked to rejuvenate the wood. Today, without any tinted varnish, the wood has found again its original color of rich dark brown. The doors seem to predate the use of firearms, since the only weapon represented is a machete.

Life with an only child is hard. Karen became one when the three oldest siblings went away to boarding schools in Europe. It was hard for the three of us. The house had been full of the wonderful music of the 1970s, such as the Moody Blues and Neil Young. To this day I cannot listen to songs by Cat Stevens without being submerged by waves of sadness. Nothing was more depressing than taking the children to the airport after their vacations. Frequently, the *Harmattan* wind blowing from the Sahara desert would engulf us in clouds of dust, matching our depressed mood. Karen missed above all Diane, who was the closest to her in age, helped her with math, and was her best sparring partner. Fortunately, Karen's social life became as busy as ours in no time. She slept over at friends' houses, sailed, played tennis, or spent days at the beach. She took piano lessons and enjoyed singing in a choir.

Riding Goldie, her adorable Palomino pony, was Karen's highlight of the week. She usually rode him after school. One day, the trainer told us that we had to give the pony back since the owner was returning. Actually, there was a shady business going on at the club, and the trainer was trying to rent the pony twice. We did find another acceptable pony after much effort. But no horse could ever replace Goldie.

In addition to her schoolwork, Karen was taking a correspondence course to cover the French curriculum. She made her debut behind the wheel in the parking lot of Ikoyi Island with me at her side. On the rare evenings when the three of us stayed home, we enjoyed playing three-handed bridge. But I guess Karen never got used to being left alone with her parents. The low point came when Alan got too busy at the office and forgot her birthday. Later, in Tunis, she wrote a moving "fiction" story about a girl who was abandoned by her parents.

Raising children is not easy, but doing it long distance is even more frustrating. Alan sent the children long, typewritten letters with lots of advice and lofty thoughts about proper behavior and life. No matter how much advice we offered, in the end the trust we had in them was our only guarantee of their doing the right thing. My letters were more on the light side, with daily accounts of our life overseas. In return the children kept us happy with a constant flow of letters. Thus we managed to keep the channels of communication open during the difficult years of adolescence.

In 1971–72, Philip was a junior at the Collège du Leman in Geneva. He enjoyed more freedom at the boarding school than Sylvia, who was a grade behind. Several months into the school year, he warned us that the pressure was on from his peers to do drugs. He kept us informed every step of the way and, finally, told us how he gave up resisting.

In 1972–73, the three older children attended St. Stevens, located on Via Aventino near the Roman Coliseum. It was a top-notch school, academically speaking, but quite permissive. I guess we will never know exactly what was going on there, but I have a feeling it was quite wild. I suspect that Campo de Fiori, where young people gathered, was not only a flower market but also a center for drugs. Studying in Rome must have been a dream for the children. Imagine studying Latin sitting on a column of the Forum!

Alan would often admonish the children, saying, "You are going to bed too late! Sylvia, why won't you take American history? Do more sports; taking dance classes every day is too much; be careful not to go to dark churches with priests; do not break the curfew time; you need to balance your budget; taking four liters of wine to watch a movie is not acceptable; and so forth." Once Alan scolded Philip, telling him it was not appropriate to visit girls in their rooms. Philip, having grown up with three sisters, saw nothing wrong in socializing in the communal dorm. But our comments were far from always being negative. We much preferred supporting them and praising their accomplishments. We fell all over ourselves to compliment Diane on her excellent report cards. We loved the comments from one of her teachers: "Diane is a typical giggly hysterical sophomore, and we are delighted with her."

Our lives in Nigeria revolved around the sports clubs we had joined. The pony club for Karen, the Lawn Tennis Club on Lagos Island, and the Ikoyi Tennis Club for the three of us. Karen was a full-fledged participant in the activities of these clubs.

The Lagos Yacht Club was located at a strategic location where the Cowrie Creek runs into the harbor. Canoes, fishing boats, and ferries filled with passengers in colorful national dresses sailed across the bay. The LYC, founded by the British about a century ago, was run like the navy. Races took place three times a week: on Wednesdays, Saturdays, and Sundays. Their rules were seriously observed and the organization of the club was strict. One afternoon, the race had generated so many complaints that the committee did not render its decision until eight at night, and no one would have dared leave earlier. The club was a lively and breezy place to meet at noon. Many of the white-collar workers left their downtown offices to come here for a scampi lunch. On Wednesdays, the special was "cheese and pickles."

Diane and Karen, respectively thirteen and twelve, had their own sailboat—a fourteen-foot catamaran, or Aqua Cat, which they had baptized *Catimini*. They fearlessly sped all over the harbor, sometimes even making a nuisance of themselves by zigzagging between the racing boats.

The girls had a terrifying story of their own: One Sunday, the two of them were on *Catimini*, and Alan and I were not far away in our old seventeen-foot wood *Wayfarer*. We were quite far from land when we noticed a black line running above the horizon. This was trouble brewing. In no time the line squall hit us with fury, howling winds, and sheets of hail. We saw their lightweight boat picked up by the wind, fly over the water, continue over the beach, and end up crashing into the thatch roof of a *paillote*. That feat, with a happy ending, was so incredibly fast that we did not have time to feel any fear for their safety. Anyway, we would have been unable to help them, since we had to anchor our own boat offshore until the storm was over.

The usual destinations of our weekly sails were Tarkwa Bay or the Lighthouse Beach on the ocean. To reach both beaches we had to follow the whole length of the harbor, then cross it. This could be an exciting experience. Lagos is an extremely busy commercial port. At any given time more than thirty freighters, container ships, or tankers waited at the entrance for a place to berth. There was barely enough room for a ship to pass another in the narrow channel, which was less than three hundred meters wide. I was petrified, in retrospect, when Philip and Sylvia described the frightening moments they experienced when returning from an outing to the beach: the *Wayfarer* got squeezed between two monsters while sitting helplessly with its sails slack from total lack of wind.

I must admit I was always relieved after having safely crossed the harbor and finished each trip by hugging the shore of Victoria Island on our way back to the LYC. One day Alan and I were on our way to Tarkwa Bay, rounding the stone sea wall jutting out from the bay, when our mast snapped. We were tossed about in the rough water and exposed to the ocean surf. We felt completely helpless. I soon realized that we were smack in the middle of the path of the maritime traffic and started to panic. As expected, a freighter was making her approach. There was no way she could slow down or engage in maneuvers to avoid us. At the last minute a police boat rushed to pluck us out of the way.

Not all my stories at sea are frightening, however. Once, while sailing near the jetty, Alan saw something shining at the bottom of the sea. He dove in and found a watch. That watch never stopped working. We hung it over the beautiful picture of him sailing near Notre Dame cathedral in Paris. It ran for a long time even after his death in April 1997. It rang at exactly the time he died, and continued doing so for several months.

I should not mention this, lest I ruin my image as a decent crew, but I really fouled up our return back to the yacht club one day. Alan asked me to throw the line, but I could not find it. He had to repeat his maneuver. I found the line the second time around, but it was all tangled up with the jib sheet. On his third attempt, I threw the line, knots and all, to a friend on shore, but I was not holding the other end! It worked the fourth time when the friend threw us the end of the line.

Another time when we were sailing back from the beach, the rollers behind us were enormous. Karen thought this was great fun. Alan said, "Rollers are all right. Only if they break over the boat, they could be dangerous." I put on a second life jacket. Our "tallest" sailing story, however, was the Badagry Race. I defer to Karen's account of that story, which appears in this book's appendix.

Nigerians eagerly play tennis and polo. The two tennis clubs we had joined had many excellent players. Tournaments took place several times a month, sometimes attracting world champions. I still remember the kind face of Arthur Ashe, who won the Nigeria Lawn Tennis Open Championship.

Every day, sometimes more than once, the three of us would go to the club. We entered tournaments at all levels: club, regional, and national. I even ended up as the number two player of Nigeria! We had many amusing experiences at the club. I recall the countrywide

Open Lawn Championship. It was a mad confusion. People were milling around, not able to find their partners and ending up with the wrong ones. On another day, I really played ghastly tennis, and my British partner remarked wryly, "I say, your game is a bit off today!"

This was the time Karen learned how to play tennis, and I am proud to say I helped her during that early stage. But she much preferred a handsome coach (whom we had baptized Robert Redford). Karen has always been a natural player with a lovely style. It did not take her long to beat me, and to do so consistently in Tunisia, two years later. After long interruptions due to back and knee problems, she played in competitions for many years.

Alan and I had found a great way to beat the humid heat of Lagos. We would play singles at the hottest time of the day. Needless to say, we would soon be totally drenched, but continued playing and felt as if we were in a sauna. Then, we would take a good shower and go on with our various activities. At cocktail or dinnertime in the evening, we would feel and look fresh and dry. The other guests would be drooping like wet mops.

I made an attempt to exercise my "little grey cells" while in Lagos, but the effort turned out to be so painful that I felt on the verge of a breakdown. I was in the middle of a protracted cycle of courses toward a master's degree in Russian studies at American University in Washington, D.C. All I was trying to do while in Nigeria was to obtain three credits by completing a reading course. The topic of my course was *The Possessed* by Dostoevsky. I would escape from the tropical heat by studying in the library of the Institute of International Relations. As soon as I left the building, I had the impression of reaching a state of deliquescence. My professor, Dr. Vadim Medish, made harsher and harsher comments on the essays I was sending him. Finally, he announced that my text was so unreadable that he needed me to send its translation into English.

It took me close to ten years to complete my Russian degree. The fact that I had skipped the undergraduate years did not help. Besides, our various foreign assignments interrupted my studies. Faculty and students joked about the student who never went away, but they also admired my efforts. Eventually I received my

M.A. with honors. Since the difficulties I encountered in Lagos, I have always felt that the African climate is debilitating and that mental activity while living on that continent requires superhuman efforts.

I was teaching French to the fifth through ninth grades at the American International School. I am not a born teacher. For me, teaching represents more of an intellectual challenge than an enjoyment. And I did get the challenge I was seeking! First of all, it was a tough age group. It would have been a miracle for them to feel the motivation to learn an unknown language. Every night, I was racking my brain to design ways to entertain the classes. The hot and humid temperatures sapped the energy from the students (and teachers). But, the main problem was the lack of teaching tools and books. I had to create most of my pedagogical props from scratch. One day, I had a brilliant idea and went to the Alliance Française and found films (videos did not exist in those days). I arranged for my classes to watch the series *Belphegor—The Phantom of the Louvre* once a week. Surprisingly, the whole student body seemed to have developed a sudden taste for the French language. The days of the showing, my classroom was filled, standing room only!

I do not have any particularly pleasant recollections of the food I ate in Nigeria. In fact, I only remember two repulsive incidents.

Dutch friends had invited us for a dinner at their home. To my horror, they served two dishes I could not even look at: octopus, followed by an eel main course. Another evening, the administrative officer from our embassy and his wife had invited us to a sit-down dinner. The first course looked appetizing, with golden morsels. As I chewed on a piece, I asked what it was. The answer made me practically choke: we were eating giant Nigerian snails! Indeed, they had nothing in common with sophisticated French *escargots* swimming in garlic, butter, and parsley. The second course arrived. This time, I was more cautious and inquired before eating. Guess what? The same "delicacy" had been prepared another way, in a delicious-looking *gratin*.

Toward the end of our stay in Nigeria, the government decided to bring changes to the driving regulations. Driving on the left would be replaced by driving on the right. Nigerians are pretty unruly

drivers in spite of the white-gloved British-trained police trying
to control the wild and noisy traffic. A joke was going around: To
make the transition from left to right easier, the new system would
apply to the cars one day and to the busses and trucks the following
day!

Lagos's population exuded an appearance of entrepreneurship. The
dynamic activity was dizzying. I often observed that the products
sold in shops or even on the sidewalks were packaged in Nigeria
or bore the name of a Nigerian company. Very few other African
countries could boast the same thing.

There was something else I observed, both during our travels
within the country and through conversations with Nigerian acquaintances. Since the beginning of the oil boom in the 1970s, the
country went through a rapid process of urbanization. Workers left
the old banana or pineapple plantations to find quick money in the
cities. Armed with transistor radios, they would join the crowd of
unemployed people living in the shantytowns of the mushrooming
greater Lagos.

The economy increasingly began relying on the oil revenues
from petroleum and less from a diversified agricultural production, hence making the country more vulnerable to the vagaries of
the world commodities market. The military government, riddled
with corruption and graft, seemed quite remote from the problems
of its impoverished population. One of the most unstable regions
was still the Niger Delta, in the Ibo region. Incidents were quite
frequent in the Port Harcourt area through which the oil transited
from offshore platforms. The population living near the pipelines
did not profit from the oil boom. Their poverty was more brutal
than anywhere else.

Obviously Nigeria constituted a strong attraction for the world
powers. Forty-two countries had opened embassies in Lagos. We
lived in a cosmopolitan world, socializing not only with Nigerians
and Americans, but also with the British, Canadians, Dutch, Ro-
manians, Canadians, Germans, and others. As had been the case
in Guinea but on a smaller scale, being bilingual in English and
French and fluent in Russian opened new horizons.

An administrative circular issued by the U.S. embassy set the rules of representational functions. The ambassador's secretary served as a central clearing point. Rules of protocol forbade us to entertain either civilian or military officials above our rank within the embassy. Before planning a function the date had to be tentatively cleared against the social calendar maintained by the ambassador's secretary.

In spite of these stifling constraints, Alan and I maintained a stimulating life and made a number of personal friends. We also managed to liven up what could have been a stilted official life. *La Fête à Montmartre* accomplished such a feat. With two other American couples— Earl Bellinger, head of the administrative section, and his wife, Michelle, and Jim and Emily Thurber—we threw the most enjoyable event of the season. It was quite a colorful and decadent event. The flavor was totally French. Our friends' lawn was turned into a food fair with booths offering onion soup, *boeuf bourguignon*, cheeses, and *crêpes Suzette*. The two other hostesses and I were dressed as Montmartre prostitutes. The best costume contest was won by a young woman wearing a paper dress eventually trimmed to a minimum by the male guests using scissors. There was a Java and Tango competition.

Our gracious ambassadress, Carolyn Reinhardt, was one of the judges and seemed to enjoy herself tremendously. We were fortunate to have her husband, John Reinhardt, as our ambassador. He was one of the first black American ambassadors. They both were wonderful people and helped make life within the embassy quite pleasant.

I remember an incident that could have been most embarrassing. Alan and I were invited to a small, formal sit-down dinner. Rushing (as was always the case with Alan) from a long sail, we arrived late, after the ambassador. This is an absolute no-no according to the "bible," *Social Usage Abroad*. But not a remark was expressed by the Reinhardts at that time or later. I could have been intimidated while interviewing Mrs. Reinhardt for our *Fancy That* local newspaper, but she put me totally at ease, telling me about her family, her several assignments overseas, and her involvement in the community wherever she lived.

At the end of two years, we started packing. It was a traumatic experience for Vania, our American cocker spaniel. We had acquired him when he was three months old. He was so adorable then that everybody would stop to pet him when we walked under the cherry blossoms by the Jefferson Memorial on Sunday mornings. Unfortunately, Vania was not made for the constant moves required by the diplomatic life. I still see him sitting beside the crates on the upstairs landing of our Lagos house. He was looking at us with his sad brown eyes, and then he forgot his manners. We decided he would be happier spending the rest of his life with a nice family in southwest France.

7

Tunisia 1973–1976

Three major events marked our stay in Tunisia. The children reached the age of young adults and became a source of pride, but they also turned Alan and me into helpless wrecks in the face of their uncontrollable independence. Alan acquired a real sailboat that totally changed his life, and mine, too. From then on, our family became a *ménage à trois*—Alan, the boat, and I. And, we happened to be in Tunisia at the time of the largest UNESCO archaeological salvage expedition ever undertaken. As a result, I became seriously interested in archaeology, a strong avocation that was to last for close to twenty-five years.

There was no house available for us when we arrived from Lagos in the summer of 1973. Actually there was, but we did not like the land-locked Tunis suburb of El Menzah, where the Admin section wanted us to move to be near other embassy residences. As usual, we chose to get away from the pack. We had our eyes on another house, located in Gammarth, the elegant suburb northwest of Tunis, and right on the Mediterranean.

Because the Gammarth house was not ready, we had to "rough it" for several weeks at the Hilton Hotel, near Tunis. Alan was going to work every day, but the children and I settled down in the hotel. We established our headquarters by the pool. Soon, the children knew everybody among the hotel staff. The members of the orchestra became their good friends, and we did not miss a single one of their rehearsals. I did not mind being confined to the Hilton without a car. It felt like being on a fantasy island in the middle of the Pacific. One problem though: the U.S. government did not pay for the food of embassy dependents. We coped with the situation by taking turns at lunch. Each day, only one person was allowed to eat, while the rest of us munched on mustard and ketchup sandwiches.

We moved into our house toward the end of September. The beginnings were not easy. The painters, plumbers, and electricians had not completed their work, and our personal effects were slow in coming from Nigeria. Besides, the political climate was uncertain due to the Middle East conflict. As Alan wrote on October 15: "There are guns thundering again in the Middle East, with each of the two Semitic tribes which live by the book again living by the sword."

This was the fourth time Alan was a witness to the Arab-Israeli wars. In 1948, he was working at the United Nations in Paris as an intern during the first conflict following the creation of Israel. He actually saw (as we all did) the French and British fleets sailing off the coast of southern Turkey during the 1956 Suez war. As political officer in Conakry, Guinea, Alan was following the tense political situation and feared that President Sekou Touré would break diplomatic relations with the United States in 1967.

The situation was worsening. The Yom Kippur war [1] was imminent. The Egyptians were advancing against the Israelis. As a result, our installation process was stalling: Would we have to pack again before even finishing unpacking? Eventually the situation quieted down, and in January 1974 Secretary of State Henry Kissinger brokered an agreement on troop disengagement.

We could now settle down. We hung our pictures and curtains, installed the embassy furniture, and had fun transforming a tiny room into a Tunisian corner with colorful blankets, a copper table, a leather hassock, and a multicolored lantern.

The house was unique, built on three levels. The entire roof was a terrace. We used the main terrace, which was off the living room, constantly. Karen's and our bedrooms were far apart on that level and sort of jutting into the sea. The dining room, the kitchen, and two other bedrooms for the children or guests were on the lower level. Young people were always welcome to eat one of my imaginative salads on the downstairs patio, shaded by grapevine. One crossed a small garden, opened a rickety wooden gate, and there was the beach.

One stormy night, one of our first in late September, Alan was invited to a stag dinner. Karen and I stayed alone, each in our bedroom, as exposed to the elements as in a lighthouse. We were scared. We could hear the waves crashing. The wind was howling. The surf was monstrous. The beach seemed to have shrunk and come dangerously close to the house. For more than two weeks we felt as if on a boat lost in a storm. We learned later that it was one of the worst storms Tunisia had ever known. To get our thoughts away from raging storms, we went to see the film *Poseidon*, about an ocean liner overturned by a tidalwave. Whose idea was that anyway?

Then, one morning we woke up in total silence. Alan asked, "Has the Mediterranean dried up?" The winds had stopped. That night we saw from our windows a romantic scene: the moon and the glistening path it created on the ocean.

Alan's position in the embassy as economic counselor fitted his academic qualifications. His total proficiency in French was an important asset in his work. His responsibilities covered all areas of the Tunisian economy, including the textile industry and the exploitation of natural resources like natural gas and petroleum. He flew by helicopter to see the oil rigs off the coast near Sfax. He was involved in a number of trade negotiations, the relations with Europe and Africa, and monitored U.S. investments. When American archaeological expeditions were launched in Tunisia, he was responsible for the implementation of the cultural agreement signed between the American and Tunisian governments.

Alan was outgoing, cheerful, and jovial, even at the office. I remember calling him there one time. His secretary answered, "Just a minute, Alan is in the middle of a joke." At dinner parties he was always the center of attention, talking nonstop. In fact, I have always wondered whether this trait explained his slow advancement. Maybe he irritated people with his directness and knowledge. Personally, I believe that the real reason is that he spent too much time away from the power center in Washington. For him, working in the field was far more important than applying his energy toward the next promotion.

The stalling of his career began to be apparent in Tunisia. I decided to confide in the wife of a senior embassy officer. From this conversation, I discovered that I was not imagining things. Who had destroyed the progress of his diplomatic career, and when? I have my suspicions. Alan continued doing his work with enthusiasm and professionalism for another decade and retired at the young age of fifty-seven.

Karen stayed with us for another year while her three older siblings studied in Rome, a quick flight away. The French Lycée of La Marsa was the best school around. She had not been in the French system since Moscow, and the adjustment was not easy. She was accepted in *quatrième* (or eighth grade) with an emphasis on languages and literature. By the end of the year, her report cards were excellent. Before starting university, she received a perfect score of 800 in her achievement test in French.

Every day she rode her bicycle from Gammarth to La Marsa, eight miles away. The up and down route offered a lovely scene over the Mediterranean, but it also had steep slopes. Karen's life was busy with private lessons in piano, tennis tournaments (she was already beating me by then), and the beach. Quickly she became part of the *jeunesse dorée* of Gammarth–La Marsa and made it to the top when she became part of Dawcer's Club. This is what I called the group of Karen's friends, usually seen on their mini 50 cc Honda motorcycles.

On November 18, I made a ridiculous birthday cake for her. It was a brown mosque surrounded by a cherry orchard. A driveway of pecan nuts, lit by blue candles, led to the top of the mosque.

I could not live in style without a sports car. I found a second-hand red Fiat 1500. It was convertible and quite dashing. It cost only 300 dinars. We had trouble going into first gear, and the shock absorbers were shot, but it became quite a hit with all of us.

One evening, Alan and I were driving through fields on our way back from a dinner party in Carthage. The top was up (fortunately). All of a sudden, I felt a heavy weight crushing me. A horse had run into us, practically sat on me, and then continued crossing the road to get to another field, where the grass was apparently greener. Alan realized immediately what had happened. He ran to the field to make sure that the horse was all right, while I sat in the car, totally numbed by the violence of the shock. Back at the house, it took a long time to pull the multiple slivers of glass from my face with tweezers.

At 8:30 a.m. on October 1, 1973, I reported for work at the United States Information Service (USIS). My office was in downtown Tunis near the St. Vincent Cathedral, avenue de France and avenue Bourguiba. I worked there part-time for eight months. Besides doing translations and writing press releases and letters, my main responsibility was to research and voice weekly reports on developments in Tunisia and the Maghreb for transmittal to the Voice of America's French-to-Africa division. The first time I was in the soundproof studio, I was quite nervous. It felt weird not to hear my own voice and to be cut off from the outside world, except for two large headphones. Apparently I had a good voice for radio reporting. I enjoyed the USIS environment, which put me ahead of the news.

During Ramadan, which fell in October that year, the Tunisian employees were dragging, as if all energy had deserted them. I suppose my presence turned out to be helpful at the office during this difficult month of fasting. On October 27, a holiday marked the end of Ramadan in a festive atmosphere. Men had been sitting all day at cafes, waiting for sundown. Everyone was dressed in bright new clothes. Firecrackers went off. People visited each other, offering the traditional pastries.

Soon after my arrival I decided that my central interest while in Tunisia would be to learn about the often-belittled history of the Punic people and understand their mysterious art. I wanted to know why a brilliant general like Hannibal, who accomplished the incredible feat of crossing the Alps with his elephants and threatening Rome, was finally defeated and his country, albeit temporarily, annihilated.

Ancient Carthage was the capital of a civilization that spread westward from Phoenicia, or modern Lebanon, all the way to Gibraltar and beyond at the end of the second millennium BC. It was a time when navigation in the Mediterranean became easier, thanks to the replacement of flat-bottomed ships by more seaworthy vessels with keels. The rich Phoenician cities needed to expand their markets and were looking for copper, gold, silver, and particularly tin.

At first the Phoenicians settled in Cyprus for more than a hundred years. Then they reached Malta, Sicily, Sardinia, Algeria, Morocco, and the Iberian Peninsula. Their trade relations extended as far as the British Isles. It was in 1101 BC that they settled in Utica, in the north of modern Tunisia.

The largest colony, and the hub of the Punic empire, was to be Carthage. Virgil in his poem *Aeneid* described the mythic foundation of the city by a legendary princess, Queen Dido, also known by her Greek name Elissa, sister of King Pygmalion of Tyre. The year was 814 BC. "Punic" was the Romans' name for Phoenician.

By looking at maps one can easily understand the reasons for the strategic importance of Carthage. First, it commanded the Sicily straits between the eastern and western parts of the Mediterranean.

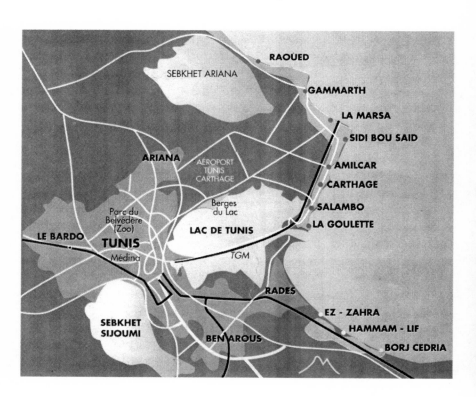

Secondly, the site of Carthage was ideal both for commercial and military activities. It is a promontory protected by two bodies of water, the Lake of Tunis in the south and the Shebkhet Ariana Lagoon in the north, with a high point called Sidi Bou Said. Ships could always find a haven, either on the east or on the west, depending on the direction of the prevailing winds. Carthage received the name of Qart Haddash, or New Town.

At the height of its power the Carthage metropolis had 100,000 inhabitants and ruled over a rich country. For centuries, it fought against Greece. Later, Rome became the main enemy. The three Punic wars against Rome ended in 146 BC.

My first encounter with the archaeology of Carthage was at a meeting with Father Jean Ferron, a Jesuit *Père Blanc*. He was a legend. He had made the study of Carthage his single passion in life. He often found himself in disagreement with other archaeologists, particularly the French, but was well accepted by Tunisian archaeologists. He was an ardent defender of Punic culture, which was sometimes scorned as "primitive" by the "classical" scholars of the Rome and Athens schools of archaeology. He was a one-man operation. His office was a small, cluttered room located in a former Beylical (that is belonging to the former Bey) palace by the sea, and now housing the headquarters of Carthage archaeological expeditions.

Père Ferron was a small and friendly man in his fifties. On that first day, he talked to me for three hours about Punic mythology and religion. Right away he told me about the topics he was working on: anthropomorphic sarcophagi, frescoes in Jewish tombs, Punic inscriptions on *cippi,* and several necropolises in the interior. A few days later, he asked me to proofread an article he was writing about funerary *stelae.* I came to his office regularly, becoming one of his collaborators. He would greet me in the morning, wanting to share his latest hypothesis. I seemed to be a useful sounding board for his new theories. He would write his texts by hand, without drafts, in small notebooks or use an ancient typewriter.

It is often said that Scipio the Younger razed Carthage to the ground and threw salt over the land so nothing could ever grow again. This is a usually accepted view found in history books. But Père Ferron never concurred. For him, Carthage was not permanently destroyed, but was rapidly resurrected to become a prosperous province of Rome and its granary.

I am very grateful to Père Ferron for making me a "puniphile" (I created that word). For five years thereafter I became more and more involved in Punic archaeology, as I became a staff member of the Oriental Institute of the University of Chicago excavations in Carthage. Well into the 1990s, Père Ferron kept sending me long letters. His enthusiasm was still as vibrant as ever as he described his many publication projects.

I feel unabashed in saying that our stay in Tunisia stands out as the most fun-loving time we had during our years overseas. It was an easy life. The official duties and our private life were not really separated. This was fortunate since the pace of entertaining, which is an important part of a diplomat's work, was unrelenting. In the course of three years in Tunisia, a total of 1,012 guests came to our house. (This number does not include our children's friends, who frequently dropped in.) Each dinner or cocktail had to have an official purpose to qualify for "representation" vouchers to be reimbursed by the embassy.

Relationships with the sophisticated Tunisian upper class were easy. This well-traveled, highly educated elite included lawyers, doctors, academics, and government officials. Ethnically, and to a larger degree than the rest of the Tunisian population, their mixed origins could be explained by history. They had always had contacts with Europeans. Three centuries of Ottoman rule had left Turks and Circassians. After seventy-five years as a French protectorate, the presence of France was still quite strong. Habib Bourguiba, Jr., nicknamed Bibi, the son of the president, had a French mother. His wife, Neila, was half French.

Tunisia's foreign community was made up of diplomats, businessmen, oil company executives, journalists, and *pieds noirs* (literally black feet, meaning French born in North Africa). Except for some official dinners in downtown Tunis, most of the social activities took place in private homes located in the northern suburbs of Tunis: La Marsa, Sidi Bou Said, Carthage, and Gammarth, where we lived.

This was an elegant crowd. The women wore black slacks and silvery blouses. Giorgio Re, an Italian fashion designer living in La Soukra, a Tunis suburb, created beautiful knit clothes worn by

many women, including me. Necklaces, bangles, and heavy bracelets made of Bedouin silver were the rage. One spoke French, English, and Arabic, sometimes in the same sentence. The use of the
familiar *tu*, kisses, and an extravagant display of affection were *de
rigueur.*

The Italians set the tone for this lively group. They loved to
dance and, under their influence, there was not a single party without dance music. The first time we invited a large group of friends,
we put on tapes after dinner. It was a total disaster, the music was
mediocre, and our guests left early. Alan and I were mortified, and
we sent an SOS to our children. With their help, we greatly improved our musical background. "I Shot the Sheriff" by Eric Clapton
brings back lots of memories. One evening our guests were taking
a breather when Philip and Sylvia, our two oldest children, spontaneously started dancing, totally oblivious of the world around
them. Their performance was superb, and every one watched them,
mesmerized.

The residence of American ambassador Talcott Seelye and his
wife is probably the most spectacular of all American embassy residences in the world. It is perched on the top of a hill facing Sidi Bou
Said. Decorated in the superb taste of the ambassador's wife, Joan
Seelye, herself a talented painter, the residence combined Tunisian
architectural features with modern artwork loaned by the State Department and the personal treasures she and her husband had collected during their several diplomatic assignments to the Persian
Gulf. These included an ornate chest from Kuwait. Examples of
wool sculpture with surprisingly modernistic designs were hanging on the walls surrounding the atrium. The nearby reddish rocks
of the vertical cliff led the eyes to the vast expanse of the Mediterranean far below.

In such a setting, official dinners were quite a spectacle. One
evening, under the new ambassador, Edward W. Mulcahy, who arrived in 1976, the guests were disappearing under heaping flower arrangements. Everything was sparkling—the chandeliers, the
crystal glasses, the silver. Waiters in traditional Tunisian costumes,
wearing the *chechia* (a small cylindrical hat) with a black pompon,
spun around between the long tables. They came out from the
kitchen as if choreographed by an invisible conductor, one holding
a soufflé, another a roast, the third a mountain of ice cream.

Toward the end of our stay in Tunisia, Philip spent several months working with an architectural firm called Taktak. I think Tunisian architecture should be on the required curriculum for all architecture students because it has so much to offer. It is characterized by the purity and simplicity of basic forms such as cubes, domes, and arches. The influence of Roman architecture remains strong. Porticoes and peristyles give lightness to buildings. Take for instance the inner courtyard (or atrium), with its basin and fountains, the heart of the residence, as it was in Roman times and still is today.

The simple lines of whitewashed buildings are interrupted only by the blue of massive nail-studded doors, wrought-iron work, and the delicately carved wood of *mashrabies* (porches from where, in olden times, the women could look out into the streets without being seen). The color blue is rich in symbolism. It is intended to keep away the "evil eye." In Turkey, horses wear necklaces of large blue beads for good luck. Blue has another, more practical reason as it is a repellent against mosquitoes. Tiles made in the town of Nabeul covered all walls, floors, pools, and built-in furniture. These tiles are an explosion of floral motifs or mythical animals.

The deputy chief of mission of the Italian embassy, Federico di Roberto, whom we knew in Moscow, and his Belgian wife, Beatrice, threw elegant dinner parties. Their residence was one of the most beautiful examples of Tunisian architecture. All the rooms opened onto an inner courtyard. One of these rooms was a bathroom lined with floral tiles and dominated by a balcony. In its center stood an ornate marble bath.

Our children were going through the really difficult age of adolescence. We had four teenagers at the same time, Karen being the youngest at fifteen! Alan wrote, "Every night, we dread the squabble about whether they can go dancing. The girls think only of freedom, boys, going out, boys, dancing, boys." Once a late night at the Baraka discotheque forced us to ground Karen for a week.

Our three older children were at the time of their lives when college was the most important preoccupation—after having fun, of course. The topics of our letters were achievement tests, advanced placements, and SATs. Philip was already in Stanford University in California. His courses toward a degree in architecture and design

sounded quite appealing and included visual thinking and relax-
ation exercise. Sylvia had applied at Radcliff, Wesleyan, MIT, Mid-
dlebury, Cornell, and Stanford. She chose Stanford. Diane, a junior,
kept us frustrated with the comments from her teachers: "She never
seems to use her vast resources of imagination, quick mind, vivid
style, interests, etc." She eventually chose University of California,
Santa Cruz because of its free lifestyle.

We lived a page of history on November 20, 1973, when "Dr.
Excellency" Henry Kissinger landed in Tunis on the presidential
plane Air Force One. He was to hold a one-hour talk with President
Bourguiba. The streets were emptied except for the police. In the
airport VIP lounge, journalists, photographers, and American
officials milled around. At six o'clock, everyone rushed to the
tarmac. The plane landed. The special guard of honor froze. A few
Secret Service men jumped on the steps and looked around. Then
the secretary came out, chewing gum. He went down the gangway,
walking fast, and was immediately surrounded by a group of
journalists. Still almost running, Kissinger, his interpreter, and
the Tunisian minister of foreign affairs were whisked away in the
first car, followed by fifteen black official cars. Led by screaming
sirens, the convoy rushed to the presidential palace in Carthage.
Kissinger's interpreter, who was of Armenian origin and probably
the best interpreter the State Department ever had, spent the night
at our house. We certainly enjoyed every word of his behind-the-
scenes stories.

Tunisia is a country rich in history spanning Punic, Roman, Van-
dal, Byzantine, and Ottoman periods. Alan and I enjoyed walking
around the ruins of Roman cities such as Dougga, Tubhurbo Majus,
and Maktar. These antique remains were totally deserted, unlike
Greek sites, which are always crowded with tourists. One day, I
picked up a handful of *tesserae*, or mosaic fragments, from a temple
floor. I could have kept them, or a slab of marble for that matter,
and there would have been no one to stop me.

The Romans lived a good life in Tunisia during the *pax romana*,
which lasted three centuries after the end of the Punic wars.
Although their cities were provincial, they could be proud of
their usual forum, temples, baths, and theaters. Roman architects

designed naturally air-conditioned residences by building them underground, with a central courtyard open to the sky. The cool temperatures and the trickling noise of the fountains must have been most comfortable during the hot summer months. To link the cities, the Romans constructed an efficient communication network. Their bridges stood the test of time, whereas the ones built in later centuries were periodically washed away during flash floods.

Mosaics in the Bardo Museum show scenes of life in Roman country estates. Around grand houses, agricultural activity takes place while the master of the house and his family lead a life of leisure, surrounded by servants. They sip wine, hunt, ride horses, and raise exotic species of animals.

In Tunisia more than in any other country where I have lived, I found a continuity of cultures through the ages. Each civilization borrowed from the preceding one. In addition to my earlier remark about the Roman influence on Tunisian architecture, I would like to give two examples to support this remark. The motifs of rugs created by Tunisian craftsmen today reproduce the designs found on mosaic floors dating from Punic and Roman times. The "hand of Fatma" in traditional Bedouin jewelry is supposed to bring good luck. This belief has its roots in the Punic religion with the representation on *stelae* of a priest stretching his hand to show his power and role as a protector.

In February 1943, the battle of Kasserine Pass in the north of the country marked a turning point in the outcome of World War II. The Panzer division of the German Afrika Corps, led by Marshal Rommel, was caught between the British troops coming from the west and the Commonwealth forces coming from the east.

In 1956, Tunisia proclaimed its independence from France, thereby putting an end to the French protectorate created in 1881. Habib Bourguiba was elected its first president. Chief of the *Neo Destour* party, he was considered a hero by the population. His first decision was to establish the emancipation of women, as formulated in the 1956 *Code Personnel*. This was a revolutionary step in the Muslim world. Personally, I never saw a woman wearing a veil or a scarf in that country. On the beach, in the streets, or in the workplace, women came and went freely. The situation is quite different today under Bourguiba's successor, President Zine El Abidine Ben Ali.

Bourguiba had wanted to make his country a modern state and create a dynamic economy. There was a free press, as we judged from talking with our journalist friends. Among these was Tanya Matthews, the *New York Times* correspondent and seemingly a permanent fixture in the intellectual circles of the capital.

The Tunisian population was conditioned to revere the *Combattant Supreme*. Every night on TV, like clockwork, one saw the president. He would be inaugurating a new plant or reviewing the military. Then the viewers would be treated to a newsreel showing the daily official meetings taking place in the Carthage Presidential Palace, with ministers or foreign dignitaries in attendance. As the years passed, Habib Bourguiba's health seemed to deteriorate. The rumor was that he had to receive enough medication to allow him to carry out even the minimum of his official duties and make his daily appearance on the nightly news.

Tunisia is a small country that you can discover by car in one day. But you would not want to do that, because there is too much to see, from the rocky Cap Bon, stretching into the strait of Sicily, down the picturesque coastline, all the way to Shott el Jerid, or salt lake, in the south where the movie *Star Wars* was filmed.

Alan and I went back and forth across the country numerous times. On one trip, we drove to the southeastern coast with Talcott and Joan Seelye. We took the ferryboat across the bay of Tunis, then went along hills clearly outlined in the November light. The winter wheat was coming out, and the leaves of the grapevines were turning red. After passing a truck with a camel sitting in it, we saw El Djem, the largest Roman coliseum in Africa.

We always enjoyed being with the Seelyes, whom we found refined but accessible at the same time. Talcott was one of the most prestigious Arabists of the State Department, as I mentioned in my Lebanon chapter. Once, as we were dining in our hotel, Talcott did not like the hotel's onion soup he was served. So he explained to the headwaiter, in his elegant classical Arabic, how the soup should be prepared.

On this trip, there was not a ripple on the deep blue sea. The fishermen were throwing their nets. On the horizon, the sparkling white buildings of Sousse, dominated by the towers of the *Kasbah* (a fortress), created a scene of incredible purity. The following day we visited the *Ribat*, a fortified monastery. Nearby was Skanes, the birthplace of President Bourguiba. We were received in the Tunisian president's sumptuous palace. It had marble walls, ten-foot-high tapestries, mosaics, swimming pools, and ten small houses for his guests and his staff. The president had also already built an imposing mausoleum for himself and his family.

During this official trip with the Seelyes, Alan managed to get away for a few minutes to take pictures of three camels on the beach. He was petting them, as he used to do with horses, until one decided he had had enough and attacked him. Alan started running, but the camel reared and pounced on him, baring his teeth. It was hysterically funny, but also scary. I was afraid the animal would bite him. Alan told me later that all he was interested in at the time was the "photo op" and that he was sorry I did not shoot the scene with my camera.

On a trip to the south of Tunisia to visit the Oasis de Montagnes, we drove with four French couples in separate cars. Alan, feeling like an Arizona cowboy, which he once was, left the paved road to drive through fields, gullies, and rocky outcrops. The Land Rover was getting rough treatment over the rocks and almost got stuck in the sand. The landscape became increasingly desolate, with rugged canyons all around. Finally, we ended up getting lost. We arrived in Gafsa after dark and met our friends, who were expressing their worry over drinks.

We reached the three oases—Mides, Tmerza, and Chebika—situated close to the Algerian border. The houses, made of raw bricks, were in ruins. For several months a year, those villages are cut off from the rest of the world by the flooded *wadis* (small rivers). The skin of the frail children was black from both the sun and the dirt. Against this desperately sad background the only color came from the flaming hues of the women's dresses in purple, raspberry, and orange.

Driving down the mountains, we reached the largest centers of the "grand Sud"—Tozeur and Nefta. While Alan and the children were exploring the salt lake, I spent two hours with our friends in the coolness of these large oases, the babbling of the water sources, and the flowers. It was easy for me to understand how writers such as André Gide and Arthur Rimbault, or painters such as Henri Matisse, would fall under the spell of such places.

Early in our stay, my brother Jean Prévost, a general in the French Air Force, announced his arrival on an official visit. Seventy persons, civilians and military, accompanied by ten faculty members, were touring Tunisia as part of a nine-month course at the Institut des Hautes Études de Défense Nationale, equivalent to the U.S. War College. His group included high-level officers, CEOs, engineers, and civil servants representing the elites of France.

Tunisian officials were at the airport to meet the old airplane of the French Air Force. One by one the visitors approached us, saying to me "You must be Prévost's sister." Then they bowed, kissed my hand, and said, "*Mes hommages, Madame.*" I was flattered by so much French *galanterie.*

A tour of the ruins of Carthage is always a must for visitors. The bus unloaded its French guests, who quickly found the pace of the excursion too slow. So, armed with my two months of exposure to the ancient city, I took over and gave my first guided tour of the site. I hoped my lack of knowledge would be compensated by my enthusiasm.

That evening, the French were invited to a cocktail offered by the Tunisian army. Jean was shaving in the kitchen, his two friends were putting on the officers' full-dress uniform, and the two women also taking the course were slipping on their evening dresses. The lower level of the house had been turned into a dorm and had never been so lively. A musical and dance interlude was offered during the reception that evening. To my embarrassment, three women of the group and I were chosen to give an exhibition of belly dancing in front of the distinguished personalities.

Early in January of 1974, Alan started his hunt for a boat. He had various leads and had made several offers when he saw a slender twenty-seven-footer, with a pale green fiberglass keel, in the Sidi Bou Said marina. She was a Ranger class, designed by Rhodes and built in Holland. For Alan, it was love at first sight. It was a boat for the hardy types. No self-furling in those days! It was impossible to stand up except in the very center of the boat. The map table was a board placed over the stove. The forward cabin was used to dump sails in a hurry.

After some work in drydock at the shipyard of La Goulette, Alan finally realized his dream. He made several trial sails in the bay of Tunis, most of them in very strong winds. One day, he tested his crew by making the boat pitch and roll. This put me rapidly out of the contest. Alan commented to the children, "Mommy prefers to go looking for Punic tombs on long day jaunts."

Throughout our stay in Tunisia, our sailboat *Philvia*, named after our two older children, remained a central element of our family life. For Alan, it was a new world. He described it as "challenging, tiring, sometimes frightening, and yet wonderfully relaxing and satisfying." Every free minute, every lunchtime, Alan was on his boat. When he received in the mail a new light he had ordered for the boat, he was so excited that he put it on display among my 300 BC Punic artifacts!

One of the side projects I enjoyed doing in Tunisia was leading a class in English language and literature. My students were wives of prominent members of society such as ministers, professors, and doctors. In our group was Neila Bourguiba, the president's daughter-in-law. The members of the group were delightful and incredibly motivated, never missing a class. I had asked a Canadian friend to be the Anglophone linguist. We studied the tales of Edgar Alan Poe and Richard Bach's *Jonathan Livingston Seagull*, among other books. The sessions were opportunities to meet with friends and to exchange the news of the week. When you make friends in Tunisia, it is forever. Although it has been years since we left, I am still in touch with these good friends.

In March 1974, Vice President Nelson Rockefeller came on an official visit to Tunisia. His trip coincided with Tunisian Independence Day, marked by popular demonstrations, flags waving, music in the streets, sport events, and more. Our ambassador suggested I give the Rockefellers an archaeological tour of the city. I was supposed to meet them at the palace of President Bourguiba. As I entered, the crystal chandeliers, the grand marble stairs, and the magnificent gilded halls dazzled me. The place was swarming with security agents. A party of eighty people accompanied the foreign visitors.

Everyone waited, pacing back and forth. I was getting more and more nervous. Then, the vice president's wife, Happy Rockefeller, appeared on the stairs. She was a tough-looking woman and had no intention of waiting for her husband while he talked to the members of the Tunisian government. She, her daughter, and I climbed into a car and headed in the direction of the ruins of Carthage. She was very interested in the history and the excavations and asked all sorts of questions.

We were admiring the beautiful mosaics of the Roman Villa overlooking the lake of Tunis and talking about Punic religion when we heard sirens. A bulletproof Cadillac was approaching, flags flying, followed by a file of official cars. It was the U.S. vice president, who wanted to join the tour! Alan was with him. After a visit to the ancient vestiges, we all piled into the Cadillac. We arrived in Sidi Bou Said in the midst of a religious feast. The streets were packed, and an orchestra was playing. Rockefeller waved. To chase the evil eye away, two men were carrying *tromblons* (short guns), using them to snap firecrackers. They pointed the guns at us and the firecrackers blew up under the car! It happened so quickly that we did not have time to panic at the sound of the explosion.

We finished the tour with a visit to the Bardo Museum, which contains the richest mosaic collection in the world. By the end of the afternoon, we were like old friends. I promised to send Happy's daughter a small coral puppy.

I was making inroads into the archeological circles of the capital. I met Dr. Beschaouch, the director of the National Institute of Art and Archaeology, toured archeological sites with specialists, and became acquainted with a number of them. We invited Dr. Margaret Alexander, the American author of the definitive "corpus" on Tunisian mosaics, as well as British and Tunisian archaeologists, to dinner. We had the privilege of being introduced to M. Dupont-Sommer, the French Orientalist and leading scholar in the Aramaic language and the Dead Sea Scrolls.

I wanted to share my interest for archaeology with others and organized a series of archaeology workshops that met regularly at our house. More than twenty women signed up. I planned topics of research, made up a bibliography, and invited distinguished speakers.

Père Ferron was a passionate excursion leader. One day he took our group of eager fans walking for hours through the uninhabited hills of the Cap Bon, looking for a Libyan necropolis dating from the third and fourth centuries BC. (Libyan in this context means the indigenous population of Tunisia.) The tombs were carved out of the face of the cliffs. It was late in April and the wildflowers displayed blue, purple, red, orange, and white. A herd of black goats contrasted with the bright yellow on the field.

Gradually Père Ferron's excursions attracted a growing number of disciples. On one Sunday, I had convinced our friends Italian DCM Federico di Roberto and Aurelio di Martin, the director of Agip Oil Company, to join us. This turned into a hysterically funny trip. We were driving in Aurelio's Land Rover. The whole way, our jolly Italians were bellowing Italian operas. They had bought thirty kilos of oranges, which the merchant dumped into the car. Each jolt of the rover on the rough dirt road made the oranges roll under our feet.

During a trip Alan and I took into the interior, we stopped by the wide Medjerda River. Recent flooding had washed up several objects on the banks of the wide riverbed, including three third century AD oil lamps, which we bought. Alan became intrigued with two objects so dry that they seemed to weigh nothing. One could see a crude drawing of a man on one of them. We had no idea what these objects were but Alan bought them anyway. I told Alan he had paid too much. But Père Ferron appeared very excited when I showed him the artifacts. He asked if he could borrow them so they could be "published." No similar object existed in the Carthage museum's collection. We learned from Père Ferron that the two artifacts dated from the Byzantine era and were a host for mass and a mold to stamp the host.

Once we were invited to a duplicate bridge party. Alan and I warned our hostess that we were strictly accidental players. She assumed we were being polite. The money stakes were high. As I displayed my totally amateurish talent, my partner's expression grew angrier with each round. When we said our good- byes, the hostess remarked with a sweet smile, "You were right, you really can't play."

A few days later we were invited to another bridge party. It was a friendly game and not for money this time, fortunately for us, since one of the players—a Master—had played against Omar Sharif, the well-known Egyptian movie actor who was the hero in the film of Boris Pasternak's *Dr. Zhivago*. Sharif, incidentally, is also one of the world's best chess players.

In 1975 we were the co-hosts of an *orgie gauloise*. The theme of the party was "Asterix in Carthage." Asterix is the national character of the most popular comic book in France. He represents the defiance expressed by the blond Gauls against the occupying force of the rather stupid Romans. The party took place in the Palais Rose, a beautiful residence built entirely of pink marble, where the American embassy political counselor lived. René Goscinny, the author of the Asterix comic books, had chosen many locations to stage his stories, including Egypt and Rome, but not Carthage. We wrote to him, inviting him to the party and suggested he choose Carthage as a setting for his next book. He declined the invitation, but indicated in a very friendly way that he might consider Carthage as the location for a future book.

We had pitched the tent of a Roman camp in the courtyard. For lazy guests, there was a *duoclinum* (dining room) with couches to recline on and eat from. A wild pig was roasting on a spit. The "magic potion," prepared by the druid Panoramix, was served to the guests out of huge earthen jars. We could not believe the imaginative costumes of our guests. Carthage had come alive again with its cosmopolitan population of Romans, Greeks, Gauls, Vandals, and nomad Bedouins! Alan was the fat Obelisk, the dolmen lover. His hair was in two plaits of coarse red wool. His Turkish baggy pants, bought in the *souks* in downtown Tunis, were filled with pillows. I had put a red mop on my head and wore a dress of brocaded fabric woven with gold thread. I looked like a Carthaginian Cleopatra.

We served some of the best Tunisian wines – Vieux Thibar, Haut Mornag, Hidalgo, Chateau Lamblot, and of course, the *vin de messe* produced by the White Fathers. This was at the risk of being anachronistic, since Punic wines had other names.

We were treated to an evening of parapsychology when we invited the Novikoffs, a couple of White Russian origin, long established in Tunis and interested in occult sciences. We wanted them to meet my sister-in-law Geneviève, who was visiting from France. Geneviève is a follower of the anthroposophy movement (a religious sect of theosophy) and is a fanatical believer in clairvoyance and astrology. She lives in a world of esoteric books, collects plants, and concocts mysterious potions.

The evening was extraordinary. Alan (who was silent for once) and I were following their conversation like a ping-pong tournament, turning our heads back and forth. Diane and Karen had refused the invitation of their friends to see a movie and rushed home afraid to miss the fireworks. Mme. Novikoff and Geneviève were talking the same language about vibrations, *shakras* (vital centers), and reincarnation. They discussed the presence of souls that gather around a dying person to take him or her away. They talked about the evil eye and the Tunisian customs to protect against it. They described séances and how the medium leaves his aura in an armchair. It was getting spooky and we felt presences around us.

One of the stories of Mme. Novikoff was called "The Cat and the Bell." A bell was placed under their dining room table, which was used to call the servant at dinner. One night they had heard the bell ring although there was no one on the ground floor. They went downstairs and found their cat with his stomach ripped open. He was waiting for them before dying. Maybe the cat had fallen from the window and come back inside and pushed the bell with its foot.

In 1975 I embarked on my second job. I became the personal assistant to Dr. Mokhtar Latiri, the director of the Ecole Nationale d'Ingénieurs de Tunis (ENIT). Once more I plunged into a profession I did not know anything about and loved it. It was a stimulating environment with an international faculty. The emerging but dynamic economy of Tunisia attracted a number of delegations from France, the United States, the Soviet Union, and other countries. A school of engineering provided a neutral ground for political and economic competition. It was interesting to observe the national power plays going on.

An important meeting of engineers took place in the spring. Soviet personalities in the field of architecture, construction, and urban planning had been invited. The amphitheater was overflowing. The Soviet lecturers were obviously trying to make a strong impression on the representatives of the host country. They had brought their model of a residential block consisting of thirty-story-high buildings to house 20,000 people. An underground network of roads, garages, and shops was part of the design. The project was scheduled to happen in the 1980s. (Incidentally, it did not happen.) A French engineer made a typically sarcastic comment, asking, "Who wants to live like termites?" A short while later the Soviet minister of education made an official visit to Tunisia and came to ENIT with an impressive group of stern-looking Russians.

My role at ENIT was to coordinate between Dr. Latiri and his faculty, report on special events, advise on the teaching of English, and organize exhibits. There was also a lot of note-taking and participation in staff meetings. The bonus, aside from my basic salary, was that I could attend courses in business and economics, among other topics. I remember in particular a brilliant MIT professor conducting a seminar on civil engineering, stressing the necessity of an economic approach for the engineer. I worked the whole academic year at ENIT.

"*Les Américains à Carthage,*" announced the headlines of *La Presse*, the daily newspaper of Tunis, when Americans finally joined the UNESCO expedition in 1976. It was about time! More than eighteen teams of archaeologists, including French, British, Danish, Germans and Italians were already at work, participating in the largest salvage expedition ever launched by UNESCO. The massive project was to excavate and preserve the ancient vestiges left in this metropolis through the centuries. The task was urgent in the face of fast-paced modern construction that threatened to seal forever the layers of human occupation under tons of concrete.

The director of Chicago University's Oriental Institute, Dr. Lawrence Stager, the director of Michigan University's Kelsey Museum expedition, Dr. J. H. Humphrey, and the head of the American Schools of Oriental Research (ASOR), Dr. Frank M. Cross, had come to the American Embassy to meet the economic counselor, namely, Alan. They discussed the cooperation agreement signed between the American and Tunisian governments.

I happened to be in Alan's office at that exact moment. The person responsible for their expedition's logistics had to cancel his trip because of a broken leg, so I jumped at the opportunity and offered my services. I became an instant driver, interpreter, supply buyer, and liaison person.

Dr. Stager was allocated the Punic *Tophet*, or sanctuary, and the southern bank of the "merchant port" in Carthage. Those were the choice areas to excavate. Dr. Humphrey's team was going to dig Roman levels rich in mosaics east of the Byrsa Hill and make probes in the circus area.

I worked with the American Punic project in Carthage for five years, until the end of our stay in Tunisia, and for three subsequent summers, from 1976 to 1979. Later, I was fortunate to join the Harvard expedition that Dr. Stager conducted in the Philistine city of Ashkelon, Israel, from 1985 to 1993. But that is another story.

It was very special to be in Carthage during the UNESCO campaign. Imagine the ancient ruins still existing on the northwest coast of the Gulf of Tunis being excavated at every street corner by teams of archaeologists. I found it amusing to note the different methods. The Germans were quite disciplined and never went down into the trenches. Each supervisor had his/her desk on the edge of the excavated areas and was protected from the sun by a beach umbrella. The Tunisian workers would shovel the debris onto a conveyor belt. The American methods were more rustic: archaeologists worked side-by-side with the local workers. The dirt was taken away in crude baskets made of recycled rubber tires. The British were excavating the circular military port. At the entrance to that port a team of blind Albanians was retrieving artifacts from the muddy shallow waters.

The French had a long history of excavations in Carthage, dating from the mid-nineteenth century. Their largest site, headed by Serge Lancel, was located to the south of the Byrsa hill. This was the only location where Punic dwellings still remained. The French archaeologists were able to expose cisterns, house foundations, walls, and streets from under sustaining walls and massive piers that the Romans had erected in order to create a huge platform for majestic public buildings.

It was striking to note the difference between the excavations taking place in the 1970s and the ones conducted a century earlier. The technique of opening one thousand tombs to find funerary goods—some described it as treasure hunting—were replaced by the meticulous study of strata and scientific recording of findings.

I loved riding my bicycle at dawn on my way to work on the dig and seeing the sun rise over the Punic port. In the distance, the twin peaks of Bou Kornine, considered a shrine by the Punics, rose above the Gulf of Tunis. On top of the hill of Byrsa stood the St. Louis Basilica, commemorating the place where the French king Louis IX (St. Louis) died in 1270 of typhoid fever returning from his second crusade. Now, the archaeological museum of Carthage occupies the grounds next to the church.

The *Tophet* of Carthage was the sanctuary where children were sacrificed. It was an area smaller than one and half acres. In his *Interim Report* on the Punic project, Dr. Stager wrote that 20,000 children, from unborn fetuses to fourteen- year-olds, were buried in the precinct from 400 to 200 BC. The Americans excavated 400 cinerary urns (that is, containing ashes) with charred human and animal bones, along with amulets and beads. The highest density of burials took place in the fourth century BC. Stager noted that child sacrifice was also practiced systematically among Canaanites, Israelites, and Phoenicians.

Gustave Flaubert, the French author best known for his novel *Madame Bovary*, also wrote *Salambo* (1862), containing an immortal and tragic description of the Punic god with outstretched arms on which the sacrificed children were thrown and then rolled down into the pyre. Flaubert had done intensive research and had studied closely the reports made by the French archaeologist Beule in 1857. He had read the historians Polybius and Thucydides, as well as the Bible.

In the March–April 1986 issue of *Archaeology* magazine I published a short article on my experience in the *Tophet* of Carthage. Here are a few excerpts of my story:

A small enclosure, peaceful and charming, spring flowers cascading over terraced walls, frolicking frogs among water lilies, in the shade of pomegranate and orange trees, clay jars nestle close to carved and often inscribed *stelae*. This idyllic place, located near Carthage, a seaside suburb of modern Tunis, was in fact the gruesome *Tophet*, where ancient Carthaginians practiced their religious custom of immolating and burning their children as a sacrifice to the god Ba'al Hamon and his "consort" Tanit.

The *Tophet* site was opened in 1976. The bucolic garden was assaulted, trees were uprooted, and six working "squares" laid out. Groundwater was soon reached and pumps had to be put in action to allow further digging. The site began to look like a sick person, with pipes, wires, and tubes hooked on as if to keep it alive.

At first, when I was not chauffeuring, buying buckets or acting as an interpreter, I was allowed to do small tasks on the dig. I was taught how to use the trowel, basic tool of the archaeologist, with a "bulldozer" action, by scraping, never digging (a heinous crime). The process of archaeology is very similar to the unraveling of a murder mystery. One of the basic tenets is to "go from the known to the unknown." The thread of deduction must never be severed. "Dig with a porpoise" (archaeologists have a sense of humor) is the golden formula. Relationships are more important than an isolated find, even of a precious object. Each change in soil texture, each structure has a *locus* number. A cross-section of the stratigraphy appears on the "balks," or walls, of the dugout squares. One of the loci, I remember vividly, was 007, which made the whole exercise more exciting than a James Bond story.

During five seasons I was privileged to dig on an area so delicate that no local labor was allowed to tread. Dr. Stager commented that the *Tophet* is one of the hardest types of excavation, because of the dense and intricate accumulation of artifacts and the continual use and disturbance of the soil over the centuries. I remember seeing Doug, my supervisor, at particularly puzzling times, staring at his square and striving to understand the sequence. He must have felt the archaeologist's panic of "losing" his square. Our square was particularly fertile in burial urns (more than 200).... Hearing a hollow sound, we would say, "Oh no! Not another one!"

We went down four meters below the modern surface, through Tanit III and Tanit II. Then, one day, amid general excitement, a potsherd with red slipped and burnished wiggly lines was found, heralding our grand entrance into Tanit I. We had reached bedrock and the natural murky silt without occupational debris—in other words, practically all the way to the origins of Carthage in the ninth century B.C.

In the early spring ferocious storms often drove us under the Roman vault built over the tragic site of the Carthaginians burials. Crashing thunder made us feel like sacrilegious grave robbers who had violated this holy sanctuary and incurred the wrath of the gods. But no matter, it was all in the name of science!

It is saddening for me to recall this story, because the main character was Doug Esse, my *Tophet* companion, my mentor, and the nicest, most brilliant young scholar I ever met. He was being groomed by Dr. Stager to become his successor as the head of the Oriental Institute when he died tragically of stomach cancer in his mid-thirties while excavating in Israel.

One summer Dr. Stager invited Karen to join Doug Esse and myself in our square on the *Tophet* dig. She had done some research at the Institut d'Art et d'Archéologie in Carthage. I was quite impressed by her interest.

Punic iconography is rich in symbolic meaning. It can be seen on thousands of votive *stelae* uncovered mainly in Carthage but also throughout Tunisia. The message carved on the stone could express a prayer addressed to the gods asking for a successful harvest or a victory in battle. It is an abstract art made up of geometric forms, such as the bottle idol, the disc-sun, the crescent-moon, and the lozenge, which all have solar and therefore religious connotations. The best-known sign, one that also epitomizes Carthage, is what is commonly called the "sign of Tanit." It is believed to allude to the goddess Astarte, consort of Ba'al Hammon, ruler of the Punic pantheon. The sign consists of a circle (the sun) on top of a triangle (the earth). Two horizontal lines starting at the top of the triangle naturally suggest arms, and this sign is easily made into an anthropomorphic figure. Pierre Cintas, former director of the French archaeological mission to Tunisia and one of the *Tophet's* early excavators, wrote in 1968: "The sign of Tanit has unlimited possibilities for the expression of abstract concepts in concrete form."

I personally loved the representations of human figures on neo-Punic *stelae* (first and second centuries A.D.). The artists must have had quite a sense of humor and could easily, I think, have inspired Picasso. In the countryside *stelae* were probably influenced by the style of local or indigenous craftsmen. They appear more crude but not at the expense of their originality.

I also associate Carthage with artifacts that are found in no other antique culture. Here I refer to terra cotta masks representing a demon with a sardonic grin or figurines made of glass paste with globular eyes, curly beards, and bright colors. These tiny objects were placed in tombs to protect the dead.

Fortunately, the children spent many vacations with us. Their visits created even more opportunities to enjoy Tunisia and its people at their best. I will always treasure the memory of the laid-back people at the Café des Nattes in Sidi Bou Said enjoying the spectacular view over the Bay of Tunis while sipping mint tea or tea with pine nuts. An emblematic sight was a man with a jasmine flower over his ear; he would walk among the tables and sell flowers from a basket. The children and I never tired of going to the *souks* in the Medina (or old town) and buying embroidered dresses, *burnous* (capes), vests, colorful blankets, and Mergum rugs. We could hear the hammering sound on brass tables or pots and smell the scents of spices or perfumes in *souk* El Attarine near the Great Zitouna Mosque.

Jewelers, selling gold and silver, were found together in one of the lanes of the Medina. I learned that unfortunately the beautiful Bedouin silver was already becoming rare. Resellers were traveling through the remote regions of the country. They would return with buckets filled with old Bedouin jewels belonging to village women. Back in Tunis, they would melt the silver and turn it into shiny brand new material.

Deep inside the narrow lanes of the Medina, the owners of each stall would call us but without being aggressive. I never had the claustrophobic feeling I experienced in the old city of Jerusalem, where I was almost caught in a terrifying stampede on a Friday after the mosque let out. Bargaining here was enjoyable. After going back and forth on the price, the merchant would say, his hand on his heart, "Your price is mine."

After one year living with us in Tunis, Karen left to study in Rome, where she joined her siblings. This was followed by a year at Millfield, a beautiful boarding school near Bath in England. There she was part of the tennis team, one of the best in England.

At that time, I turned into a full-time consultant for the kids. I did all sorts of research on tennis schools or camps for Karen, on ballet and modern dance opportunities for Sylvia, and on-the-job architecture training for Philip. This occupation went on for many years.

For months, Alan had been making summer plans to take the children sailing on his first long adventure, to Bizerte, Sardinia, and Corsica. As they were getting ready for the first big crossing, a violent *mistral* started blowing at an easy forty knots, with gusts up to sixty. They set sail nevertheless. I drove up to the highest point of Sidi Bou Said and saw our tiny sailboat *Philvia* bobbing up and down in the immense expanse of rough water. My heart sank. For me, Alan and the kids belonged to a race of giants, while I remained on shore, too afraid to go on that uncomfortable vessel.

My relationship with *Philvia* was complex. I hated her and was angry at Alan for sailing her through dangerous waters with the children. Surprisingly, however, I was in a state of shock when, a few months after we left Tunisia, I received in the mail a fragment of pale green fiberglass. It looked familiar, and I soon realized that it was a piece from *Philvia!* The new owners, a couple of French "*coopérants*" (comparable to Peace Corps volunteers), had sailed her from Tunis to La Galite, off the town of Bizerte. The couple had tied her to the rocks on the protected lee side of the island. But she broke loose during a storm that night. *Philvia* had committed suicide after twenty-four hours! I felt very sad.

Some time later, friends offered me a passage to Sardinia on their Arpège-made sailboat, and I initially accepted. I changed my

mind ten times, thinking I could never do it. On the eve of departure I went to the ambassador's for cocktails. This was a bad idea;
from far above, the whitecaps and waters in turmoil looked even
more ominous.

After two hours of sleep, I got up at 4:00 a.m. to go to the Sidi
Bou Said marina. Our friend's boat, the *Moby Dick,* was an efficient,
bulky, fiberglass vessel. By two in the afternoon the wind had really picked up and reached force seven. We went through rough
seas. Fortunately I trusted the skipper totally. He was a former navy
commander, calm and a bit taciturn. He only once appeared an-
noyed and mumbled a curt *"merde"* when the wooden flap of the
automatic pilot broke off.

I survived the crossing to Sardinia and regained a bit of my self-
esteem. I had done it! *Moby Dick* was sailing back to Tunisia, and
I continued north toward France. I flew in a small biplane across
Sardinia. A day later, I sat down on the Bonifacio marina, waiting
to hitch a ride along the coast of Corsica. Some friendly people on
a lovely sailboat offered me a lift. The only problem, one that I discovered later, was that they did not believe in wearing bathing suits
on board.

In January 1976, I started my third job, this time in the corporate
world, and continued until the end of our stay. I became the administrative assistant of Thomas Pierpont Grose, Bankers' Trust vice
president, who was opening a regional office that covered the area
from North Africa all the way to Mauritania. I was a one-person office helping him and his family get settled. I was supposed to know
about insurance, income tax, customs, legal contracts, banking, and
many other things. I created filing cabinets out of cardboard boxes.
My office was on the ground floor of a seaside villa next to the Punic port. The Tunisian owner of the house had admirably preserved
a Punic murex dye factory dating probably from the sixth century
BC. (Note: The purple dye from murex gave the Phoenicians and
the Punic peoples their names.)

In the spring of 1976, the whole family left for home leave by
ferryboat to Italy. After a great crossing we had a mishap that could
have created a real mess. We were driving into Genoa in a pouring
rain. It was getting dark. We had stopped for gas, and Alan put our

six passports on the top of the car. As we drove off, he immediately realized what had happened and stopped. Of course, it was too late. The passports were gone. We went into a police station and explained the situation. We braced ourselves for the prospect of filling out tons of forms. It was awful. We all felt most depressed.

A short while later, a policeman came in from the rain holding our passports! Someone had found them on the street. It was a miracle! We all thought Italy was the greatest country ever, despite the pouring rain.

Photo Gallery II

The *paillotte* and pool, with Logan children and friends, Conakry, Guinea, 1966.

Diane (left) and Sylvia starring in my production of Tom-Clownery ballet, Conakry, 1967.

(from left) Diane, Sylvia, Philip, and Karen at a birthday party on the grounds of Ambassador Robinson McIlvaine's residence, Conakry, 1967.

Reception for African diplomats, Washington D.C., 1963. (L. to r.) Kadiatou Conte, wife of the Guinean ambassador, Nicole, and Mrs. G. Mennen Williams, wife of the assistant secretary of state for African affairs. Credit: U.S. Department of State.

Diane at the Lagos Yacht Club, Nigeria, 1973.

Ambassador and Mrs. John Reinhardt at the Montmartre party, Lagos, 1973.

(From left) Goldie the pony, Sylvia, Nicole, Philip, Diane holding Vania, and Karen at the Lagos riding club, 1973.

Gammarth house on the beach, Tunisia, 1974.

The age of teenagers: Philip and Diane in our living room, Gammarth, 1976.

Economic Counselor Alan Logan on an official visit with President Habib Bourguiba, 1976. Credit: Government of Tunisia.

Four elegant women represent Tunis high society, 1975. (From left) unidentified, Monique El Memmi, Zinah El Goulli, Claire Bellagha.

Skipper Alan on *Philvia,* Sidi Bou Said, near Tunis, 1975.

The Logans in Sidi Bou Said, 1973

Official delegation of archaeologists on the *Tophet*, Carthage, 1976. (From right) Dr. Frank Cross, head of the American Schools of Oriental Research (ASOR), Nicole Logan, Dr. Lawrence E. Stager, Oriental Institute of the University of Chicago, Dr. Bachaouch, Tunisian Minister of Culture, and unidentified staff. Credit: Oriental Institute expedition to Carthage.

Doug Esse and Nicole recovering a cinerary urn containing ashes of sacrificed children in the *Tophet*, Carthage, 1976. Credit: Oriental Institute expedition to Carthage.

Karen in front of the Brussels American School, 1976.

Living in a roof, Uccle, Brussels 1976.

The U.S. Consul General's residence in Durban North, Natal, South Africa, 1979.

Alan Paton, with Alan Logan (standing), Durban, Christmas 1979.

Zulu warriors, on Shaka day. King Good-win (center left), and Chief Minister Gatsha Buthelezi (center right), Natal 1978.

The Logans in safari clothes. (From left) Sylvia, Diane, Philip, Nicole, and Karen, Durban, 1981.

‎

Nicole at the Cape of Good Hope, South Africa, 1981

Residence and private beach of the U.S. ambassador to The Gambia, 1983.

Alan, sailing through Paris on *Katy II,* Notre Dame in background, 1990. Credit: Karen Logan

8

Belgium 1976–1979

An assignment to Belgium, in the heart of Western Europe, was a totally new experience for us in many respects. At first, it seemed overwhelming to be in a town where museums, universities, cinemas, libraries, and concert halls were readily available. A cosmopolitan atmosphere reigned in Brussels, which was not only the capital of Belgium but also the headquarters of the European Union. After all these years in Africa and the Middle East, the pleasure of seeing leaves turn in the fall or of waking up in the morning to a cover of snow and the simple change of seasons was a pure joy.

Something else was different: the proximity of other countries. Instead of harrowing flights from deepest Africa separating us from the children, all we needed was a short drive by car, bus, or even a bicycle, and bang, we were in another country. I remember a particular weekend when I went to buy my croissants in Paris, Karen spent a couple of days in Amsterdam with a friend, and Alan went skiing in the Alps.

I must admit I had misgivings when we moved from Tunis to Brussels. How could the easy and relaxed life we had known in Gammarth among wonderful friends possibly be matched in this large, impersonal city? But it took less than six months to make the transition. I ended up loving the differences and had no trouble making adjustments.

The American embassy in Brussels did not provide its personnel with housing nor with furniture, as our embassies did at other posts. We were on our own. Hunting for a proper house took a few weeks. So guess what? We started this new assignment living in a hotel again. The twenty-seventh floor of the Sheraton became our temporary home. We really did not mind. The accommodations were most comfortable. They even provided daily laundered terry cloth bathrobes to lounge in. There was an internal TV that showed the same movie called *People Next Door* several times a day. So we watched it several times a day. Our hotel rooms overlooked the large Rogier Square near the railroad station. The red light district, with its prostitutes seated in the windows, was not far. One avoided walking in that direction. The square opened onto the ring road. I loved taking the tram following that road because it went in and out of tunnels, and it reminded me of Boston.

Alan was part of the economic section of USEC, the United States Mission to the European Community. There were two other American embassies in Brussels, one to the Kingdom of Belgium and a third one to NATO. USEC was probably the most important of the three because its role was to work with the very large European government apparatus. Alan was responsible for several areas, including law of the seas, nuclear power, and energy. As usual, his bilingual talent facilitated contacts with diplomats from different countries. Not the least of these contacts were established and nurtured over a hot tennis court.

The USEC ambassador was Deane R. Hinton. Both he and his wife, who was of South American origin, were quite distinguished. Between them, they had ten children. Their stay in Belgium coincided exactly with ours. Our embassy colleagues were pleasant, but we never felt part of a tightly knit group as we had in Tunisia.

We had arrived in midsummer. Philip was already at Stanford University, and Sylvia and Diane left for California not long after. Karen was to spend a year at the International School in Brussels attended mainly by children of the very large civilian and military American community. I do not know whether Karen will agree with me, but I think her best memory of that school was a bus trip we took together to the French Open tennis tournament at Roland Garros, in Paris. A young John McEnroe was playing in doubles and entertained the public with his fits of anger.

During our early weeks in Brussels, Karen and I spent a great deal of time walking around, discovering places, looking at people, in other words, getting a feel for our new home town. We were struck by what jolly *bons vivants* the Belgians are. They love to eat and drink beer and are the highest consumers of beer in the world. Among hundreds of brands the most potent one is called *Mort Subite* (sudden death).

To celebrate the inauguration of the Métro, Brussels became even more festive than usual. Concerts and illuminations were everywhere. From our upper floor, we could see people dancing in the streets. In Antwerp, which Karen and I visited early in our stay, we saw placid tourists walking calmly, stopping for a *cornet* (cone) made of newspaper and filled with French fries topped by a large spoonful of mayonnaise, for waffles covered with confectioner sugar, or for pastries disappearing under globs of whipped cream. Karen discovered in Brussels a *festival du poisson* (fish festival) and a *marché du fromage* (cheese market) where everything was free.

One month later, a giant food fair attracted apparently famished mobs. It was a scene of collective *grande bouffe*. (*La Grande Bouffe* is the name of a Franco-Italian movie, released in 1973, where a group of friends gather with the purpose of eating themselves to death.) Every possible product from Belgium and around the world was on display. We tasted cheese, chocolate, and cakes. Little old ladies were sampling small glasses of liqueur and looked quite happy. Families were sitting around tables laden with sauerkraut and lobster with mayonnaise as early as ten in the morning.

A pleasant way of ending a day's walk around town was to sit down at the terrace of a café on the Grand Place and enjoy a *kir* (white wine with black currant liqueur).

In the process of our house hunting, we remarked how extremely bourgeois the Belgian middle class is. They want large houses, but mainly they want to show they own large houses. They give the appearance of being solidly entrenched in all aspects of the material comforts of life.

We also noticed the enormous displays of food in shop windows. It seemed that the sheer quantity of products mattered more that the subtlety of an artistic arrangement.

To celebrate Karen's seventeenth birthday on November 18, we had dinner in a Russian restaurant on the Place des Sablons. While melancholy gypsy music played in the background, we sipped our *riumki* (Russian for liquor glass) of vodka and ate *zakuskis*, or appetizers. Karen opened Sylvia's gift containing a fragrant candle and read the telegrams sent by Philip and Diane with emotion.

The house hunting intensified. We had arrived in August, found the perfect house in October, and finally moved in on November 24. We proudly announced to our friends: "We are going to live in a roof!" Our next home was to be a duplex in a large house in Uccle. The landlord and his wife lived on the ground floor. We had the two upper levels built in the huge sloping roof, though with regular windows. We were very proud of our *oeil de boeuf* (small circular window). The owners loved gardening, and it was wonderful to look down at the flowers, bushes, ponds, and lawn without having to do any work. The living room alone was about six hundred square feet, had a beautiful fireplace, wood panels, built-in bookcases, and hardwood floors. Large French windows opened onto a balcony. We had five bathrooms with ten washbasins. From the country kitchen we enjoyed a plunging view on what I used to call the "little house in the woods." Its owner became a close friend and taught Karen how to make sourdough bread. Karen established her private quarters in the several small rooms and bathroom on the upper floor.

The last hurdle was bringing our own belongings. For the first time since Ankara, in Turkey, we had the pleasure of being surrounded by our personal effects: the carved Nigerian door, the gazelles from Mali, the paintings from dissident Russian artists, our piano, the Henredon walnut-finish dining room set bought in San Francisco, and the Danish teak furniture that had survived four active children.

While Alan was working on the oh-so-serious matters of energy or law of the seas, and while Karen was thinking of SAT exams, achievement tests, and university applications, I was getting ready to discover what made Brussels unique.

Living in Brussels one felt close to the center of power. I thought it would be appropriate to take a course on European organizations that was offered at the ULB (Université Libre de Bruxelles). The construction of Europe was still in its early stages.[1] The EEC (European Economic Community), as it was called then, included only nine countries: the six original members—the Benelux (Luxembourg, Belgium, Holland), West Germany, France, and Italy—plus Ireland, Denmark, and the United Kingdom, which joined in

1973. Negotiations were taking place for the accession of Greece, scheduled for 1981. Borders and annoying customs formalities still existed between each country.

For me, the course on the European institutions was the beginning of a long-lasting interest in the construction of Europe. It has been a gradual and difficult process that started in 1951 with a handful of countries and was limited to specific sectors like steel and coal. In the 1970s, governing nine countries was a complex task. The EEC was already a huge bureaucratic establishment. Its cluster of modern office towers contrasted with the low Brussels skyline of small buildings and houses surrounded by gardens. The European Parliament's deputies traveled every week from Strasbourg to Brussels. The "Eurocrats" enjoyed a prestigious status; they were exempted from taxes and were rather envied by ordinary diplomats like us.

The European government became an unwieldy bureaucratic machine as the number of member states grew to reach twenty-seven by 2009; the areas of competence became ever larger, ranging from agriculture to taxes, from immigration policy to defense. Two attempts to draft a constitution, one in 2004 and the other in 2007, failed after vetoes from France, Holland, and Ireland. Two years later, the Irish voted again in a second referendum and this time approved the treaty.

In November 2009, the Treaty of Lisbon was formally ratified by all twenty-seven-member states of the European Union, as it is called now. The objective of a constitutional framework, contained in the treaty, was to strengthen the European Union's government and facilitate the decision-making process. The key changes included abolishing the six-month rotation of the president of the council and replacing it with a two-and-a-half-year mandate renewable only once; modifying the system of majorities to put an end to the gridlock stagnation resulting from the unanimous votes usually required; increasing the role of the European Parliament as the democratic representatives of the European population. The treaty was also intended to affirm and clarify the "principle of subsidiarity," which defines the limits of the authority of the central European government versus the rights of the member states.

The extent of the help that the "old Europe" has provided to the "new Europe" has not been sufficiently acknowledged. The inclusion of new members less economically developed required important financial aid from the older members to raise them up to the European Union level. This was a success story, at least for a while, in the case of Greece and Spain. At the writing of these memoirs, Europe is shaken by the worst financial crisis it has known since its inception. Greece is on the verge of bankruptcy, with possibly other countries to follow, and can only be saved with the help of the more solvent European partners. In more recent years, Poland, even prior to acquiring membership, benefited from financial subsidies, and its economy has grown by leaps and bounds. Poorer countries such as Bulgaria or Romania, however, will need a great deal of assistance for their economies to catch up with the rest of Europe.

Turkey, which geographically has only a foothold in Europe, with less than one percent of its territory on the European side of the Bosporus, has been knocking at the door to become a member of the "club" for many years. However, the endless negotiations have so far not been successful for Turkey. The majority of Europeans are against membership for this country of eighty million inhabitants, which continues to grow at a rate of one million people per year. A widespread opinion is that Turkey should be a close partner with a privileged status. Turkey has been a crucial member of NATO since 1951.

Another interest I pursued while in Belgium was in Russian language, literature, and art history. I grabbed at any chance of pursuing my Russian studies, albeit in a scattered way. I hoped that this would help me toward obtaining a masters' degree in the future. I attended an evening course in Russian offered by the Belgium Chamber of Commerce every week. Karen and I found a number of activities at the Institut de la Langue Russe de l'Association Belgique–URSS. Karen joined a Russian choir and learned folk songs. I signed up for a class on Russian literature.

ULB had an active Russian department, where I studied during my whole stay in Belgium. Even though I was not seeking a degree, each of my courses required writing papers and taking exams. The head of the department was Professor Jean Blankoff, an authority on Russian art history and an author. For many years he took part in the excavations of medieval Novgorod in northwest Russia. Archaeologists have uncovered more than fifteen levels of wood layers of human occupation there. Blankoff published papers on the expeditions and particularly on the fifteenth century inscriptions found on birch bark. Born to a Russian father and a French mother, Blankoff had an owlish look. He was an unforgiving professor and demanded high results from his students. I remember one afternoon when he called me to his office to discuss my latest exam. He did not mince his words and made caustic comments on my fumbling performance. I also attended a course in Russian philology taught by Madame Onatsky.

One of my fellow students was Helen Ramsay, a delightful woman who has been my friend ever since. Helen's mother was Boris Pasternak's sister. Her family emigrated from the Soviet Union and never used the Russian language as a matter of principle. Therefore, although she had Russia in her genes, Helen was a total beginner in the language. She later worked on her mother's archives in Oxford and published them.

Every week, the largest amphitheater of ULB would overflow with students and the general public to hear Professor Hadot give his master class on early Christianity. He and his twin brother were part of the faculty of the Institut Catholique in Paris. He made the trip from France once a week to teach in Brussels. I particularly remember one of the opinions he expressed: Jesus was probably a composite figure, and there was no historical proof of his existence. Professor Hadot believed that Jesus was just one of the many messiahs and preachers living in that part of the world at that particular time. What made his presentation brilliant was that it was learned, objective, and at the same time inspiring. I found it pretty amazing to hear a Jesuit express these opinions.

Alan met with his foreign or American colleagues over frequent business lunches downtown. Our entertaining consisted of rather formal small dinners resembling a miniature United Nations, including Dutch, Swiss, French, German, British, Russian, Greek, and Belgian acquaintances.

I was always a little nervous in preparing these dinners. Belgians are connoisseurs of food. I found a way to fake good cooking: I used exotic dishes from countries where we had lived. From Beirut, I brought the recipe on how to make Lebanese *hummus* and *taboulé*. (Nowadays we can find these ready-made in supermarkets.) Other dishes were Turkish grape leaf *dolma*, cheese *boereks*, or Russian *pirojhkis* and borscht, and also Tunisian *briks*.

Tennis occupied a lot of our time. I played singles with a regular partner at the Castle Club. Alan was so determined to find courts downtown that sometimes he played at three in the morning! One day he played for five hours straight (two singles and three doubles). His back went out. For a long time, he had to wear a steel corset and was in constant pain.

During the weekend, La Rasante tennis club was quite a social place for friendly matches and tournaments. Karen was on the tennis team at the International School. She entered tournaments in Antwerp, Holland, the NATO Shape military base, and many other places.

My life in Brussels was different from every post I had lived in until then. Since my obligations as a hostess had diminished, I found myself with plenty of time to soak up the culture of Belgium; and there was plenty of it. In fact, it was usually hard to make choices. I attended the *Mardis de la Poesie* at the Brussels Royal Museum of Fine Arts. On one program poems of Baudelaire, Verlaine, and Rimbaud were recited to Debussy's music; another day, a Russian prince delivered a brilliant lecture on Chekhov, the Russian playwright. During the *Midis de la Musique,* I recall listening to piano recitals and to a Bulgarian quartet playing baroque music. Music and poetry, it seems, are two art forms that Belgians and Russians cherish above all. Only in those two countries have I attended so many poetry readings or piano competitions. One of the big events of the season was the Queen Elizabeth piano competition, with superb young soloists.

We happened to be in Antwerp when it celebrated the 400th anniversary of the birth of Peter Paul Rubens in 1577. Special tours of the town's architecture were offered. The sixteenth century came alive again, thanks to large exhibits of paintings by Rubens, who brought the *joie de vivre* of baroque art following the Reformation and Counter Reformation movements. From the late fifteenth century on, Antwerp had been the center of merchant banking, the first international port in the world, and Europe's richest city.

Antwerp today is known for the famous *Bal des Rats Morts* (Ball of the Dead Rats), which takes place every year in March. It is a tradition, and a pretty wild one at that. Three orchestras played nonstop. Some of the costumes were incredible, for example, those of a group of transvestites took our breath away. They were lavish and turned the young men into beauties. We stayed until the early morning hours. I did my best to keep Alan awake at the wheel on the way back to Brussels.

Ballets, concerts, and plays were running every night in the capital. The *Ballets du XXe Siècle*, created and directed by the French choreographer Maurice Béjart, attracted crowds of dance lovers at the Théatre de la Monnaie. I have never become tired of watching his marvelous creations, such as the *Rite of Spring, Firebird*, or *Bolero*. After twenty years in Brussels, Béjart moved on to Switzerland, where he created the Béjart Ballet Lausanne, which he headed until his death in 2007. We also had a chance to see the Hamburg Dance Company, directed by John Neumeier, perform a ballet based on Gustav Mahler's Third Symphony. The choreography, the moving forms, and the lights were superb.

Brussels, being mostly a French-speaking town, has no real cultural borders with France. Plays from the Paris stage often came to Brussels. We enjoyed the series of *Comédies du Boulevard* at the Théatre des Galeries. One evening we saw Gerard Depardieu, the ubiquitous French movie star, on the stage. Somehow I found him crude and almost repulsive in the flesh. We left the play before the end.

Alan and I were also great moviegoers. We had a chance to see the latest French films such as *Cousin Cousine* and *Lucien Lacombe*. We enjoyed the Russian movie classics shown at the *Musée du Cinéma*. The Festival of Women's Cinema, however, totally turned me off, for several reasons. Too often female directors exaggerate their feminist stance. Besides, I usually find it demeaning for women to be treated as a separate group in films.

Our stay in Brussels was not an easy time for Karen. Once more, her siblings were away and she was alone with her parents. Her relationship with Alan became strained, and I was caught in the middle. After she left for university, Alan commented on her "lovely and fulsome letters." He was sorry to learn that the two years in Nigeria and Tunisia had been so lonely for her and confided that he had felt quite lonely himself as a child. Their rapports warmed up tremendously after this exchange of letters. Several years later, he saved her from a possible depression. I was in Russia at the time, but Alan's presence and close contacts helped her come out from a deep emotional turmoil.

Karen's first year in university was split between the American University in Rome and the American University in Aix en Provence. Then she decided to pursue her studies in the United States. She looked into Redlands, California, where Alan had been an undergraduate, but finally chose Georgetown University, where she was admitted as a sophomore and remained for one and a half years. Alan and I were most impressed by her acceptance at this very selective university. By the time she graduated two years later from the American College in Paris (ACP), today called American University of Paris, she had studied in nine different educational institutions: the American International school in Lagos, the Lycée de la Marsa in Tunisia, St. Stevens in Rome, Millfield in the UK, the International school in Brussels, plus four universities. I think this personal history of extreme adaptability shows the resilience of so-called Foreign Service brats.

The three older children studying in California were wavering in their determination to complete their undergraduate studies, which worried Alan and me. Philip was to graduate in 1977 from Stanford and had applied to several graduate schools without success. Sylvia toyed with the idea of leaving Stanford for a while to dance full-time at Purchase University in New York. Diane was dragging her feet at the prospect of staying at Santa Cruz, but fortunately she transferred to the American College in Paris, where she graduated. Alan and I kept writing to the three children, exhorting them to complete their B.A., using all the arguments possible. Looking back, I can say we succeeded since they all graduated, but I assume that they must have found our many letters indigestible at the time.

Something personal happened to me in the winter of 1977. I met a young British Anglican minister who welcomed me into his church. I had been attracted to the Episcopal religion for several years. In the 1960s, we had our four children baptized in Arlington, Virginia. I began to attend the services regularly at the English and American Episcopal Church in Brussels and liked it more and more, although I had been brought up in the Catholic faith. When I was in primary school in Paris, catechism took place on Thursday mornings in the cavernous crypt of St. Honoré d'Eylau Church in the sixteenth arrondissement of Paris. We were almost terrorized by the priest for whom we had to regurgitate answers memorized by rote. I also remember the unwelcoming attitude of the Catholic Church when we were living in Africa in the 1960s.

I found the environment of the Anglican Church totally different. For the first time, I had a chance to read the scriptures directly from the Old and New Testaments without their being predigested by the priest. The ordeal of confession did not exist. The liturgy was a flexible compromise between informality and ritual, depending on how "high" or "low" the church was. I was one of a handful of adults who met regularly with the minister. We discussed religion and were eager to learn. I made the decision to leave the Catholic Church and become a Protestant—a decision I never regretted.

In early April, I went to Tunis for three weeks to excavate again with Dr. Lawrence Stager's team on the *Tophet*. Carthage was fragrant with honeysuckle and pithoscorum, and wildflowers covered the fields. I wrote to my family abundantly about my experiences, and I was definitely bubbling all over. It is only now, looking through old letters, that I realize how hard it must have been for Alan to be alone. I still feel bad about this.

When not compiling reports, monitoring his stocks, or ordering spare parts for his boat, Alan was an excellent writer with a sharp sense of humor. Here are some excerpts from his letters:

Life is getting very complicated. Here I sit all alone, with everyone scattered almost all over the world, having a great time [Philip was rafting down the Salmon River, Sylvia and her friend Dick were living in a Greek cave, Diane was staying with friends in Brittany, Karen was exploring her old battleground of Rome], while I slave away trying to earn enough bread, butter, and glue to hold the family together. I can't make enough carbon copies for every one. [It was a tradition with Alan to make copies of his typewritten letters and to distribute them among the whole family, including his mother and brother. The last one on the list was out of luck, since the text was barely legible by then.]

I can't find anything in the kitchen. Finally, I found the dishes and the silver in the dishwasher, dirty! [Three days later, he wrote:] We are having a lousy spring in Brussels, while Nicole cavorts in the Tunisian sunshine. She is returning Wednesday, thereby putting an end to the joy of being miserable.

By early summer we were already thinking of our next summer in the United States. Alan went for a routine checkup at the Brussels hospital before going on our next home leave. The doctors found something "suspicious." For anyone who has known Alan, it was not surprising that he took this news in stride, so much so that we almost forgot about it. We had a busy few months ahead of us, attending Philip's graduation at Stanford University and chartering a sailboat in the Virgin Islands.

When we returned to the United States, Alan was admitted to Middlesex Hospital, in Connecticut, for a battery of tests. I drove every day to Middletown from nearby Essex to visit him with Harriet and Frank. He had quickly adjusted to the life in the hospital and made the nurses laugh. If he was anxious, he did not show it. Neither did his mother and brother, who preferred to talk about politics or literature rather than moan. The existence of a cancer in the prostate was confirmed. But the good news was that the cancer was small and localized. We were all so excited that Harriet, Frank, Alan, and I decided to celebrate by having a lobster dinner in the best restaurant in town.

As soon as he returned home, Alan decided to get in shape physically before the operation. He inspired all of us to go boating, jog, and play tennis every day. The surgery took place at the end of August at Yale–New Haven Hospital. The young surgeon was pleased to say that he had found no bad surprises during the two-hour-long procedure. Alan described his prostate gland as being turned into a "pin cushion," with thirteen nuclear implants, or "seeds." In 1977 this method was barely out of the experimental stage and was only available at a handful of hospitals throughout the country. Alan recuperated for four weeks in Essex and resumed his active outdoors life before returning to Belgium in the fall.

I enjoyed a two-day trip to Berlin by bus with the wife of Alan's immediate boss in the USEC and a jolly group of American tourists. The drive was only one day long, but the crossing from the West to the other side of the Iron Curtain made us feel as if we had landed on another planet. At dusk, we reached Helmstedt, the border town with East Germany. A nervous tension rose in the bus. Guards were looking at us with binoculars from the top of watchtowers. Powerful searchlights, barbed wire, and dogs were bringing on a feeling of fear. A "corridor" of about 120 miles was the only access to West Berlin. The road was narrow and full of potholes, and the countryside seemed deserted. In contrast with the darkness in East Germany, the lights of West Berlin looked even brighter when we arrived.

It was a Saturday night and carefree crowds were strolling on the Kurfürstendam, Berlin's main avenue. Gaudy shops, bars, and discotheques were full of people. I still remember the inelegant restaurant where we had dinner. The unsophisticated service was so bad that they brought our plates one at a time and, as a result, we had to eat in shifts.

In the evening, our guide took us to a noisy beer hall. We were amazed by the incredible strength of the waitress, who carried ten huge mugs of beer at a time. She laid the tray at the end of the table and made the mugs slide to the other end. The beer was flowing, everybody was singing, holding arms, and standing up on chairs.

After this rather decadent evening, the view of the Wall was a sobering shock. Erected in only one night in 1961, the Wall was in fact a no-man's land, about fifty meters wide. The West Berliners could visit the East six times a year, but nobody could go from the East to the West. We were nervous at Checkpoint Charlie, where the *Volkspolizei* (People's Police) took the passports of our group. They returned some time later and compared each picture with the passengers.

(Twenty-eight years later, the Berlin Wall came down in amazing circumstances. Mikhail Gorbachev, the Soviet head of state, had been engaged in rounds of intensive diplomacy to bring an end to the communist regimes of Eastern Europe. He happened to be on an official visit to East Berlin in November 1989. The news came out on the East Berlin radio that the gate would open between the two divided Berlins. Gorbachev gave orders not to be awakened for any reason. The East German border guards were at a loss, not knowing what to do, and just watched the crowds getting larger and larger. Finally, the pressure was too much and a flood of tens of thousands of the GDR (German Democratic Republic) population poured into West Berlin. Pick axes started dismantling the Wall.)

In East Berlin, we saw dreary apartment buildings and giant empty squares, contrasting with imposing historical monuments. Our guide, a pleasant young woman, showed us the huge museum created to house the ruins of the ancient city of Pergamum in Turkey. I could sense her dedication to the job and could not help compare her apparent sense of purpose with the dissolute impression I had of West Berlin.

A "tornado" hit us in late October. It was Karen returning from her university tour in Rome. She arrived with her bags and, literally, set up camp in front of the fireplace. She slept on a mattress surrounded by her books, an apple, and some fruit juice. The stereo was not far. She was in a good mood and had had a good meal of pasta. We spent a few wonderful days together.

Late one Sunday night, Alan and I were driving our small Renault on the highway from Lille, in northern France, to Brussels. The fog was thick and the visibility bad. In front of us we noticed the red brake lights of cars that were either stopped or braking. We realized that there had been an accident; the police were there, and the traffic was blocked. Alan slowed down before coming to a full stop, leaving a safe space between us and the car in front. Then, things happened very fast.

Alan shouted, "Watch out!" I did not know what to watch out for, but he knew. We felt a violent shock from the rear, and our car almost jumped toward the car in front of us. I was in a daze. The police sirens came closer, voices surrounded me, and someone helped me out of the car. I was like a zombie, unable to comprehend, traumatized and shaking. An ambulance took me away, but Alan stayed with the car. Only much later was Alan able to find me, and somehow, I do not remember how, we returned home in a rental car.

This is what had happened: The man behind us was driving a car that was not his, had no driver's license, and was drunk. He rammed into our car, causing a chain reaction of several wrecks in front of us. The impact was so strong that the suitcases at the rear of our station wagon had landed on my back. In those days there were no headrests, nor seatbelts. Alan had seen that crazy driver coming and had had time to brace himself. I had not. Our car was totaled. Doctors found nothing wrong with my back. However, less than ten years later, I was diagnosed with a *meningioma.* To this day I am convinced that what caused my near-severed spine had been that violent shock.

Some of the most enjoyable ten days I spent in Belgium were in Kierbergen, organized by the Association Belgique-URRS, as part of a Russian language and literature seminar. We were staying in a nondescript dorm in the middle of a forest. I felt like I was in Russia again. This was total immersion into Russian culture, with a hilarious amateur show at the end. In the evenings, we gathered in each other's bedrooms with our instructors. A Belgian friend would play the guitar, and we would sing Russian folk songs and "romances" and drink tea. Those were my dreamy days of nostalgia for a mythic Russia that has certainly faded away today.

I had my own "May 1968" during our stay in Brussels. Like the demonstrators in the streets of Paris, I fought for a cause I believed in. We were in the 1970s, and the time was ripe for militant women like me to help bring about drastic changes to the status of U.S. Foreign Service spouses (90 percent of them wives in those days).

From the 1950s until the mid-1970s, I had lived in a system that did not recognize women as equal human beings. We were not allowed to work inside the Embassy. Laws of the host countries also made it impossible for us to seek employment. We had to follow the rules of hierarchy and protocol and were often subject to the whim of the ambassador's wife. We were assigned functions and instructed to behave at all times in a manner corresponding to our rank in the embassy. In one extreme case, the wife of a junior career diplomat was asked to take the coats of the guests at the door during a reception at the ambassador's residence. That really was the last straw! I already mentioned in my Lebanon chapter how I committed a breach of the rules myself by sitting on the right side of a sofa—a seat assigned to the ambassador's wife.

Largely as a result of our task force's proposals, the U.S. government abandoned the system whereby it was getting "two for the price of one." From then on, few demands were to be put on the spouses. Many wives took the Foreign Service examination or opted to pursue their own careers. Because spouses became frequently unavailable, they had to be replaced by fully paid personnel.

Regarding jobs, I must stress that I was able to beat the system and work in every single country we lived in. From my employment in the Chinese-American information office in Taiwan, to a position with Banker's Trust in Tunisia, or as Student Advisor in South Africa, I never ceased to work. All I needed was a little imagination and lots of determination. I found the variety of projects available unlimited, especially when considering the volunteering opportunities I have described at length throughout my story.

To make up for our having been unable to attend Sylvia's graduation at Stanford University in California, Alan and I invited her to take a trip to the Soviet Union in 1978. We were traveling under the best conditions possible, given that we had diplomatic passports and were the personal guests in Leningrad of U.S. consul general Thompson Buchanan, and in Moscow of the French chargé d'affaires, Jacques Dupont. At the same time, we were traveling independently.

Before leaving Belgium for the Soviet Union, however, I felt nervous. I went to the Soviet Consulate to obtain my visa and was immediately taken to a room. The windows were painted over, so I could not see outside. The consular officer closed the door. He had a round face and scrutinized me with his small eyes. "I know you *Gospoja* (Madame) Logan, we were in Guinea together." Somehow, since the time we lived in Moscow, we always had the feeling of being followed by the Soviets at all times.

The panic attack started again when we got on the train from Paris to Leningrad and were stripped of our passports, visas, and tickets. We felt a growing sense of fear when we crossed the border in Grodno, because it was not the usual point of entry for foreigners, which made us feel even more isolated. Again, we had the distinct feeling that the police and the customs officials not only knew us but were expecting us. After waiting five hours for the train to be lifted onto the wider Russian tracks, we were on our way to the Leningrad railroad station.

The Residence of the U.S. consul general in Leningrad was the elegant green and white palace of Grand Duke Constantine Constantinovich, the great-uncle of the last tsar, Nicholas II. It had grand marble stairs, beautiful reception rooms, painted ceilings, and sculpted stucco with gold. Sylvia could not contain herself and started doing *grands jetés* across the room. The Residence was complete with a couple of servant-spies who took care of us. Our good friends Consul General Tom Buchanan and his wife, Nancy, had graciously offered their home to the three of us while they were on leave.

Alan, Sylvia, and I spoke Russian, which made contacts most interesting. We used public transport, stayed in ghastly hotels when stopping in small towns, and went off the beaten tracks. We crossed Lake Onega to visit Kiji Island, with its beautiful wooden churches from the sixteenth and seventeenth centuries. It was cold and damp. In Petrozavodsk, we dined in the newly restored governor's residence dating from Peter the Great's time. The waiters were wearing costumes from that period. Sylvia engaged in conversation with some young people around us, and we had a delightful evening. Like everywhere else, people were eager to talk and ask questions and were incredibly friendly. The young girls invited Sylvia to visit them in their Leningrad dorm, and she accepted.

Continuing with our travel as normal Soviet tourists, we made a stop in Novgorod with its beautiful twelfth-fourteenth-century churches. We had lunch in the vaulted rooms built in the walls of the Kremlin. The restoration had been done with a great deal of taste to recreate a medieval atmosphere. We ate delicious *blinis* swimming in butter and served in coarse earthenware pots with wooden spoons. We returned to Leningrad after an exciting bus ride without headlights. Young women in trim navy uniforms and white gloves were standing by each car of the train to welcome us on the overnight "Red Arrow" to Moscow.

The U.S. embassy in Moscow did not greet us as warmly as the Leningrad consulate had; in fact, it did not greet us at all. We were not even allowed in the snack bar! In contrast, our friend Jacques Dupont, the French chargé, made us feel most welcome. He had arranged an evening at the Bolshoi Theater. George Kennan happened to be there. When the Russian public found this out, there was a standing ovation for the American diplomat.

The European Union requires the largest contingent of interpreters in the world—more than the UN and more than any other international organization, a real tower of Babel! During my last year in Brussels, I thought I would try out my possible skill at simultaneous interpreting. I enrolled at ISTI (Institut Supérieur de l'Etat de Traducteurs et Interprètes) in Russian/French. We had to learn the jargon used during international conferences dealing with the nuclear nonproliferation treaty, disarmament, and the like. It was an interesting experience, but I found it too difficult. I quit after a while.

In 1975, the World Federation of Friends of Museums was legally founded in Brussels and staffed by volunteers. I am proud to have been a part of this organization during its initial years. Today, the federation groups national associations from thirty-four countries and represents two million individuals. "Friends" has become an indispensable institution that provides financial and other forms of support to museums around the world. I was fortunate to be appointed as the person responsible for international relations. My job was to coordinate and stimulate existing Friends associations and also to contact potential new members. I remember, for instance, my exchange of letters (in Russian) with Irina Antonova, the director of the Pushkin Museum in Moscow. The WFFM headquarters were located in the elegant district next to the Musée des Beaux Arts and the Royal Palace. I worked several months in those pleasant surroundings with people full of ideals.

We heard the good news that Philip was accepted at Columbia University for graduate school in architecture. Sylvia spent the summer with the Tanzproekt dance company in Vienna before moving to Salt Lake City and joining a company there.

Diane was now a student at the American College in Paris. She rented a *chambre de bonne* (maid's room) in the seventh arrondissement on Rue de Rennes. The room was on the seventh floor with no elevator. The primitive toilet was down the hall. Incidentally, such *chambres de bonne* are worth a fortune today. It had a great view over probably the most spectacular traffic gridlocks in Paris.

During all that time, Alan was boat-hunting. He explored shipyards in the UK, Holland, and all over France. He was desperate to go sailing. A Dutch couple had invited him to join them on a sail along the Mediterranean coast. Alan's spirits lifted. However, our female skipper friend canceled the trip at the last minute, because a witch doctor had said the weather was too dangerous.

Taking advantage of being in a European post, we thought it was a good time to plant roots in France. At first, we bought a beautiful piece of land in Provence with an orchard of almond trees, with the intention of building a vacation house. It had a panoramic view over the Durance Valley and the hills near Mont St. Victoire, so often painted by Cezanne. When this project did not work out, we decided to buy a property on the Mediterranean.

We found an apartment in a private villa surrounded by umbrella pines in the small fishing village of Sanary-sur-Mer, located in the unfashionable part of the Côte d'Azur. The location was great, but the apartment was in abysmal condition. It had the ugliest yellow flower wallpaper, a huge bathroom with a dining room table in the middle, a tiny kitchen stuck under the stairs, and small rooms with lots of doors. What's more, short-term summer renters had wrecked it. Fortunately, Superman Philip, the budding architect, stepped in. He spent the winter months of 1979 in the frigid place without water, heat, electricity, or even a toilet. He worked with carpenters, plumbers, and electricians. It was great on-the-job training for him. Later his sister Diane gave him a hand laying the gorgeous hand-made bathroom tiles.

Eventually, our seaside apartment became a bright and comfortable place to spend a vacation. We loved what I called our "Matisse window," because it reminds me of the several paintings Matisse made of his artist's studio in Collioure from 1905 on. Our wide and old-fashioned window overlooks the Bay of Sanary, dotted with sailboats and windsurfers. In the distance, one sees the Island of Embiez.

In the spring of 1979, Alan received a cable from the State personnel office in Washington, announcing his appointment as deputy chief of mission in Bamako, Mali. Everybody congratulated him. Alan started dreaming: "Imagine sailing down the Niger River by moonlight to Timbuktu!" He was quite pleased to return to a continent he knew so well and to a post with more freedom, a post Washington had little interest in. Researching through his abundant correspondence, I realized then how hard the past three years spent in Brussels had been for him. A few weeks later, as we were getting ready for our move to Mali, another telegram arrived: Bamako was off. The new ambassador was a thirty-year-old woman with no diplomatic experience and a friend of Andrew Young, former ambassador to the United Nations. Apparently, the ambassador-designate wanted to choose her own deputy chief of mission, and Alan was discarded.

It was an example of the total lack of communication within the State Department: Nobody had been notified by the Office of Personnel of Alan's appointment. And this illustrated a more worrisome trend—the appointments of nondiplomats as ambassadors to African posts. This has been demoralizing for career FSOs who work very hard all their lives to reach the top echelon of the hierarchy. A few years later, while serving in Durban, South Africa, we heard a rumor that the post of ambassador to the mountainous state of Lesotho had been offered as a favor to someone from Colorado who loved high altitudes.

After this big disappointment, Alan obtained an extremely interesting assignment as consul general to Durban in the province of Natal in the Republic of South Africa. This change of plan may actually have turned out for the better, as I will try to show in my next chapter.

9

South Africa 1979–1982

For an FSO (Foreign Service officer), the next assignment is always the source of hope, anxiety, and sometimes disappointment.

Toward the end of our stay in Brussels, we still did not know where we would be sent next after the cancellation of the Mali posting. The rumor was that it would be Constantine, Algeria. I was not too excited at the prospect of moving to a provincial town built on the edge of a geological chasm. Then, the rumor faded until, in September 1979, Alan learned that he was appointed consul general in Durban, in the South African province of Natal.[3]

My first reaction was a moment of panic at the idea of going to the other end of the world, on the Indian Ocean. And it was not even in an embassy! As it turned out, this was to be one of our richest assignments: a spectacular country, a gorgeous Residence, but more important, a crucial time for American diplomats to help work toward the end of apartheid. Our home was going to become a neutral ground where leaders from all ethnic groups and political parties would meet to discuss and lay the ground for future changes. As for me, I used my official position to become involved in the development of all forms of arts—dance, plastic arts, music, theater, and handicrafts—which gave a chance to all races to work together for the first time.

The post of consul general in Natal Province offered Alan more independence than he had ever experienced in his thirty-year diplomatic career. Far away from the ambassador's authority in Pretoria, he was in charge of a huge geographic area,[4] home of the country's most powerful black political group—the Zulus—and a large Indian community living in Durban. In 1994 Natal Province changed its name to KwaZulu Natal at the end of apartheid.

We did not choose the most direct route to reach South Africa. We first flew to Rio, where we spent two days discovering the decadent splendor of old buildings with overgrown vegetation, the exuberant multiracial population, a thrilling ride up Sugarloaf mountain, an uncomfortable glimpse at the *favelas*, followed by a ride through the lush surrounding hills.

A pleasant seven-and-a-half-hour flight on Brazilian Airlines took us from South America to South Africa .We were pampered by courteous flight attendants, who served us stylishly on a white linen tablecloth with silver and fine China. As we made our approach toward Johannesburg, we saw highways and a modern airport.

Our new life, as the U.S. consul general and his wife, started the minute we touched ground. Whereas our fellow passengers had to wait in a long line to pass through police control, we were met by a protocol officer from the South African foreign ministry and whisked to an official limousine to be chauffeur-driven to Pretoria, the capital.

In those days, anyone moving to South Africa had to be given a general introduction to the race relations existing in that country in order to understand what apartheid really meant. The American ambassador, William B. Edmondson, and his wife—our marvelous hosts in Pretoria for three days—were kind enough to give us that introduction.

The situation, they explained, was complex and evolved constantly. Some provinces or towns were more liberal than others. In a Johannesburg coffee shop, you might be sitting next to a black, or "African," as they were called here. No such thing in Pretoria, however. Pietermaritzburg, the seat of Natal's government, boasted about its liberal views. Most of the South Africans we talked to were well aware of the core problem of race and fell over backward to assure us that things were improving.

In a recent speech, the prime minister, P. W. Botha, had announced the projected changes in the racial rules: no more discrimination in restaurants, Africans' right to join black trade unions. Also, the government was ready to consider changing the Immorality Act and the Mixed Marriage Act. Botha did not look at mixed marriage as a sin but considered it undesirable. Many types of discrimination remained: no mixing in dancing places or swimming pools, an interdiction against different races living under the same roof. In Durban, as we were to discover soon, there were separate beaches for whites, Indians, Coloreds, and blacks. The largest group of Coloreds lives in the Cape Province and their ancestry there is a mix of Hottentots and Dutch. The nonwhites lived in communities and "townships" on the outskirts of large cities.

The strategy of the South African government toward the black population was the "consolidation" or "constellation" of the Homelands. By grouping and increasing the areas of the Homelands, making sure they had mineral and agricultural resources, the government thought that they would become economically viable. The government envisioned South Africa as a federation of white and black states. This idea was totally rejected by countries around the world, including the United States.[5]

We said good-bye to Bill and Dona Edmondson and started our long drive to Durban, Natal Province's largest city. At first, the landscape was flat and monotonous. Then we drove through rolling hills and had a glimpse of the grandiose Drakensberg mountain ridge. We left Transvaal and entered Natal. We reached Newcastle, the center of a coal mining and heavy industry region. Round Zulu huts covered with thatched roofs replaced the brightly painted adobe houses of the Transvaal.

As the official car was right-hand driven, I had prepared a large sign for Alan, reading *"Hou Links,"* meaning "drive left," lest he forget the driving regulations. We followed a series of plateaus stepping down toward the Indian Ocean

We crossed the Tugela River, many times mentioned in relation to Rorke's Drift Battle between the British and the Zulus in 1879. The name of that battle is as well known here as are Waterloo and Borodino in Europe.

Then the fog closed in on us. It was getting darker. The scenery became more rugged. The road was dropping steeply by now. I thought our descent would never end. Finally, we arrived in Durban, greeted by the wonderful sight of lush hills and comfortable residences nestled in the midst of luxuriant vegetation. The apartment buildings looked quite modern. Several skyscrapers announced Durban's downtown area, bordered on one side by a huge commercial port and on the other, by the Indian Ocean and its beautiful beaches. Tourist hotels and amusement parks lined the waterfront avenue.

A highway led us to the affluent neighborhood of Durban North. The Residence of the U.S. consul general at 20 Monteith Place lay up a hill. The large house dominated a series of several terraces following the incline of the slope. I saw well-kept lawns, an orgy of rosebushes, and a variety of trees, including jacarandas, papayas, and bougainvilleas. Through the giant cypress trees, the city lights shimmered on the horizon. One could hear the faint sound of the crashing waves of the ocean far below. It was dusk by now.

I was taking in the impressive aspect of our future home when I heard an eerie sound coming from the several ponds. Hundreds of frogs and toads were greeting us in a loud bacchanal. The cry of the *ladidas* birds added to the cacophony (the name of *ladidas* imitates the cry these birds make.)

One entered our house through a large foyer. The elegant staircase had an elaborate wrought iron railing. The entertainment rooms were spacious and included a double living room, a formal dining room, and a cloakroom with a guest toilet. Off the living room was a den with a large picture window. There were three guest bedrooms upstairs. The master bedroom suite was surprising: It was separated from the rest of the house by a metal bulletproof door that looked fit more for a submarine than for a family home. Everything had been painted white and cream, creating a feeling of clarity and cleanliness. The view from the upstairs windows was even more beautiful, as I discovered the following day. Off the huge and stark white kitchen, a series of small white buildings lined up along an alley constituted the servants' quarters.

Jim Bumpus, Alan's assistant, and his wife Mary Reeber, head of the branch public affairs office, greeted us warmly. "You are going to be very busy," they announced, showing a pile of invitations lying on a silver platter in the entrance. Alan had been named vice president of the Natal Baseball Association and several other organizations. He was scheduled to be the guest of honor at a men-only consular corps luncheon at the Durban Country Club. The following week, we were expected to be the hosts at an American-Canadian "genuine curry dinner." I thought this was rather ironic, since I had no idea how to prepare curry, especially for eighty guests.

In spite of the grand allure of the Residence, I had found the taste of the decor, particularly in the choice of upholstery and furniture, frankly atrocious. That problem was pleasantly solved soon after our arrival. The U.S. government had decided that it was time to freshen up the looks of the house. A budget of $15,000 had been allocated for the renovation, with me in charge. The only problem was that we had only four days to allocate the money.

My initial stay in Durban was therefore spent happily in an ambitious decoration project. I plunged head first into the commercial life of Durban. My center of operations became the elegant Berea district. Never in my life, before or since, have I had the privilege of spending time in fashionable boutiques, with rolls of upholstery material rolled out for my pleasure.

My objective was to get rid of the living room's yellow flowers and our bedroom's dark green colors, as well as the purple and brown motifs of one of the guestrooms. Not only was I in charge, but also I had *carte blanche* to express my taste. I wanted to recreate the luxuriant atmosphere of a primeval African forest. My plan called for the living room upholstery to be turned into giant orchids in shades of coral, browns, and almond green. The chintz curtains and lampshades were going to be in matching colors. The dining room remained a formal room for official sit-down dinners. In contrast, I decided to decorate the den to make it a modern, more personal room: all white, with a bar, shelves full of books, a stereo, and family pictures. A designer's glass coffee table was to rest on a shaggy white rug. The window opened onto the veranda and the distant view of the ocean. Every morning, I could not wait to go down and check on my team of decorators, carpenters, and painters. Quite a rapid way to meet professionals anxious to please Madame the Consul General!

It was early October, a month marked by rain showers. Ferocious winds picked up suddenly, the way they do on the Mediterranean. People strolled on the waterfront to watch the reckless surfers ride the mountainous waves.

One of the first things Alan did was to check the yacht clubs, thinking vaguely of buying a boat to replace the twenty-seven-foot *Philvia*, which had committed suicide on the rocky coast of Tunisia. Finally, he decided not to buy a boat, realizing that his official duties would take too much of his time. Besides, sailing is difficult here: the coast is inhospitable, as evidenced by the presence of numerous wrecks, and the surf one of the roughest in the world. Even sailing small boats like Lasers would be difficult in the Durban commercial port, the busiest in the country.

The U.S. Consulate General was on the twenty-ninth floor of the Durban Bay House, right downtown. Alan's office was large, commanding an impressive view of the harbor. The furnishing was severe. Hidden behind closet doors one found a bar and, more important, a pair of powerful binoculars. I suspect Alan liked to follow the activities of the Point Yacht Club located just below his windows and the likely arrival of round-the-world "yachties" seeking protection during the hurricane season. The friendly and chatty consular team included Americans, South Africans of British origin, Afrikaners, Indians, and blacks.

When we first arrived, Alan said he was looking forward to relaxing times in his new position. His work at USEC in Brussels had been intense, embroiled in complex matters such as nuclear power or the deep-sea fishing wars. But even in South Africa, Alan never lost that hurried look. He got up even earlier than in Belgium, and kept on running. Every night, he returned from the office with a bunch of official papers to work on.

For me, this was an interesting change: Unlike the previous post where I had often been shut out from Alan's classified work, in South Africa I was able to follow what he was doing, as I will show in detail later.

The U.S. consul general was a prominent personality in Durban who appeared at every single official event. His title of Dean of the Durban Diplomatic Corps sounded impressive, but was in fact somewhat ironic since, except for himself and his British colleague, all the consuls were honorary—that is, not career diplomats.

The day after our arrival, Alan had to present his credentials to the administrator of Natal Province in Pietermaritzburg. After driving fifty-five miles to Natal's capital, we were received by J. C. G. Botha, his wife, and members of the executive committee in a sumptuous residence. With much ceremony, we were treated to hors d'oeuvres of game meat, a milk tart, and plantain fritters. The conversation touched on politics regarding the current situation in

South Africa. The officials were telling us the things we wanted to hear. The situation was improving, they assured us. Progress is being made regarding women's condition, as well, they added.

For an outsider like me, the place of women in the South African society was reminiscent of the situation existing in America and Europe thirty years earlier. A few months later, I was to be the keynote speaker at a large gathering of women and had a chance to research this topic. Career women were a rarity here. There was only one woman in the parliament. Divorce laws were unfavorable for women. If a university professor married, she lost her job immediately. Even women who were high-level officials entered private clubs through a side door. Women were only allowed in bars during "ladies' nights." Useless to say the situation was even worse for the African women.

The first official ceremony we had to attend was the Annual Military and Civic Church Parade. The city's VIPs were present, including several parliamentarians. The mayor wore a wig; the members of the Municipal Council were in robes, and the military in full-dress uniforms. The women's attire included hats, gloves, and outfits usually worn at formal balls. After a sermon, the honored guests gathered for a reception at the city hall.

A nonstop round of official visits and travel began in earnest. We accompanied the agricultural attaché from the American embassy in Pretoria for three days on an informative visit to several farms run by whites—Afrikaners or South Africans of British origin. The farms could be as large as ten thousand hectares. Modern equipment, scientific methods, and irrigation were used on cattle and grain farms alike. The dairy output was enhanced by the use of computer technology. Research had led to the production of ethanol long before it was even mentioned in the West. The farmers lived in comfortable houses with swimming pools and tennis courts. The country club was never far. The wives were elegant, and the children studied abroad in expensive boarding schools.

I was struck by the paternalistic attitude the white farmers had toward "their blacks." One of the wives made a comment about their farmhands that I found characteristic: "We know them well, we have grown together on the same land, we played together as children! We consider ourselves as their parents. Whenever they have personal problems, they are welcome to come to us." A village for the black workers had been created on the farm, including a school where the boss's wife would volunteer her help. It was not unlike life in the American Deep South many years ago.

On this first trip, we also visited a meat-processing plant making bacon, sausages, and ham. The facilities were spotless, and the black workers dressed in impeccable white blouses. I saw fifty of them at a long table putting bacon strips in plastic bags. A machine could have done the work in five minutes! But then, what to do with this mass of unskilled workers? Increasing productivity would no doubt create unemployment. The resulting social unrest would be worse. I found out later that there were practically no skilled black workers in this country. For generations, the Africans had been kept in the lowest positions. They were not allowed to create or join a trade union. Needless to say, strikes were out of the question.

Continuing our trip, we drove though the sugarcane region and were given a tour of a technical school and an experimental station. Only Indians were employed or trained there. Indians had arrived in the nineteenth century as "indentured servants" to work on the sugar cane plantations. They could rise up the social ladder and become "artisans," a qualification not accessible to blacks. The most important sugarcane company was in Tongaat. The plantation owners lived in majestic buildings with columns in the classical style, reminiscent of Williamsburg. The Indian workers were housed in what looked like a model village, with small white homes in "Cape Dutch" architecture, manicured lawns, and flowerbeds. We visited a decent-looking school where the students wore black and white uniforms. We finished our tour of the sugar industry by looking at the terminal located near the Durban Harbor, which exported one million tons of sugar a year.

On a Sunday, Alan and I were the guests of honor at the Orient Club. Close to half a million Indians lived in the Durban area. Entire streets in the city were lined with Indian shops. When my children came to visit at Christmas, one of the first things they wanted to do was to shop in the open market fragrant with a multitude of spices. I learned that the market had been even more colorful before the great fire of 1972.

The Indians occupied a special place here. They had their own newspapers and their own culture. Their university, which was located in the suburb of Durban Westville, had a high academic standing. At the graduation ceremony we attended, a degree in philosophy was awarded to a distinguished female student. The university was also an active cultural center. This is where we saw an excellent adaptation of *A Passage to India*. The playwright was the daughter of E.M. Forster's Natal-born collaborator. The Indian community was tightly knit, observing traditions and religious practices. To be the guests at a Hindu wedding felt like a total immersion in a culture far from Africa. They also had their own temples. About 20 percent were Muslims and gathered in mosques.

The Indians played an important role in local politics. One felt their presence at all administrative levels. It was logical that they would fear the breaking loose of the blacks. They definitely had more affinity with the whites. For them, the motto "One man, one vote." and majority rule were frightening prospects. In spite of this somewhat privileged position, the Indians could also fall under the harsh rules of apartheid. It was during our stay that a renowned sociologist named Fatma Meer, already under house arrest for a long time, encountered serious legal problems for breaking the rules by attending a public event. The Indians had learned how to cope with the Special Branch, or secret police, which could harass them.

They formed an industrious group, active in commerce and even liberal professions, and showed definite signs of wealth. Almost always, the foreman in a factory, farm, or mine was an Indian. Some of their houses were extravagant in size and style. It was not uncommon for an Indian to own a sports car. They traveled extensively and sent their children abroad to study. The mayor of Durban organized frequent functions for the Indian community. In 1980 one particularly brilliant banquet marked the 120th commemoration of the arrival of the first Indians as indentured workers on the sugarcane plantations

An anecdote will illustrate the Indians' entrepreneurial mentality. I was visiting a black "reserve" near Durban. More than fifty women were waiting by the roadside with plastic buckets and drums.

"What are you waiting for?" I asked.

"The owner of the water is expected at 11: o'clock," a woman answered.

Sure enough, at 11:00 sharp came a dapper little Indian in an immaculate white suit. He was wearing a white lace skullcap and had a well-trimmed, thin beard. He looked like a shrewd money-lender displaying generosity toward the poor people. As the water started gushing out, the Indian businessman explained that he had drilled a well eight years before and that since then he had shared the bounty with the populace at his own expense. He owned a service station, a shop, and a thriving clothing factory. He pointed at the lush field where a few horses were grazing. This was only a fraction of the two-hundred-hectare property he owned.

Mahatma Gandhi was Natal's most illustrious son. Born in 1869, he came to Durban from England as a lawyer of modest rank in 1893. He rapidly became shocked by the terrible living conditions of his compatriots. One day, riding the train to Johannesburg in first class, he was rudely moved to the third class. When he complained, he was simply thrown out of the train. From that moment on, his personal mission became the emancipation of the Indian population. In 1894, he created the Natal Indian Congress. Jailed several times, he went through twelve years of struggle until he left for India in 1915. It was in Natal that he first applied his philosophy of passive resistance. Phoenix Farm, a community near Durban that retains Gandhi's ideas and principles of simplicity, self-sufficiency, and love, became a shrine opened to tourists.

The Schlebush Commission, named after the minister of justice, was hearing "testimonies" in order to bring constitutional changes to the status of Indians and Coloreds. Members of parliament and public law jurists spent many hours around the discussion table. In theory, these hearings were open to the public, but since there was little publicity in the press, the public was absent. The central question was whether to create two new parliaments for Indians and Coloreds, or accept the two groups into the existing Parliament.

Unlike Johannesburg or other large towns where the black areas, such as Soweto, were remote and totally separate from the white city, Durban was an intricate ethnic patchwork: the black "townships" were not far from the city center and its suburbs. Some of our friends whom we invited frequently to our house belonged to the black middle class. They were doctors, lawyers, and business- men. But life was not easy for them. During one of the dinners we gave at the Residence, a young lawyer explained in detail the in- tricacy of the legal system that repressed the blacks, as well as the restrictions imposed on trade. They could own property only in a few areas.

Migrant black workers were housed in hostels. The poorest of all were the 350,000-odd squatters who lived on the most desolate hillsides among overgrown weeds and mounds of garbage. There was no electricity. The few points of communal city water were not provided free to the people. It was dangerous at night, and there was tension between the squatters and the inhabitants of the black townships. The Zulu Homeland, or KwaZulu, was made up of dis- connected enclaves scattered throughout Natal. Also called "black spots," they were situated on poor and steep land.

In spite of the bleak condition of the Africans, there was a sense of expectancy among the entire population when we lived in Dur- ban. More and more people were looking forward to the changes promised by P. W. Botha as the beginning of a new area. A climate of approaching changes was mentioned every day in the press, but the task ahead remained enormous. Critics characterized reforms as "cosmetic," saying they only rectified details and made the hu- miliation suffered by the blacks even harder to bear. Signs like "Eu- ropeans Only" in the railroad stations were disappearing. Blacks were allowed to wait in line to buy their train tickets along with the whites, but once on the train, segregation ruled again. Sports events were not segregated anymore in theory, but an African could not buy beer in the sport stadium.

University libraries, hospitals, theaters, concert halls, wedding receptions, congresses, clubs, drive-in theaters, circuses, cafes, and restaurants could now ask, once and for all, for an "exemption" allowing them to admit all races. However, the rules concerning the alcoholic beverages in these premises were not modified. The liberalization was conditional upon noninfringement on the public order.

Had I been a black, I would have been infuriated by the expres- sion often used by the whites: "It takes time." Actually, the changes that were supposed to be just around the corner, when we lived in Durban, took another fifteen years to take place.

I found the feelings strong, even visceral, on both sides. The whites wanted to hold onto their superior rights for dear life. The blacks were full of hatred and bitterness. One could have expected the end of the apartheid regime to be marked by a bloodbath. I am still amazed that it did not, due to the god-sent presence of Nelson Mandela.

The racial problem could easily turn into an obsession. It seemed to obliterate all other topics of interest (cultural, economic, political) such as existed in other countries around the world. Many whites played the ostrich. When I once asked a white farmer whether he was obsessed or not by the ever-recurring question about race relations, he answered: "You, and the outside world are obsessed, we are not. We are doing just fine!" When we talked to liberals, academics, journalists, writers, and intellectuals, it was a different story. They were worried and felt the burden of responsibility for this unjust situation. Many progressive whites believed they were sitting on a time bomb ready to explode. Many would have liked to leave, but the South African government made it impossible to pull one's capital out of the country.

Our own situation as Americans was not always easy. We were being attacked from all sides. If we mentioned human rights, they would shoot back "What about Vietnam?" If we supported the great efforts of philanthropy carried out by the whites, the blacks expressed their resentment for any form of "do-goodism." All these first impressions hit me with a bang upon our arrival, and they did not go away. During the entire time we spent in Durban, Alan and I faced the heavy burden of an inescapable guilt mitigated by our efforts to help bring about changes.

My house renovation project was beginning to take shape. Our home looked like an anthill with workers everywhere. In our bedroom, a thick, soft white wall-to-wall carpet was installed. Walking barefoot on it was a pure delight. The armchairs and sofas returned, reupholstered in an extravagant motif of giant orchids. Alan made a horrified face when he first saw it. The last touches to the renovation of our living room were two lamps: an enormous white lamp and another *sang de boeuf* (deep red) color. Teams of electricians took over the whole house like termites, made holes, laid wires under rugs. Hygiene services came to spray closets, drawers, and every corner of the house with insecticide. The living room carpet was Scotchgarded. For twelve hours, we had no access to the room. How much times have changed! As I am writing this text years later, the thought of all these chemical treatments that are so harmful for the environment make me shudder.

Five weeks after our arrival, our small Peugeot showed up in the port of Durban in pitiful condition: rusted, with a broken window, full of scratches and bumps. All the spare parts that Alan had carefully collected in France had disappeared.

Since I could not drive the car yet, I used the time to read about the history of the Bantus, the generic name given to blacks in South Africa. *The Washing of the Spears: A History of the Rise of the Zulu Nation Under Shaka and Its Fall in the Zulu War of 1879* by Donald R. Morris was just the book I needed. It is a monumental and informative work and reads like a brilliant novel. The migration of black tribes from the north occurred over many centuries. When the Portuguese navigator Vasco da Gama sighted the coast of Africa, on Christmas day 1497—hence the name of Natal—it was already inhabited. Some historians mentioned the twelfth century or even earlier for the arrival of blacks in Southern Africa. In the 1770s, the Dutch were slowly moving away from the Cape, where they had first settled in 1652, looking for more grazing lands. The Bantus were going south at a leisurely pace. When these two groups met each other on the Great Fish River in the Eastern Cape, both were equally surprised. Until then, the only indigenous tribes the whites had ever known were the weak tribes of Bushmen and Hottentots. For the first time, Bantus and whites realized that the "limitless open land" had limits. The question as to who was there first has been hotly debated for a long time in South Africa. Obviously, the answer had an impact on determining the legitimacy of the blacks to own land. With dry humor, Morris wrote: "History had offered the blacks a continent and 10,000 years to fill it, and they had dallied a little too long."

The Bantus consisted of two main tribes: the Sotho, who remained in the west, eventually settling in Lesotho, Botswana, and parts of the Orange Free State; and the Nguni, who migrated down the eastern seaboard. In the nineteenth century, three important tribes dominated southern Africa: the Basutus, whose descendants live today in Lesotho and were led by Moshesh, a just and peace-loving man and a good diplomat; the Ndebele, who followed a long odyssey, destroying entire regions of Transvaal and northern Natal to end up in what is today Zimbabwe under their cruel chief Nzilikari; and the Zulus.

The Zulus were the most powerful. Led by a brilliant chief, Sha-ka, they were organized into a well-structured political state and military society, with a royal hierarchy. The land they took over was exceptionally rich. Diseases like syphilis, smallpox, chicken pox, and tuberculosis had not yet made their way from Europe, and their population grew rapidly. The aggressiveness of these tribes brought a bloody turmoil to the region. The weaker tribes were absorbed, wiped out, or forced to flee to the mountains and the poorest lands.

The Zulus were warriors. During the Zulu War of 1879, they wiped out the major white columns at the Battle of Isandlwana. Some 3,500 British and 2,000 Zulus died. At Rorke's Drift, a handful of British troops beat off thousands of Zulus.

Old illustrations show the men carrying spears and shields while the women bore domestic implements on their heads. The clan would live in a *kraal*, or corral. The hive-shaped huts, made of saplings with thatched roofs, were situated in a circle, protecting the cattle in the middle. The "great wife" had her personal hut situated the closest to the chief. The other wives were positioned according to their place in the group's hierarchy.

To return to the beginnings of our life in South Africa, the investigation of the tennis club scene was on our priority list. We found the clubs' facilities fairly poor compared to those in Brussels, a fact that surprised me, given the world-class level of South African tennis players. Besides, we could not find any clay courts. The Durban Country Club had the best facilities. On weekends, "round robins" were the rule. A club official kept a book and called the players. The sacrosanct tea ritual served by Indian waiters highlighted the social atmosphere. Sedate in their white clothes and straw hats, the bowlers here were quite different from the loud and animated French crowd playing *boules* on the Mediterranean coast. Finally, Alan joined the Berea Club. The players there were good, in fact, too good for me. Once in a while, I was tolerated to make a fourth at doubles game. At 6:00 p.m., everyone would gather in the tiny clubhouse and discuss politics over several beers.

My search for the right tennis club continued for a while, until I found the delightful Morningside Club. The setting was pleasant and the players were either my strength or a little better. Just perfect! I made good friends there. Toward the end of our stay, I invited my partners to the Residence for lunch. It was a heart-warming experience. The ladies were so grateful and touched by my gesture! I told them about my long "career" in tennis. I provoked a roar of laughter when I said, "You may not have noticed but I have won many tournaments in my life." I clarified my statement by saying that the frequent reason I had occasionally won tournaments was the lack of strong opponents. I told them about the *faux pas* I made by winning against the American ambassador's wife in Conakry, Guinea.

One of our neighbors, who lived in a grand mansion and raised horses, was involved in charity work with Africans. One day, she invited me to join her on a visit to a poor town south of Durban. Our guide, who lived in that town, was an admirable person and the only woman on her city council. She was dedicated to improving the living conditions of her black compatriots. Among many other projects, she created nurseries.

We drove to KwaZulu, down into deep valleys and up craggy hills. Our destination was a high school built on a steep ridge. We saw seventy students per classroom, no equipment, and a "library" consisting of a few books on a table. After completing their years of schooling, the Zulu children obtained a "senior certificate," but not the "matrix," which is required to go to university. The buildings were run down, there was garbage thrown on the grass. The principal's office had bars on its window and door. The week before, students from another school had made a hole in the corrugated iron roof. The principal said with humor: "Now we have to put bars on the roof." She added, "Violence and petty crime are rampant in the village. At night, they come and rob vegetables from my garden."

Alan and I had a chance to discover northern Natal as we accompanied Jay Taylor, political counselor at our embassy in Pretoria, and his wife Betsy. At first, we drove along the Indian Ocean coast through the sugarcane country. It was October and the cane was almost full-grown. The harvest is staggered over a period of four months. During that time, the landscape looked like a lush lawn as far as the eye could see.

Once more I was struck by the sharp contrast between the lands occupied by the whites and the lands occupied by the Africans. In the white areas, on top of each hill, dwellings that looked more like manors than farmhouses nestled among flowering trees and bushes. Well-disciplined eucalyptus trees lined the approach roads.

It looked as if the rainfall had never reached the land on the other side of the road, which happened to be in KwaZulu! Crushed by the constant trekking of goats, the hillside crumbled down in dust. There was not a single tree in sight. On uncultivated fields, skinny cows munched weed. Near the tiny houses built of dry mud, a tentative corn crop grew. The quality of the land and the quantity of rainfall were identical on both sides of the road, but one side was lacking fertilizer, good seeds, water, and agricultural equipment. Something else was missing: manpower. The men worked in the mines and factories of western Natal or Transvaal. Women were left to till the land by themselves.

Our first stop was Richard's Bay. In the midst of a moonlike landscape, disfigured by chemical pollution, we were shown the active commercial port terminal exporting coal, aluminum, and phosphoric acid. We walked through mounds of black dust. This was not coal but titanium extracted from coastal sand dunes.

At that point we were more than ready for a refreshing, ecological stop and spent the night at St. Lucia Reserve. The hotel corresponded exactly to the idea I had of safari accommodations: the rooms were located in individual grass huts shaded by red frangipani trees, rubber trees, royal Poinciana, or flaming trees. Jokingly, we asked the hotel manager if we would have a chance to see "real" hippos. In an utmost serious tone, he answered: "Yes. Harry comes by every evening at 10:00 p.m." The following morning, guided by two friendly game rangers, we visited the park, the beach, the estuary, and the campsites. At the crocodile farm, we could have learned all about crocodiles' family and sex life had we had more time.

As we sailed up a lagoon in a small motorboat, our young guide suddenly turned his boat around and pointed at a huge brown mass with tiny ears. It was Harry, barely six feet away from us. By the end of our trip, we had seen more than thirty hippos. They keep cool in the water, in family groups of five to seven. They can stay seven minutes under water. They submerged halfway, perhaps thinking we could not see them.

We reached Hluhluwe Game Park under threatening black clouds. The following morning, I had my first experience of big game. We fell upon a group of white rhinos.[6] They had been on the endangered list, with only sixty left. Now the breed was doing much better. In his typical fashion, Alan immediately got out of the car to film them. With apprehension, I noticed that the group of rhinos was slowly cutting off Alan's way back to the car. I imagined them rushing toward him all of a sudden. But no, with apparent indifference, they went about their business and disappeared among the trees.

I was caught in uncontrollable fits of the giggles when I saw a few giraffes in a field. They were towering over the trees. As soon as they saw us coming, they moved closer. They seemed to walk in slow motion but actually moved extremely rapidly. Twisting their necks like a periscope, they examined us with curiosity, as would gossipy village women. During that first visit to Hluhluwe we saw crocodiles, baboons, monkeys, wildebeests, warthogs, buffalos, birds, all types of antelopes, kudus (as tall as elks), impalas, and nyalas. I did not like the "hunting dogs," who are vicious killers and not as cowardly as hyenas. Fortunately, they were in captivity.

To our great disappointment, the British consul left. Her Majesty's government had decided to close the office for financial reasons. Now Alan was dean of the consular corps for life. A farewell dinner was given in the beautiful British Residence. The guests, mostly intellectuals, liberals, and academics, were entertained in high-ceiling rooms and sat on the veranda opening onto the quiet night redolent of fragrant flowers.

Alan had to make his official presentation to the Zulu govern-ment, headed by Chief Mangosuthu Gatsha Buthelezi, chief min-ister of KwaZulu. It was an unforgettable day. Alan and I drove through spectacular scenery. After we crossed the Tugela River, we entered the heart of KwaZulu. Leaving the coast, we veered north-west and reached an abrupt escarpment where the road climbed in hairpin bends. From the ridge, we could see far into the rugged Zulu landscape with its *kraals*, or compounds. Then we dropped into the Umfolozi River valley. On the arid land, only scrawny bushes and thorn trees grew.

Ulundi, the capital of KwaZulu, was a brand new town. The ministries occupied two- story brick buildings. white officials, dressed in pastel safari outfits, moved discreetly from one office to another. They were the "advisors." While Alan presented his credentials, I spent a pleasant few hours with Princess Irene, the chief's wife. Unlike her husband, she was not of royal blood, but a commoner. A nurse by profession, she came from Johannesburg. She explained to me how hard it had been for her to adjust to her new position. She took evening classes to learn the Zulu language. Both the chief and the princess were Anglican, but they had to ac-cept the Zulu traditions and customs.

It was particularly important for Alan to meet with the Zulu government and be introduced to their 300,000-strong political movement, Inkatha, representing more than seven million people. This was by far the largest black political force in the South African Republic. Gatsha Buthelezi had just returned from England to meet the Patriotic Front and the ANC (African National Congress). This political movement, of Marxist tendency, lived in exile. For us, to be in Ulundi meant being in the midst of intense political activity that was crucial for the future of South Africa. While driving from Durban, I had been reading Alan his "briefing papers," and on the way back, would write down his conversation notes. For the first time in my "diplomatic career," I felt I was part of Alan's job. Dur-ing our stay in Natal, Alan became an expert on Zulu affairs—what I would call a "Zulu watcher."

The festival of French films was a welcome break in the never-ending debates about racial problems. We saw great movies, such as the 1973 film *The Passengers* with Jean Louis Trintignan and *The Purple Taxi* with Fred Astaire, set in lush, green Ireland. The funniest film was the 1978 Franco-Italian production of *La Cage aux Folles*, which the South Africans just loved. To a select audience, the festival offered, a chance to see uncensored films, something very special in a Puritan-minded country where all events had to be approved lest they shock the public. *La Cage aux Folles* had everything to shock; not only were the main characters homosexuals (which is not acknowledged in South Africa), but there were blacks and whites living in the same household. We enjoyed the uninhibited laughter of the South African audience so much that we had to see the movie a second time.

We saw our first horse race at the Pietermaritzburg Turf Club. Watching races became a favorite weekend pastime of ours. South Africans of all colors are horse race *aficionados*. Holding our handsome red and gold engraved invitation, Alan and I joined the other distinguished guests on the special grandstand. The event started at noon with two races, and afterwards lunch was served. Three more races, and it was time for tea. At about 5:30 p.m., we gathered for a cocktail reception, after which the prizes were awarded. Ten diminutive jockeys represented South African provinces. One of the best American jockeys, McNargue, raced for each of the local stables as a visitor. In an elegant gesture, he offered his own first prize to the South African with whom he had tied for first place. It was particularly interesting to observe the intensity of the public, whether they were in the "Bantu enclosure" or the "Indian enclosure" or the "Colored enclosure." Toward the end of the race, the clamor became increasingly ferocious. Even the elegant ladies and proper gentlemen around us could not contain themselves any more, and shouted for their favorite horse. Being chauvinistic was a bad idea, since I bet three times for the French horse, which lost all three times.

Fortunately I was able to control the gambling urge in my DNA—a bad habit my father had acquired during the twenty-odd years he spent in Indochina—and limited my bets to ten dollars each time. I found it fun to study the horses in the paddocks, to dig out tips, to listen to "whispers," and write down complicated calculations of probabilities in a little book. Later in the year we saw the July Handicap, the most important event of the year, attended by 50,000 people and remarkable for the daring hats of the women.

We found that the South Africans wanted very much to be loved. They would frequently ask how we liked their country. Their image abroad was of concern to them. One had to have a diplomatic answer ready when our South African acquaintances asked us if we were impressed by the changes made in the racial tensions. Once, I took my cue from Alan who said: "Mao Tse-tung said, if you want to travel 1,000 miles, you have to start with one step." The woman he was talking to was a good sport and laughed. Quite often, at the end of an official dinner, guests would ask Alan how he evaluated the solutions to the racial problems. Silence would set around the dinner table and Alan, speaking in a learned tone, would draw an in-depth picture of the situation

As Christmas approached, the social life seemed to become more and more frantic. We met the same upper class several times a week at the Lions Club, the International Tennis Tournament sponsored by the Sugar Association, and the end-of-year ceremony at Sultan Technikon (an Indian technical school). Whether the occasion was an art *vernissage*, a play, a dinner, or a meeting at the town hall, Alan and I had become an institution, part of the scenery. People we met were more than friendly; they were deferential. Nine times out of ten, protocol assigned the honor seats to us.

During our first two months in Durban, our only house servant was Bennett, a subdued little guy. He worked around the clock and slept in the servants' quarters. We had a young South African woman do some catering for us whenever we had a party. We were going out so much that we did not really need a cook at first. We had inherited Bennett from our predecessor. That was the easy solution, but not necessarily the most exciting. I remember one morning when we came down for breakfast we looked with astonishment at Bennett's head, which was bald like an egg.

"What happened Bennett?" we asked.

He answered, "I thought it would be cooler this way." As I recall, it was the only personal decision he ever made.

The story of Grace is something else. When we started entertaining, we really needed a servant to wait on the table following all the rules of etiquette. I had a sit-down dinner for twelve. Grace had been given instructions to follow Bennett and do exactly as he did. But, oh horror, she was one of those people who take initiatives. She was practically throwing the food on the table. Seeing that two guests did not want seconds, she assumed that nobody else was hungry and proceeded to take the plates away. Poor Bennet panicked, and mixed the order according to which he was to pass the dishes. I wrote in my diary: "Grace is a pure disaster. She has been with us for ten days, and she is stubborn and lacks the slightest bit of intelligence. To her credit though, Alan and I have become more religious, since we say Grace before, during and after every meal," I concluded.

To our astonishment, Grace turned out to be the best servant we ever had, cheerful, efficient, and learning our ways very fast. I taught her how to make scones, and her skill is still remembered by our family today. She was a lovely, smart person in her own right. With her savings and our help, she was able to build her own house in KwaMashu, a black township close to Durban. As private property was not available to all blacks, she thereby reached a middle class social status. I can still remember her expression of pride when she showed us the work site of the new home for her and her children. I felt then that I was looking at the bright future of South Africa

All of a sudden, our life changed: Our youngest daughter Karen was visiting for Christmas vacation. She arrived on December 14. Our life became a happy whirlwind, pleasantly upsetting our existence of staunch bachelors. She discovered South Africa with a voracious enthusiasm. Seeing through her eyes, the country and its people became even more appealing. The aseptic kitchen became alive. Karen cooked her first dish, a delicious lasagna with spinach. My Osterizer, which had not left its box, started running nonstop to make cold soups, juices, and "smoothies."

Thanks to Karen we made new friends among artists, musicians, and journalists. The most interesting and lasting relationship we established was with two women, Betsy and Dina. The first time we met them was while jogging on the racetracks. Betsy had come to South Africa eighteen years before, to work as an *au pair* with a family. The few days she intended to stay turned into years. She pursued her studies in musicology, obtained her Ph.D., and became the head of the music department at Natal University. For her, to be in a place where Western and Asian music met with the innate musical talent of the Zulus was unique. She was also the conductor of the multiracial choir of the Berea Catholic Church. Her friend Dina was a former Carmelite nun who had escaped the convent with the help of a confessor priest. She turned to a passion of hers, wood sculpture, while completing a Ph.D. in theology. Since then she has become a leading artist in South Africa.

Karen rapidly turned her bedroom into a workshop. She bought sarong material at the Indian market. Dress patterns covered the floor. She started knitting a sweater using natural wool from Greece. The sewing machine, books, and vases full of roses cluttered the room pleasantly. For the first time, Alan enjoyed going into the kitchen, where Karen was concocting delicious spaghettis with pesto sauce made from the wild basil growing near the house. She loved picking the papayas, mangoes, pineapples, lemons, and avocados growing in our garden.

We spent Christmas and Boxing Day at a friend's farm a one-hour drive from Durban. We felt like part of the family during a festive dinner and long, leisurely conversations. Just before Christmas dinner, we went to see the African staff celebrate their Christmas. Low cuts of meat had been distributed to them. With the help of two cases of brandy, the atmosphere was more than lively, and they danced for us.

One of the leaders of the progressive NRP[7] (New Republic Party) had invited the three of us to greet the New Year. In a relaxed atmosphere, guests gathered around the dinner table. Among them were a few politicians, lawyers, writers, and a former opera diva. At one point, I noticed Karen engrossed in a conversation with a small elderly gentleman with alert eyes. She was talking to Alan Paton! At the end of the evening, the famous author of *Cry the Beloved Country* got up and read a poem in his striking Irish accent, with humor and a twinkling in his eyes

Alan and I drove with Karen all the way to the borders of Swaziland and Mozambique. We drove first through Umfolozi Reserve, the oldest game park in Natal, created by Shaka Zulu in the nineteenth century, and spent three nights in Hluhluwe Reserve. We were given a comfortable thatched-roof cottage with a cook and even a bathtub. As in all Natal parks, visitors can both drive and walk, and we chose to walk for five hours with a ranger. A new experience for us was to sit very quietly and patiently in a "hide" to watch the animals come and drink at a small pond. The crocodiles looked deceptively sleepy until an approaching prey made the reptiles slide full speed into the water. One of the most beautiful moments was during an approaching storm. The yellow cork of the fever trees contrasted with the black sky. The reeds, swept down by the wind, were leaning toward the water in ebullition.

Next, we drove through Pongoland. I remember the road going straight up along the vertical face of the cliff, creating an unreal feeling of vertigo. From the top of the Lemombo mountain range, one could see the Mokatini Flats, a marshy, sandy area stretching all the way to the Indian Ocean. We stopped to have dinner with a group of jolly Catholic priests. Over a bottle of wine, they told us about their years spent with the Zulus.

The mission stations staffed with Western missionaries, mostly Methodists and Anglicans, were usually located at high elevation. Historically, they felt more protected from possible attacks and also away from the unhealthy malaria-ridden lowlands. The Zulu government took over most of the hospitals founded by the missionaries, but kept the Western doctors.

Torrential rains and mountainous waves eroding the beaches marked the end of January, in the midst of summer. Around-the-world boaters were getting ready to sail to Cape Town, avoiding the cyclones erupting near Mauritius Island. After the winds subsided, Alan and Karen were invited to spend a day on a giant catamaran, thirty feet wide

A constant stream of official visitors came to South Africa: top State Department officers, members of Congress, Rockefeller Foundation officials, and journalists. Natal had always been considered a "backwater" and rarely been included in visitors' itineraries. But this was changing with the growing political influence of the Zulus—a phenomenon Alan closely monitored and reported. Thanks in part to him, I believe, Durban was now on the map of intense power plays.

At one point, we gave a politically important official dinner at the Residence for a meeting between Richard Moose, under secretary for African affairs, and Chief Buthelezi. The location and object of this meeting had been kept secret from the press. I served as hostess and, with Alan's permission, became the invisible, silent witness to substantive discussions held between the Zulu leaders and the State Department's top officers. I observed how hard it was for such exchanges to produce results. Each side was solidly entrenched in its own position, while perfectly aware of the other side's position. The chief appeared suspicious, bitter, and aggressive, probably because he was on the defensive. At one point, the tension was such that sparks began flying between Buthelezi and Moose. The latter broke into a language that was crudely American and rather insulting. The chief grew increasingly nervous, even furious. This was when Alan intervened, with great diplomatic skill, in a calm and clever manner. The explosive atmosphere was defused. The interlocutors regained face and the conversation resumed with much more courtesy. A beautiful performance, I thought.

The visit of Franklin E. White, the associate director for the White House domestic policy staff, was an occasion to gather lawyers, journalists, and jurists. During this typical "working lunch" for eighteen, between the curry dish and the ice cream, Alan interrupted the general conversations and reminded his guests of the topic at hand. Mr. White gave a brief historical summary of human rights in America. He included information on the methods used by the blacks (such as sit-ins) and the whites (the Civil Rights Act of 1964, affirmative action), not only to abolish discrimination but also to make amends for the past. It was an impressive presentation made with a great deal of clarity and objectivity. During that lunch, I was wondering whether the persons in attendance were really "listening." In order to defend their own system, South Africans were always quick to stress the negatives in America. They would point out the violence in the streets, or the ghettos in inner cities. Our mission was to relentlessly expose South Africans to the American experience on how to end discrimination.

Early in 1980, the U.S. Consulate General opened its doors to an arts and crafts exhibit sponsored by the Natal Society of Art. Pottery, paintings, beads, baskets, wall tapestries, wood sculptures and creative fashion had been tastefully displayed throughout our home. Training centers for black artists had long existed in South Africa under the supervision of missionaries. These centers produced a variety of handicrafts, including baskets in Vukani and beads in Msunga Valley and Tugela Ferry. Probably the most famous was Rorke's Drift Center of Handicraft and Fine Arts School, created by the Evangelical Lutheran church and supported by the Institute of Race Relations. I had a chance to buy and now own an oversized basket made in KwaZulu. It is so tightly woven that one can store beer in it. The shape and pattern are so beautiful that this object deserves a place in the Metropolitan Museum, I think. I noticed how much the visitors who had come to admire the craft show seemed to enjoy the social opportunity to mingle freely and, most of all, make new acquaintances across the color bar. This may seem normal to you, the reader, but it certainly was not in the 1980s in South Africa.

This was when I understood how much art can bring people together. After Karen left on February 1, 1980, I felt rather depressed in a house that, all of a sudden, had become so neat and so quiet. Besides, in spite of my interest in Alan's work, I was frustrated by not having yet found a project giving my own life a direction and purpose. My objectives, at first nebulous, gradually became more focused. I began to see what contribution I could make to the country. It was time for Natal to emulate the more dynamic provinces of Cape Town and Transvaal, particularly in the areas of performing and visual arts, and encourage artists from all races.

As I started to make inroads into the world of the arts in the first few months of 1980, I joined the committees of several organizations: NSA (Natal Society for the Arts), SAAA (The Natal Branch of the South African Association of the Arts), the Durban Art Gallery, the Friends of the Durban Art Gallery, and the Institute for Race Relations. All of these groups were working toward the Durban Arts festivals to take place in 1980 and 1981. I will describe these major events and the role I played in them later in this chapter.

The University of Zululand was founded in the 1960s. It was located 142 km north of Durban near the town of Epangemi. When we visited it, the student body numbered 1,500. All the students were blacks, and the faculty was composed of whites. The president was an African with aristocratic bearing and sound ideas. Wasted space, poor acoustics, and erratic air-conditioning jarred with the modernism of the buildings. The campus was situated on a picturesque hill, overlooking a lake surrounded by pine trees. It seemed to us like an ideal place for aquatic sports. We asked why the place was deserted. The answer was surprising: the students believed that a curse had been put on the lake and were afraid to come near the water.

The courses were only offered during the morning. Most of them dealt with humanities, law, and political sciences rather than science, engineering, or technology. A perfect breeding ground for the next generation of bureaucrats, I thought. We attended one course given by an American professor on civil rights. The class was docile. A few questions were asked in belabored English.

Alan engaged in a conversation with the student association's representative, who poured out his bitterness against the brainwashing contained in the courses. But the main reason for his dissatisfaction was that the creation of a black university had further reduced the chances for Africans to enter white universities and receive a higher education comparable to that offered to the Whites.

Alan had been going to Ulundi every week. The seven-hour drive was routine for him by now. When the Zulu Legislative Assembly convened, he suggested that I accompany him. We had a chance to listen to the debates and speeches in the Assembly. The Ulundi government was dissatisfied with the stagnation in the political progress, and Chief Buthelezi was making a proposal to improve the system allowing Zulus to express their demands.

The most memorable event took place during the projection of the 1977 television miniseries *Roots: The Saga of an American Family* by Alex Haley. We had borrowed the tapes from the U.S. cultural center in Durban. For three days, we watched episode after episode as the only whites in the midst of the Zulu audience of ministers, parliament members, and general public. The audience, caught up in the action, expressed its outrage during the harrowing crossing of the Atlantic by the African slaves. The Zulus around us were getting angrier and angrier as the plot unfolded. "Kill the white men!" they shouted. I did not feel particularly reassured. At one point, Chief Buthelezi, who was sitting in front of me, turned around and laughingly told me, "Don't take this too personally." (During our next assignment, to the Gambia, we had a chance, to visit the purported birthplace of Kunta Kinte, the hero of the story.)

We attended Speech Day at Hilton College, probably the swankiest boarding school in the Republic. In a gorgeous setting spreading over several thousand acres, 440 boys were receiving an education preparing them to join the ranks of the privileged class. We sipped sherry on the lawn of the lovely headmaster's house, overlooking the bottomless hole of the valley of the "Thousands Hills"—an obscene anachronism, to use Alan's words. In his speech, the Rt. Revd. Michael Nuttall, bishop of Pretoria, commented on the sentence, "Happy be the peacemakers who will be called the sons of God" (the Beatitudes, according to Mathew). The South African church during the apartheid period typically remained cautious and involved itself more in charity than in political action. Food baskets placed at churches' entrance doors were full every Sunday.

The next speaker that day was a high official in the Department of Education. He made a noble pronouncement, saying that the improvement of education for the blacks had to start with the very young children. Indeed, I thought, there was room for improvement, given that it costs forty times more to educate a white child than a black child! Then came the turn of the all-around, clean-cut boy, who spoke of tolerance. Alan shocked a guest by saying that tolerance consisted of accepting someone with green hair and a ring in his nose. A letter to the editor of one of the local newspapers expressed outrage for the school's having served champagne and caviar at a graduation celebration at a time when the Zulus were starving. The author of the letter continued: "Do you know what the reaction of one mother was? She said 'Yes, this is terrible; we should have brought the leftovers to the Zulu village.'"

A roving government commission on constitutional problems was in the process of conducting hearings throughout the country. After months and months, the mountain delivered a mouse: the creation of an advisory body (a black council) to advise an advisory body (the president's council) to the Parliament.

One year after my arrival in Natal, I started my new job as a student advisor at the U.S. cultural center. In the course of the year, I talked to dozens of individuals interested in studying in the United

States. I explained the American system of higher education, how to apply, how to choose a field of study, and how to obtain financial assistance. Our office was located at the street level for easy access––a location that would be unheard of today because of possible acts of terrorism—and attracted a lot of interest. I found it gratifying to see that so many young people were not discouraged by the large quantity of material they had to go through and were determined to fulfill their dream. I enjoyed this position that gave me an official status in the local community.

A few weeks later, the cultural affairs officer asked me to be part of the selection process for Fulbright scholarship candidates. For two days, we had to make decisions on the fates of about thirty people from all colors, between the ages of 29 and 59. Among them were artists, actors, physicists, social workers, pedagogues, and others. A Pretoria USIA officer, a professor of geography from the University of Zululand, and a young Indian lawyer were the other members of the selection panel.

The country continued to be in a turmoil of projected changes discussed by commissions and working groups. The Lombard Report proposed to study "Alternatives to the Consolidation of Kwa-Zulu," which amounted to abolishing it. A bill of rights for urban blacks, easing the "pass laws," was under discussion. For the rural blacks, however, the "influx control" regulations were going to be more strictly enforced. This was more a side step than a forward step.

Alan wanted the visit of Ambassador Bill Edmondson and his wife to Natal to be a success, especially the important trip to Ulundi to meet Buthelezi and his cabinet of ministers. "It went superbly," Alan said enthusiastically after the meeting. Very unusual for Alan, I thought. I could appreciate this accomplishment since I knew how hard the chief was to work with, and how unpredictable and slightly paranoid he could be. As a typical politician, he always turned toward where the power was, and could be ruthless, if necessary.

Dinner at the fortress residence of Gatsha Buthelezi and family was quite a memorable event. It was a small, informal party. The chief was attentive and served the drinks himself. Also present were a minister, two pleasant officials from the Inkatha Women's Brigade, the chief's mother and wife, and an old princess who was one of the sixty-five wives of the former Zulu King Solomon. The three daughters of Buthelezi cooked and served the dinner, kneeling in obedience in front of their father and grandmother. (I noted in my diary that I should introduce this custom to my family.) Throughout the evening the television was blasting, drowning the conversation. During a lull in the TV decibels, the chief's daughters sang a Zulu ballad.

I had my first experience of cricket. For six hours our guide, the president of the Natal Cricket Association, patiently explained the terminology of the game, which usually lasts three days—wickets, fielders, bowlers, and batters. Although I far from understood the whole thing, I almost began to like it.

This was our second Christmas in Durban for just the two of us, with no children around. So we decided to spend three days in Johannesburg with old friends from Tunisia, Selim and Earline Azzam, an oil executive of Palestinian origin and his absolutely ravishing Canadian wife. We were swept away in another life style between the tennis courts and the swimming pools. People invited each other for *brai*, or barbecues. With the stereo on, spontaneously the guests would get up and start dancing. At midnight, the buffet was served. It reminded me of the carefree life we had led in Tunisia. Quite different from the serious existence we were leading in Durban, entirely absorbed by South Africa and its problems, and always in the public eye! Our hosts did not seem to have a care in the world, whereas Alan and I felt as if we were carrying apartheid like a cross. Many of their friends were journalists who had been in Vietnam, the Soviet Union, or the Middle East. Their exciting conversations touched on topics so remote from race relations!

In February 1981 we made a 5,000-kilometer trip by car. We drove through the Orange Free State and its capital, Bloemfontein, then reached the Eastern Cape Province, following the "garden route" along the coast toward Cape Town.[8] Distances are vast in South Africa, and it took us three days to reach our destination. The town and its surroundings are spectacular. There are beautiful beaches, small bays with ultramodern apartment buildings, and villas reminding me of the French Riviera. To reach the Cape of Good Hope, we walked through a natural park and saw some wildlife. We climbed a last cliff, and there, next to the lighthouse, standing at the highest point, we were struck by the immensity of the ocean, the terror of sailors under windy conditions.

We strolled around the city center enjoying the cosmopolitan feeling of the Sea Point Promenade with its many shops and the active waterfront. I remember trying to cross Adderley Street, but the wind was so strong I had to hold onto a lamppost until the gust abated. The fort of Kaapstad (Cape Town), dating back to Jan van Riebeeck, the Dutch merchant who rounded the Cape of Good Hope is the place to soak in the history of the early settlers in the seventeenth century.

After driving through the Cape Flats, we entered the idyllic wine country of Stellenbosch. A group of French Huguenots had arrived at the Cape in 1688, settled among the Dutch, who soon assimilated them. The *Franschhoek* vineyard attests to its French origins. The farms and public buildings are blindingly white, and their Cape Dutch architecture stands neatly around the *Braak*, or green. It was wonderful to travel in this wine country, dropping by cellars and tasting wine. The visit of the Delheim wine production cellar, with its fermentation, stabilizing, and storage areas, was fascinating. The town of Stellenbosch was like a museum with historical houses dating back to the early eighteenth century.

While lunching at the Parliament, [9] we had the privilege of meeting Helen Suzman, member of the PFP or Progressive Federal Party. She was an activist and a courageous opponent of the government's policies. For thirty-six years, she fought against apartheid as a member of Parliament and was nominated twice for the Nobel Peace Prize. She died in 2009 at age ninety-one. We found her very direct and quite an amazing woman. The Parliament was bubbling with the upcoming general elections called by President Botha for April. The three parties were about to start their electoral campaign.

An amazing incident happened to me at the end of June. We were in Ulundi, the capital of KwaZulu, to attend the annual conference of Inkatha, which was attended by three thousand people in khaki uniforms and black paratroopers berets. We heard long speeches, interrupted by prayers. The audience reacted with raised arms and clenched fists, shouting in unison, *"Amandla"* (literally meaning power, and standing for a call to power for the black population). A few outside guests, journalists, Red Cross officials, and diplomats were also there. Buthelezi introduced the honored guests and gave each a present. When it came the turn of the United States to be honored, he invited me to receive my present—a beautiful sculpted cane. I struggled to climb onto the stage with my narrow skirt, and Buthelezi kissed me on both cheeks. Then, I raised my cane to the audience, and along with Buthelezi, shouted, "*Amandla!*" Three thousand voices yelled along with us approvingly. This was my strongest memory of South Africa!

"Shaka Day" is the most colorful event of the year in Natal. It is a real dream for photographers. In 1981, all the Zulu chiefs were present in their leopard skins and ostrich feathers, proudly holding their *assegai*, or spears, their cowhide shields, and their heavy clubs. Chief Buthelezi and King Goodwin were the most magnificent. I noticed the beautiful profile of the youngest of the King's four wives. We were standing with the high officials and the royal family under the tent. The loud and excited crowd was closing in on us. I thought I would suffocate as the human tide encircled the tent in spite of the *impis*, or bodyguards, until we retired to the hotel's air-conditioned dining room,

Her Worship, Mrs. Sybil Hotz, the mayor, gave a reception for mayors and municipal counselors of the black townships in greater Durban. Mrs. Hotz was the second woman in 150 years to rule over the city hall. She was an outstanding mayor and held that position from 1980 to 1984. Her personality and outreach policy contributed more to changes taking place in Durban than those experienced by any other city of South Africa. It was moving to see black and white municipal officials meeting together for the first time. I was impressed by the exchange of powerful speeches that revealed a mutual knowledge and desire to cooperate to solve the problems of local politics. This was a historic moment. I am sure the Mandela transition many years later was prepared by such moments.

The 1980 Durban Arts Festival was a new experiment for Natal's largest city. Durban was still culturally lagging behind the other main cities of South Africa. Cape Town had a modern dance company (Jazzart) with a brilliant colored lead dancer. It also had a ballet company, the Cape Arts Performing Arts, of international level.

Transvaal had its ballet company, the Performing Arts Council, based in Johannesburg.

The events of the 1980 Durban Festival were modest: music in the streets, the parks, and a few performances of the Durban ballet school. My personal participation, given my interest in dance, was to become a member of the dance subcommittee. The international film festival and a national sculpture competition were probably the most successful events. But the festival grew in intensity the following year, and took on national importance to become the Durban Arts 81 festival, a national event marking the twentieth anniversary of the South African Republic.

The preparations for Durban Arts 81 began in earnest, and their feverish pace culminated in the early spring. The scope of the events had little in common with the preceding year, and I found myself fully involved. Durban now had its own ballet company. My daughter Sylvia and her husband-to-be, both Stanford graduate students, were invited by the University of Natal to give a lecture/demonstration of classical and modern dance.

Dance performances were the most popular events in Durban. They included street and professional dancing, war dances, Zulu dancing, Indian ethnic dancing, flamenco, disco dancing, and more. The activity on all fronts was incredible. Except for a few problems, such as the Port Natal administration's refusal to provide transportation for the blacks, everything went smoothly.

I offered my services at the dance gala held at the city hall. I became the official dresser of Margaret Barbieri, prima ballerina of the London Royal Ballet. I loved the high level of panic reigning backstage. I had seen the Bolshoi dancers during their workout in Moscow, but never had I been so close to one of the best ballerinas in the world minutes before she went on stage. During a ballet, dancers look like they've come out of a fairytale book. Close by, Barbieri was all skin and bones, a real skeleton. She had to endure the ordeal of costume changes and false curls glued or pinned to her head. Every piece of her costume had to be tightly attached to her so that she could move on the stage without risking losing part of her attire. And yet, after a ballet is over, the moment is magic. The dancer smiles, looks dreamy, fresh and rested, as if liberated from matter.

As part of USIA staff, I organized the projection of the PBS *Dance in America* series in black townships, cultural centers, YMCAs, the University of Zululand, and Indian communities. These documentary programs were received with enthusiasm. I followed up the projections with a distribution of questionnaires. The feedback from the public constituted an important piece of information for USIA.

Performing arts by the whites had always been active in Durban. But the type of audience was undergoing changes, in great part due to the dynamic University of Natal. The noon-hour plays the university organized made it possible for blacks working in downtown Durban to attend short programs, and it was not uncommon to sit with a multicolored audience at the lunch-hour performances staged at the Elizabeth Sneddon Theater. This was a real breakthrough.

Although the black theater was still in its infancy in Natal, there were signs that things were changing. In 1980, we had a chance to watch a play written by a black and produced in the only nightclub existing in a black township. The play was pretty bad, full of clichés and swear words. The actors were wallowing in garbage, both figuratively and literally speaking. The main character, Hobo, a bum, was in fact a medical doctor who had made the choice to live on the margins of society and dwell in its misery. He ate dog food, which he found more nutritious than "mealy meal," the staple food of the blacks. The play showed the degradation and inferiority of the black population, a recurrent theme of the black theater at that time.

A year later, the situation had changed. Several black plays were staged. The best one, *Ozza Albert*, enjoyed a great deal of success, which continued abroad. Like Johannesburg and its multiracial Space Theater, Natal wanted to acquire new venues. Two theater halls made their appearance in former churches intended for cross-cultural productions, one a Methodist and another Presbyterian.

Rick Wakeman made a stop in Durban and was a hit, particularly among the young. I dragged Alan to his concert titled "Journey to the Center of the Earth" at the city hall. On the stage was a small jazz orchestra, a symphonic orchestra, and at the very top, hanging from the great organ, a choir. Electronic equipment consisting of synthesizers and other high-tech machines occupied the center of the stage. Rick Wakeman appeared in a golden jumpsuit. Turning his back to the public, he played a few notes on one keyboard and then another, producing the maximum of decibels. I had liked his first records, but in Durban I thought he was trying to fool the audience. Part of his music was really catchy, but most of his concert consisted of orchestrating noise.

If music and dance were easily accessible to large multiracial audiences, the hardest barrier to overcome between the races was in the field of visual arts. The whites were accused of elitism for judging black art as "low in quality." Many of the black artists had been trained in missionary centers like Rorke's Drift and had a tendency to be chained to strictly ethnic art

The intense cultural activity tied to the Durban Arts 81 Festival created a flurry of opinion pieces in the South African press. On August 29, 1981, the Natal Society of Art (NSA) convened a multiracial conference on the topic of "Art and Society." Alistair Sparks, former editor of the *Rand Daily Mail*, was the main speaker. A reporter for the NSA newsletter "Newsdart" wrote: "Alistair Sparks maintained that the social involvement by the visual artists was sadly lacking in impact, particularly when compared to the commitment made in the field of drama and literature by authors such as Nadine Gordimer, Athol Fugard or Breyton Breytenback."

As a USIA staffer, I attended this conference and reported on it in an airgram forwarded to Washington by the U.S. consul general. I also sent an opinion paper on the "Arts in South Africa" to USIA with recommendations on the role the United States might play.

In South Africa, it was impossible to disassociate the festival activities from politics. Sylvia Kaplan, the first woman to be appointed to the prestigious position of president of the South African Association of the Arts, resigned on September 1981. A prominent South African artist, Professor Walter Battiss, also resigned from the Durban Arts 81 exhibition. He declared in an interview in the *Mercury* of Pretoria: "I am tired of all the bickering and disturbances." The Cape Association of Arts withdrew as well from the Republic's festival. In other words, art was a pivotal element of the society. It could bring the people together, but at the same time become a form of protest.

When all our children came to visit us at Christmas, we wanted to show them northern Natal. We drove again all the way to the Mozambique border. We flew in a four-seat plane over the Zulu landscape, the five lakes of Kozi Bay, and the ocean looking for giant turtles and sharks swimming close to the shore.

On our way back to Durban, after driving for hours on rugged dirt tracks and through the desolate countryside, we reached Sodwana Bay and were surprised to find dozens of camping cars, Land Rovers, and other four-wheelers lined up on the beach. It looked as if half of Transvaal had come there for a weekend of deep-sea fishing. This was a tough and healthy- looking crowd. I became fascinated with the efficient and brutal technique used to get the motorboats out of the water. The skipper would start his engine and reach maximum speed, whistling the whole time. Swimmers had to get out of the way, or else. By then, the boat would be flying above the water and would end up gliding on the sand, pulled by a metallic cable. African women, probably accustomed to these Afrikaner tourists, had set up the largest basket market I ever saw. A white family was selling pineapples and litchis off their truck.

If Alan and I enjoyed living in South Africa, I think the children enjoyed it just as much. They made their own discoveries. For instance, Diane worked for two months as a reporter with the *Sunday Tribune*. Thanks to this hands-on opportunity, she learned about the country and was able to draw her own opinions. The children made close friends among the University of Natal circles and a family of artists and architects. They traveled extensively, slept in a cave on Drakensberg Mountain, visited the Cape, admired the modern architecture, and gave a try at the wine tasting. Tennis and escapades in downtown Durban filled their days. They also enjoyed body surfing in what some see as the best waves in the world, without any bad encounters with sharks. Incidentally, Durbanites have a particular method to protect themselves against sharks. They let the predators swim very close to the shore then lower their nets. The sharks remain trapped and unable to swim back to deep water.

The children still remember Saturday nights at the elegant Durban Country Club with its incredible buffets, where one had a wide choice of many different cuisines.

Our third and last Christmas in Durban was very special. We all knew by then that Alan had decided to resign from the Foreign Service soon. He appeared more relaxed than he had in years and just wanted to have a good time with the family and close friends. The house was full of music, people dancing, talking, and playing bridge. An artist friend of the children had designed wild clothes for the holidays, which we all wore in an undiplomatic fashion. We revisited the reserve and national parks of Hluhluwe and Umfolozi, which we liked so much.

In early March 1982 we said our goodbyes to Durban and the diplomatic life. Friends and acquaintances, who appeared sincerely sad to see us leave, all asked us the same questions: "How did you enjoy your stay in South Africa? What are you going to do now? You are much too young to retire!" We were both amused and touched by the parting letter Chief Buthelezi sent us, which had a great touch of humor: "I am sorry your youngest daughter Karen had to leave. I was about to offer a few cows so she could join our family."

Yes, we were sad to leave such a beautiful country, with a political situation full of suspense and expectations. We had led a privileged and independent life, and it was inconceivable to accept a lower status in a large embassy. In one of his farewell speeches, Alan remarked: "After Durban, where to go but away from the Foreign Service?"

We spent a few weeks of feverish preparation toward our departure, a nonstop series of official functions. At the Residence, we entertained a large group of businessmen, representatives from the political and art worlds, from all the ethnic groups, from the press, and elsewhere for the last time.

The media orchestrated all this activity, reproducing Alan's declarations and statements. The liberal press congratulated him for declaring how abhorrent he thought apartheid was. The conservatives, on the other hand, appeared pleased that the new American ambassador had indicated he would not express his opinions about the internal affairs of South Africa. It became quite apparent toward the end of our stay how hostile the Nationalists had been toward Alan for his freely expressed liberal views. The utmost way to denigrate him was to qualify him as "Carter's man."

We accidentally discovered the degree of their hostility at an official dinner shortly before we left. In the middle of a light and friendly conversation, our host, an official from the ministry of foreign affairs, started to engage Alan aggressively out of the blue. This was when we realized to what extent we had been watched, criticized, and even slandered all this time. To be criticized in this manner in South Africa, as we had been in the Soviet Union, is a real *tour de force* for a diplomat, commented Alan as we returned home.

As a backdrop to these weeks prior to our departure, the political atmosphere in Durban was intense. The Steyn Report, published a few weeks earlier, asking for stricter control of the press, had enraged world opinion after the "suicide" of Steve Biko, an imprisoned young trade union leader. For many years, Biko had been an activist against apartheid. He created the Black Consciousness movement. The time was particularly volatile following the hijacking of an Air India flight to the Seychelles. It looked as if South Africa, by turning Steve Biko into a martyr, was testing the disapproval of world opinion in a bout of provocation.

"Dr. No" Treuchnicht, the Nationalist leader from the Transvaal, refused to support the formula of coresponsibility and the idea of "reasonable power sharing" proposed by Prime Minister P. W. Botha. As a result of its vote of no-confidence toward the government, the Nationalist Party split in two.

I felt we were leaving at a particularly difficult time for South Africa, when it was struggling to make progress toward the end of apartheid, still another thirteen years away. On a purely personal level, I must say that the friends we had made in Durban could not have been more delightful. I was most gratified to see all my efforts to contribute to an active and multiracial art scene rewarded by kind words of gratitude and appreciation.

We had expected that leaving the South African posting would mark the end to our thirty years of diplomatic life. Unexpectedly, our departure from the U.S. Foreign Service was briefly interrupted by another assignment, in the Gambia.

10

The Gambia 1983–1984

The Gambia turned out to be a pleasant interlude before returning permanently to civilian life. A few months after completing his
South Africa assignment, Alan was unexpectedly recalled by the
State Department to become ambassador ad interim to Banjul. The
U.S. government must have been desperate to find someone to fill
this position since it went through four chargés d'affaires during a
period of eighteen months.

Perhaps it is because The Gambia is such a small country — less
than four fifths the size of the state of Connecticut — that rare are the
people who ever heard of it. It is frequently mistaken for Zambia.
Located in West Africa, it is a strip of land 30 miles wide by less
than 300 miles long, hugging the Gambia River and its estuary. Its
unusual geography partially explains Gambia's agitated history.

Alan arrived in Banjul in November 1983 and spent six weeks
alone feeling quite sorry for himself. Just before I left to join him on
New Year's Eve, I received a gruesome letter that I found to be the
best piece of black humor Alan had ever produced. It deserves to be
quoted at length. Alan wrote:

> I have just set a new record for my Foreign Service life, a
> rather grotesque record that few people can match in or out
> of diplomatic life. I have three dead British sailors stacked
> in my refrigerator. ... One was drowned in the strong surf
> and riptides off the residence; the other two were killed in a
> horrible car accident that also killed a Gambian driver and
> injured four other sailors. The sailors were all off the HMS
> *Battleaxe*, a frigate on its way home for Christmas from the

Falkland Islands. You may be wondering what they were doing in my fridge along with my soft drinks and beer. The reason is that I have the only large walk-in freezer in town. I guess I am overly squeamish, but I do have a hard time adjusting myself to living alone with three houseguests on ice. It's not that they are particularly demanding, or noisy or rowdy. I am fearful that they will wake me in the middle of the night to make a fourth for a cold hand of bridge.

So, it was with a feeling of panic that I boarded the Pan Am flight from JFK to Dakar on December 30, 1983. Fortunately, Alan's horror story vanished from my mind as soon as I saw the coast of West Africa. We made our approach by flying over Gorée Island, settled by the Portuguese in 1450 and infamous for being one of the main departure points of the slave trade. As my plane landed, Alan's orange shirt on the tarmac was a welcome sight.

I had been in Dakar before and enjoyed seeing this buoyant city once again. Under the twenty-year rule of the first president of Senegal, Leopold Senghor, this West African country had enjoyed the continent's most stable government. The city was a hub for numerous international organizations. In addition, Dakar's cultural scene was important enough to attract such institutions as Maurice Béjart's Mudra School of Ballet.

Downtown Dakar was a mixture of modern and run-down buildings. I saw elegant Senegalese women doing their shopping in expensive boutiques, which contrasted harshly with the presence of young, blind mothers with their babies strapped to their backs. Begging children swarmed around us like locusts. Alan and I stopped for coffee and *croissants* along with some French families having breakfast. Alan got a haircut from a young Lebanese in a barbershop run by a Frenchman.

Dakar was really jumping for New Year's Eve, with hundreds of tourists escaping cold and dreary Europe. French President Jacques Chirac and prominent member of the French parliament Simone Weil apparently loved to come incognito to Dakar at this time of year. Around the pool of the Diarama-Meriden Hotel on picturesque Ngor Island, I could see French, Italians, Germans, English, and many Swedes. It had a jolly "Club Med" atmosphere of organized activities, sailboarding, windsurfing, tennis, games of *boules,* and, of course, lavish buffets. A disk jockey entertained children at their own party.

I had my first glimpse of diplomatic social life in Dakar at a cocktail given by the head of USIS (United States Information Service). The handsome residence had patios and high ceilings. The host, an elegant African American in a smashing red velvet suit, introduced us to his guests, mostly other African Americans as well as Africans. His amazing collection of African art was well displayed. We met the blond, German wife of the deputy chief of mission obviously wanting to shine. Her flow of name-dropping was impressive. She was talking about the seventy-seven women of the American embassy she had to "take care of." Soon she left with a flourish to go to another "function." I felt she was a caricature of what a professional diplomat's wife should not be.

It was New Year's Eve and every one was getting ready for a long, hard night. We were invited to join an American gathering near the water. We passed the lighthouse that marks the western-most point of Africa. Alan reminded me that General De Gaulle and the Free French Forces tried unsuccessfully to land there in 1942 to upset the Vichy government, which greatly humiliated De Gaulle. The British had to come to his rescue by heavily bombing the town. De Gaulle and the British had spent several months in The Gambia, preparing for the attack. At midnight, a cup of champagne in hand, we saw the New Year in, accompanied by aborted homemade fireworks. The night was beautiful, and it was fun to be in Africa again.

The drive to Banjul, the Gambian capital, took about four hours on the paved road. Mounds of sand reminded us that the Sahara desert was not far away. The "mammy wagons," or minibuses, were soon replaced by light carts on tires, pulled by small, thin horses. Fences were cleverly made of rubber flip-flops. The vegetation, which started out very dry, gradually became greener and then lush. I saw generous mango trees, elegant and a bit forlorn palm trees, and *flamboyants,* or flame trees. I had never seen baobabs before—the trees so beloved by St. Exupery's *Petit Prince.* I found their huge trunks and dwarfed branches quite eerie, as they stretched against the sky blackened by the sand during the *harmattan* season, when the wind blows in from the Sahara Desert. The baobabs seemed to be growing upside down, with their roots at the top. The villages were neat clusters of tiny round *paillotes* with thatched roofs, huddling behind wood fences. Once we crossed the Gambian border, the ubiquitous corrugated iron sheets covering the houses appeared, as in the other Anglophone countries of Africa.

At three in the afternoon, we arrived in Barra, at the mouth of the Gambia River. The tide was low and we had to wait for the ferry. This gave us time to explore an old fort still standing nearby. In the sixteenth century Portuguese gold diggers and slave traders had settled in the lower river area. The fort had round towers, *meurtrières* (narrow windows used by bowmen in the Middle Ages to shoot their arrows), vaults, and kilns. A cannon was pointed at an invisible enemy.

The crossing of the Gambia River was colorful and exciting. We first went through one hour of chaotic bad planning to load the ferry. Goats, people of various ethnic groups, and assorted costumes piled up on board: fierce-looking Narrs from Mauritania, with long robes and turbaned heads, Senegalese women in lovely dresses, Gambian women in duller outfits, Europeans in indecently short shorts, which I always find an insult to the local population. The ramp was finally lifted after trucks and cars (one of them half hanging overboard) were squeezed on the deck. At that moment the captain decided there was something wrong: two huge trucks were on the same side causing the boat to list dangerously. A decision was made to unload one of them. The ramp was lowered again, cars pulled out to make room for the truck to back up. Impossible! So, the ferry turned around to allow the truck to drive off. "Ah, those Senegalese," muttered the Gambian captain. "They always try to sneak in. This truck was loaded with cement and it had no right to come on board."

After reaching the other bank of the river, we drove toward the sprawling suburb of Serrekunda, population 120,000, where the American ambassador's Residence was located. We passed a groundnut-processing factory, a prison, various cemeteries, and low, fairly ugly houses. Then we headed off toward the Fajara cliffs jutting over the ocean. As we approached a long white wall, Alan honked his horn. The majestic gate opened, and we entered our home.

Men in khaki uniforms and dark green overalls rushed toward our car. I saw a lovely garden and a small gazebo covered with vines and clusters of pink flowers. The house was a one-story building with several wings and small courtyards shaded by trees. The inside was unexpectedly grand, with high ceilings and spacious entertainment rooms leading through archways to a glass porch that opened onto the ocean. The residence had private access to one of the most beautiful beaches in the world. For miles and miles white sand stretched along the coast; the water was clear and the surf gentle.

I met the servants. Allen, the cook, was fat and jolly. He seemed intelligent and spoke good English. He was on duty for breakfast and dinner. I was told he made excellent *crêpes Suzette, crème caramel,* and grilled fish. I soon discovered that he spiced up his meals with tender vegetables from our garden, such as tomatoes, corn, green beans, and beets. The two stewards worked in shifts. The only time we were without help was Sunday until two in the afternoon. This was no hardship because we could enjoy breakfast with flaky *croissants* from Dakar or chewy French bread baked locally. Both stewards were tall and slender. One was very new and seemed nervous. The other had an interesting but fierce face. He moved silently like a feline and stood behind my back unbeknownst to me.

Fancy tourist hotels surrounded our home. The closest one was called Sunwing. It had a pool packed with bleached-blond Swedes. They had their own Swedish hour on the radio. Nearby were a golf course, tennis courts, squash courts, and even a noisy nightclub. As we arrived, the windsurf coach was going into the water to fetch a lonely surfer.

My first impression was of the great number of expatriates in the elegant coastal stretch of the promontory located west of Banjul. About thirty British doctors and nurses worked in the Medical Research Center. In addition to the 170 official Americans, including embassy employees, USAID, and the Peace Corps, there were a number of European businessmen, merchants, international organization members, airways staff, and others. If you included all the Western tourists off cruise ships, touring the bird reserves, staying in hotels, riding their bicycles, or enjoying the beach, you had a surprisingly non-African picture.

Banjul was a typical African port and a rather sleepy town, "awakened by independence" (to use Alan's words), which occurred in 1965. The embassy Chancery was located in a three-story unfinished hotel where Alan and his staff rattled around in an orgy of space. Buildings were never taller than four stories high. Remnants of elegant Portuguese architecture, such as arcades, covered porches, and verandas, could still be seen, particularly in the Quadrangle area near the presidential palace. I also noticed the adorable small Anglican cathedral of St. Mary.

Less than one week after my arrival, I was invited to sail on the *Laurentian,* an oceanographic research boat. We started out in a leisurely fashion through the inlets and mangroves from Serrekunda to Banjul. A delicate white egret was watching us. A fisherman in his rowboat did not even turn his head as we sailed by. At the next bend in the river, I expected to see, the *African Queen* with Humphrey Bogart at the helm. The research expedition was launched by the Organization de Mise en Valeur de la Gambie (OMVG), an international group made up of neighboring countries working on the development of the River Gambia. Biologists, public health officials, socioeconomists, and environmentalist were studying the mineral and nutrient contents of the river to assess the advisability of building dams for irrigation against salinity—brackish water can be found for 200 kilometers upriver. It was an expensive project of $15 million.

From my conversations with a doctor from Michigan University, his PhD-holding wife, and other members of the team, I learned that many, including OMVG members, had doubts as to the worth of this project. Alan also had many objections. The main arguments against the project were that a man-made fresh-water lake would be a breeding ground for mosquitoes and would bring the disease bilharziasis (also known as schistosomiasis) into the area.

The *Laurentian* was a large tugboat with state-of-the-art scientific equipment on board. The crossing from the U.S. Great Lakes took more than seven weeks. The boat ran into all sorts of trouble, hit a bridge, and suffered a severe storm. The natural richness of the Gambia River reminded me of the estuary of the Connecticut River. I realize now that this environmental project was quite ahead of its time.

The essential role of the American chief of mission in the Gambia was two-fold: support the Confederation of Senegambia and oversee U.S. economic assistance to the country through USAID and the work of the large contingent of Peace Corps volunteers.

On February 1, 1982, a treaty had brought the Confederation of Senegambia into existence between Senegal, a former French colony, and the former British colony of The Gambia it totally surrounds. The treaty called for combined military and security forces and envisaged a monetary union. The two countries were joining efforts to build a bridge. It was essential for the American ambassador to be attuned to the cultures and languages of the two countries. Again, Alan had the expertise required to play that role.

I learned more about the key issues of the region during the call made on Alan by the Australian ambassador to Accra, Ghana, who was also accredited to The Gambia. During the visit Alan commented on the political and economic situation. For me it was like a fascinating briefing.

An old friend of ours, Alasan Diop, a former minister from Senegal, whom we knew during our Guinean days, had traveled seven hours from Dakar just to visit us. During the night he spent at the residence, we covered all possible topics, from politics to history to culture. Our guest was a highly sophisticated "black Frenchman" totally at ease in his "negritude."

Diop drew an impressive picture of Senegal, a country proud of its multiparty system. He explained that the political equilibrium was mainly due to the coexistence between ethnic groups, heirs of ancestral empires. He contrasted Senegal with Nigeria, for instance. For him, Nigeria did not have a real federal political system: whenever a government was overthrown, a totally different ethnic group replaced it. In Senegal, Diop was telling us, the opposition could express itself freely; it even had a humorous newspaper whose satire did not spare the politicians. Just one year before our arrival, in 1982, President Senghor had left the government with elegance. An outstanding poet, he was elected as the first black member of the Académie Française, in Paris, the most prestigious assembly of French intellectuals and writers. Diop added a little-known detail: the mother of King Hassan of Morocco was born in Senegal; hence the close ties between the two countries and the involvement of Senegal within the whole region.

Whenever we hosted an official dinner at the residence for high-level Gambian officials, Alan expressed his deep convictions with directness. He had spent so much time in Africa and been exposed to the problems of assistance to developing countries for so long, that he could speak from time-tested experience. He may have rubbed some people the wrong way, but I admired his sincerity. I remember him saying: "Africa has become a welfare continent, where the policy of the outstretched hand is the solution to all the problems." He would give as comparison the example of the Far East, where every square meter of land is cultivated. As he was speaking, I recalled the marvelous Australian film *The Year of Living Dangerously*, which takes place in Indonesia. The rice paddies undulating in the setting sun were the product of an exhausting manual labor. So different from Africa! During several official field trips into the country, we were going to collect more examples to support Alan's opinions.

During one of our official trips we visited a village about two hours from Banjul. We stopped by a sad-looking garden. Because of a lack of water the seedlings could not be transplanted. We saw four wells being dug by hand, one of them eight meters deep. Fortunately the soil was hard and the sides of the well were holding up. Come the rainy season and everything would collapse. The elders of the village, after showing us the work in progress, started asking for financial and technical assistance to dig those wells. The whole thing seemed odd to me. After all, farmers around the world have been digging wells for thousands of years! Just before leaving, Alan congratulated the elders for the wonderful work the women were doing. I do not know whether they caught his sarcasm.

In another village I noticed bags of imported rice from America with the typical USAID logo of two hands clasped to show the importance of "self-help." This was another instance of how outside assistance is destabilizing for a country. For many centuries the Gambian economy was an equilibrium adapted to the climate and the rainfall: fishing was the source of income during the rainy season when the land was flooded; then planting rice was carried out during the dryer season. Very rapidly the farmers realized that it was much easier and cheaper to count on the imported rice.

Some time later, Alan and I were invited by two Gambian ministers to visit a model village where the whole population, as a collective, was growing vegetables. The ministers were anxious to show their foreign visitors self-help in action. It was a whole-day expedition with a long drive and a ferry crossing. The whole village greeted us with enthusiasm, singing and dancing. They led us to a large vacant lot that, at first sight, seemed full of weeds. In fact it was a field of tiny tomatoes. "Isn't that wonderful?" commented one of the ministers. "We have to help those hard-working people and give them money to grow fences!" We returned to the village square. A spectacle had been prepared for us, with dancers wearing the usual raffia, feathers, and bells—always a tourist pleaser.

Then came the time for speeches. In fact, they had tricked us. First, the women's committee presented me with a goat. I was forced to take the microphone to thank the crowd. Then it was Alan's turn. The minister introduced him, saying the ambassador had come all the way from America to bring them assistance (which was not in the cards). But the worst was to come, because the Gambian officials seized the occasion to turn the visit into a political rally in favor of the ruling party. This was putting Alan in an awkward position; diplomats are never to meddle with the internal politics of a country in the public place.

Many years later I came across an example of a successful collaboration between the West and the emerging economies of Africa. I was attending a conference at Columbia University with my son Philip, who is an architect, on development projects taking place in Africa. One of the guest speakers, Diebedo Francis Kere, was an architect from Burkina Faso (formerly Upper Volta). It was impressive to hear this talented young man, educated primarily in French and a graduate of a Berlin university, making his presentation in English.

In a country where more than 90 percent of the population is illiterate, Kere's objective is to build schools, using local materials and labor, while applying the modern techniques and handsome designs he learned in Germany to his country's harsh climate. Starting from the small school for a hundred pupils he built in his home village of Gando, he went on to build a larger one for a thousand pupils, then to more ambitious creations. The whole village supported his projects with enthusiasm. For Kere the building process itself constituted a stimulus to the social and economic development for the area.

Philip and I, who have spent many years in Africa, were laughing our hearts out at the speaker's humor, which felt so familiar to us. With a great deal of honesty, Kere stressed that he needed the information and education available in the West. But his primary goal was to return to his native Burkina Faso and share his knowledge with his countrymen.

The day after the Columbia University's forum, the Museum of Modern Art in New York opened an exhibit entitled "2010 Small Scale Big Change: New Architecture of Social Engagement" in which Kere's architectural projects occupied a prominent place. I thought that a person of Kere's stature and ideals was the best thing that could happen to Africa.

Gambia had quite a large contingent of Peace Corps volunteers, considering the small size of the country. To the number of forty, who were already there when Alan arrived, was added a group of twenty a short while later. As chief of mission, Alan was overseeing their activities—a duty he greatly enjoyed. Whether visiting them in the bush or opening his house for Thanksgiving and Christmas, or giving barbecues on the beach, his informal and warm attitude made him popular with the volunteers.

The PCVs lived in rugged conditions. Before my arrival Alan visited the small village of Diabugu on the north bank of the Gambia River, where he inaugurated a new school for which the U.S. government had supplied cement and other material. He spent the night on the little bamboo bed of a volunteer. The mud and thatch hut had no electricity. The toilet facilities consisted of a hole out in the back. Buckets of muddy water were used to drink and wash.

One day Alan, the director of the Peace Corps, and I drove about one and a half hours out of Banjul, where the new contingent of volunteers was undergoing a training course. Alan addressed the group as we sat under a huge kapok, or silk cotton, tree. After making everybody laugh by introducing me as his "first wife," Alan gave an interesting introduction to U.S. foreign policy. He continued by explaining the role of the embassy in the country, how to handle the main issues of U.S. foreign policy, such as South Africa or the Middle East, when talking to Gambians. Alan had always been good at this type of exercise. He kept the talk on a high level in order to appeal to this well-educated audience. The superior attitude typical of these young people began to thaw, although a few remained on the defensive and did not hide their antiestablishment feelings.

Lunch was served on a straw mat stretched out on the ground. Volunteers plunged their right hand into the food, which consisted of large tubs of rice, and a soup in which dubious pieces of meat were floating. Alan joined them. I retired discreetly to a corner and ate some bread with a piece of *vache qui rit* (laughing cow—a type of French processed cheese).

Now I come to a particularly exciting part of my story: the "private" visit of Her Royal Highness, Princess Ann of England. As the president of the Save the Children Fund, she traveled extensively around the globe. She flew from the UK with her lady-in-waiting, her personal secretary, her lady's maid, her secretary, security officers, and others. Her visit coincided with the celebrations in commemoration of the independence of Gambia. A small and select group of high officials and ranking diplomats were to meet HRH at the residence of the British high commissioner. The guests were waiting, glasses filled from the well-stocked bar. Suddenly conversation stopped: the princess had arrived. She was tall, wore a long, pink *kaftan*, her hair severely pulled up in a chignon. The Coke she was holding with her long white gloves would last an hour and a half. Led by the British high commissioner, she started her rounds, moving calmly from group to group. She was poised, shaking hands while giving a lengthy look at the person she was meeting. She stayed as long as ten minutes with each group, asked a lot of questions, an occasional smile relaxing her face. Whereas Alan acted quite debonair in such circumstance, I was petrified.

The following day, 2,000 guests gathered on the lawn of the president's state house. The Senegalese army officers looked smart in their black uniforms, high collared with double rows of buttons, not unlike the American Civil War uniforms. Sir Dawda Jawara, the president of The Gambia, appeared on the steps of the elegant whitewashed building. He wore a stiff pastel *boubou* with wide sleeves, which made him look like a Japanese *shogun*. A few inches behind him, Princess Ann wore a very feminine half-length dress. Then came Lady N'Jamie, one of the president's two wives. We did not linger at this mass event because we had met the princess the day before. Besides, Alan was not feeling well since he had shared the common pot with the PCVs. I felt fine, and rather smug.

The following day was Gambian Independence Day. Alan was trying to hold his stomach with coal medicine. The radio announced that twenty-seven political prisoners (out of thirty-five) had been amnestied from punishment for their participation in the 1981 coup. The main event of the day was a grand parade in the football field near the state house. Alan and I, driven by our smartly dressed chauffeur, sped to Banjul, flags flying in the wind. At 8:53 the vice president arrived, at 8.55 Princess Ann, and finally, at 8.59, the president. The ceremony, amazingly, followed the precise schedule.

The honored guests sat right in front of us. Journalists and photographers were all over the place. A correspondent from *Figaro Madame* sat beside me. The parade consisted of Gambian military and police and thousands of schoolchildren. Each school had a different color uniform. The girls seemed to be dancing rather than marching. Her royal highness looked stiff. She and the female members of her party wore flowery hats. At 11 o'clock I was "off duty" and headed for the beach. Alan had to stay on and attend the inauguration of a bank.

Ocean fishing is one of the main sources of income for The Gambia. Our beach was a busy place, when dozens of heavy dugout canoes returned from the high seas. A crowd of women and children waited for them, ready to help unload the catch and set up stalls to sell it. It was always a lively scene. Some fishermen were repairing their nets, others freshening up the colorful decorations on the prow of their boats. Our cook would have only a few steps to walk to fetch our dinner: a lobster, a sole, a large grouper, or huge scampi shrimps. Further down the coast, fishing villages were busy with people salting, smoking, or packing the fish for export.

A sail upriver is one of the highlights of any visit to The Gambia. The first stop is usually on the tiny (less than three acres) St. James Island. It stands in the middle of the river, which is ten miles wide at that point. The island, sometimes called the sentinel of the river, has witnessed a rich history since the pre-colonial days. Portuguese, English, Germans, French, and Dutch fought for it, razed it to the ground, and then rebuilt it. The handful of people who had lived in the fort were colorful groups: in 1580, convicts and refugees from the Inquisition; Moors and Jews in 1609; in 1703, the dregs of London's taverns. The fort's inhabitants and visitors were a mixture of privateers, merchants, military garrisons, and aristocrats looking for slaves to work on their plantations.

The British held on to this tiny fort for several centuries. This is where they planted their first Union Jack in Africa. Today the fort on St. James Island shows a hodgepodge architecture of crude mortared masonry. The roots of baobabs towering above undermine its twenty-foot walls. During our walk on the bastion, Alan, curious as usual, picked up fragments of pipes and pieces of crude glass. Water was not available on the island and one had to take a boat to fetch it from the onshore wells. As a result, the garrison relied principally on Napoleon brandy and rum.

France and Britain struggled continuously for political and commercial supremacy over The Gambia, which was finally granted to England by the Treaty of Versailles in 1783. An 1889 agreement with France established the present boundaries. Gambia remained a British crown colony until its independence in 1965.

In West Africa, the slave trade was concentrated on Gorée Island and Port St. Louis, Senegal, but the main conduit was down the Gambia River, until the trade's abolition in 1807. It just happened that we arrived in Gambia not long after the hugely successful TV series *Roots* appeared on American television. The film was based on the 1977 Alex Haley history of slave trading originating in The Gambia. Haley had created a mythical village, where he believed his ancestors had lived, and the birthplace of Kunta Kinte, Haley's hero.

The village was called Juffure and was a prime destination for tourist boats. One landed in a dusty, treeless village, and was immediately assaulted by small children. Each child would zero in on one tourist, grab his or her hand, and ask for *bonbons* and Bic pens. As we approached the village, an old woman was sitting well in evidence. She was supposed to be a descendant of Kunta Kinte. The explanations of our guide, a smart young journalist, did not seem to convince even himself. I quickly learned the reason for his feelings. He was upset that so much expectation had been created for his people. Haley's myth, bearing little relation with the historical facts, had not fulfilled the hopes of the population. Money to be generated by tourism never materialized. The unfinished walls of a mosque were the only remains of an unrealized dream.

The Gambia is an ornithologist's paradise. Close to four hundred types of birds can be found in this tiny country. Many visitors join tours originating in the United States just to watch the birds. They come by cruise boats or land at the family-size Yundun airport, with their cameras, tripods, and telephoto lenses. Mangrove and marshes bordering the Gambia River are a particularly rich habitat for herons, cormorants, egrets, storks, eagles, ospreys, kingfishers, and others too numerous to list. Some of the birds had amusing names, such as the bulbuls, the red-billed Senegal, the cockney sparrows, and the caroline bee-eaters. Birds are the subject of many experts' works.

Shortly after his arrival in Banjul, Alan described the wild life surrounding the Residence: "There are some large graceful buzzards roosting, and during the right season, nesting in the palm trees in front of the house. These are also inhabited by hundreds of bats. At night huge red and yellow crabs that wave long claws guard the house. Flocks of quails live in the bushes nearby."

"The big game has all but disappeared in The Gambia," we were told by Mr. Breur, the British founder of the Abuko game park. "Less than twenty-five years ago, Serrakunda, occupied today by tourist hotels and their golf courses, was a thick tropical forest. One traveled around on horseback, watchful of hyenas crossing the dirt road. The last elephant disappeared in 1991, and so have the ostriches."

Among our diplomatic colleagues, we enjoyed the company of the Chinese. I had decided to refresh my long-forgotten knowledge of their language, acquired in Formosa, by exchanging a few French lessons with the chargé's wife. We became good friends.

One evening, the chargé, the first secretary, and their wives invited us for dinner. We were first received in the large living room of the Chinese Embassy. All the seats were aligned against the walls, in the Chinese fashion. The only concession to the West was the absence of spittoons. We passed a beautiful black lacquer and nacre screen and reached the dining room. A "lazy Susan" was loaded with exotic dishes specially flown from China for us. The 100-year-old eggs did not have to be sent airfreight, I thought to myself. Each of the hosts in turn got up to bring the new dish. I realized the four of them had been cooking.

Our hosts and their wives all worked. The foursome plus a driver constituted the full embassy staff. I found it amazing that such a small group would be able to administer a vast program of economic aid, such as the construction of a 30,000-seat stadium. I could not help comparing the size of this operation with the huge administrative section that would have been involved had a similar project been undertaken by the American embassy and its related agencies.

At the risk of being accused of nepotism, the American ambassador appointed me as head of the United States Information Service office in the Gambia. I enjoyed the work tremendously, even though it was for only a few weeks. As it is in every country around the world, the role of USIS consists in making available to the general public, as well as to candidates applying to U.S. universities, the best possible information about America and to organize cultural and educational events. My responsibilities were basically to revamp the "country plan" to meet the interests of The Gambia and to widen the United States' "target audience."

The ambassador seemed pleased with my work. I never had a chance to see whether my recommendations were implemented. I have a suspicion that, as it happens in any bureaucracy, the next person would undo everything I had so carefully elaborated.

The few months in the Gambia were over before we knew it. We left our life in the Foreign Service, this time for good.

Postscript

It was hard to leave the Foreign Service, but I found that tearing ourselves away from this incredible life was a chance to undertake new projects. After thirty years, it was time to break the "routine of change" that had been our wandering diplomatic lifestyle.

Alan fulfilled his passion for sailing on *Katy II*, logging more than 80,000 miles. He crossed the Atlantic twice (even with a broken centerboard!), was caught in a wind shear with ninety-mile wind gusts off the bay of Kotor on the Adriatic coast, was followed by a Soviet stealth submarine in the Baltic, and was boarded several times by the Soviet Coast Guard in the Black Sea. He sailed as far north as the White Sea and braved the monstrous waves of the North Sea. His favorite playgrounds, though, were the Aeolian Islands north of Sicily and the southern coast of Turkey. Taking a break from sailing, he did some wild heliskiing in the Caucasus with our friend Tom Buchanan. Always interested in undertaking new projects, he contributed energy and expertise while working with nonprofit organizations for retired executives, both in the United States and abroad. In addition, he devoted much of his time to a cause he believed in: the opening of the Russian inland waterways and coastlines to foreign pleasure boats. One outstanding result of his efforts was the opening up of the northern province of Karelia to visitors from the West.

The nineteen years of remission from his cancer became increasingly painful. I recall seeing him limp with difficulty on the quay of a Danish marina. Despite unpleasant medication and several operations, he continued with an active and full life until the very end on April 24, 1997.

As for me, archaeology remained my main interest. I was fortunate to be invited again by Dr. Stager, head of the Semitic Museum at Harvard, to join his archaeological expedition to the ancient Philistine city-state of Ashkelon in Israel. I excavated there from 1985 to 1993. I then decided to combine my field experience and my knowledge of the Russian language to design my own archaeological project in Moscow under the auspices of Earthwatch, from 1993 to 1996. The project enabled more than ninety foreign volunteers to excavate side by side with Moscow archaeologists. Our successive sites were Manege Square, just below the Kremlin walls, the Arbat Street area, and another medieval site, *Za Retchie*, which means "beyond the river."

There were so many new things I could do! Auditing art history courses at the Ecole du Louvre in Paris was one of them. Discovering Malevich, Kandinsky, and many other masters has become a great joy during the past decade.

For the children, Alan, and myself, being "forever on the road" has been the most enriching experience one can imagine. We have been so marked by our wandering life that even today we continue to "commute" between the USA and Europe: two of my children and their families live near Paris, the other two in New York City and Williamstown, Massachusetts. I divide my time between Paris and Connecticut, spending as much time as I can with my children and grandchildren.

Today very little remains the same in the countries where we lived and worked. The modern world's uniformity has often replaced the cultural variety we found so exciting and exotic. I am glad my memories remain so vivid.

Appendix

The Badagry Race

(This is the logbook written by Karen (age 13), first mate of the Logans' Wayfarer.)

The longest dinghy race through an inland waterway in the world, Lagos, Nigeria, October 1972.

10:10 – We start off from the Lagos Yacht Club with around thirty-four companions. Here with us is Peter Summers and his two-hull homemade boat. Now, we are ahead of five boats, but it is hard to know because we keep tacking.

13:30 – We have come around a point and now we can see the Whitehouse boat.

13:40 – Coming about we hear an ominous sound, and looking towards it see that the starboard stay has snapped loose from the side of the boat. "Pull it down!" yelled the skipper. "What, the mast?" asked the crew. "No, the sail!" answered the skipper.

13:55 – The sail up and everything is repaired. It is discouraging to see all the boats ahead of us now.

14:20 – Hornet 221 capsizes. Phew, it got up. Oops, there it goes again.

15:28:30 – We ran around Ibeshe. I relieved the skipper for an hour and took the helm myself.

17:06:30 – We pass Abaja. We are fighting to pass a GP 14 and a cat, but they are still too far.

18:30:30 – The sun is nearly—It's down. The clouds are streaks of red and yellow, the sun turns pink and so does the water. It looks like a stroke of paintbrush swept across the sky. The ocean roars over yonder but here it is quiet and calm. The wind is going down but there are "miles to go before I sleep."

19:40:30 – We stopped for dinner. We heard far away what we thought was from a village, but soon picked out the shape of fishing canoes. They were probably singing to keep themselves awake.

21:13:35 – We started again and passed T20, which was caught in fishnets in the creek.

22:12:45 – We stopped for the night at mosquito heaven. We noticed ghoulish white shapes gliding across the water. A voice came from one of these shapes and asked, "Can we share your berth?" It was good old T20 again.

05:11:55 – We started before dawn and left T20. It is very hard to see, since the moon is gone and daylight has not yet come. We cannot find passage near the swamp, but the loyal fishnet lookout on the bow spots two anchored boats and gets us back on course. We passed Topo Island on which a small village is situated. All the children are swimming and waving their hands and yelling "*Owebo!*" By the water's edge are fishing boats. The fishermen are plunging their long sticks into the water. The sun is shining on the all-green reeds behind the boats.

7:45 – We reached our destination: BADAGRY. Now we are on our way back to Lagos with the spinnaker flying high. Unfortunately, the closest boats are miles away and we only catch a glimpse of them every time we come around a curve.

11:43:45 – We passed Agaja. The water supply is running low and the sun is beating on us. The skipper dips his towel in the water and then puts it on his shoulders and screams "Great, why didn't I do this before?"

13:20 – We passed Teneco and ate lunch while moving. The rough waters of the Apapa creek create a panic when we try to get the spinnaker down.

14: 58 – We arrived at LYC. The crew enters chronometer time: 15 hours 15 minutes in the race book. It is exciting to see all the other competitors flying on the "hard" with an exhausted look on their face.

So ends our great race to BADAGRY. Physically, it is all over but mentally I still think I'm in the boat, rocking away our day.

Notes

7 Tunisia

[1] Yom Kippur is the Day of Atonement, for the Jews, roughly equivalent to Ramadan for the Moslems. The Arab oil-producing countries decided to cut down their production as long as Israel continued its occupation of Arab lands. Saudi Arabia imposed a total embargo on military aid that the Americans airlifted to Israel. On October 6, 1973, Syria and Egypt attacked Israel. The EEC issued a statement to placate the Arab world. The resolution of this crisis was marked, on March 18, 1974, by the end of the oil embargo.

8 Belgium

[2] A short History of the European Union:

1951 ECSC (European Coal and Steel Community) is inspired and established by Jean Monnet and French Foreign Minister Robert Schumann. Jean Monnet becomes the President of the High Authority.
1957 EURATOM (European Atomic Energy Community) and EEC (European Economic Community) are created by the Treaty of Rome.
1967 The institutions of the three European communities are merged.
1986 Spain and Portugal join Europe.
1992 EU (European Union) created by the Treaty of Maastricht.
1995 Austria, Finland, and Sweden become members.
2002 A single currency is adopted: the Euro.
2004 Ten new countries become members.
    A convention produces a proposal for a new European constitution. Valéry Giscard d'Estaing, former president of France, headed the convention and strongly influenced the content of the draft.
2005 Referendums conducted in the Netherlands and France. Both countries refuse to ratify the proposal for the new constitution.

2007 Bulgaria and Romania join the European Union. There are now twenty-seven members.

2007 A second attempt at the acceptance of a constitution, and the Treaty of Lisbon is voted down by Ireland.

2009 On November 13, the ratification of the Treaty of Lisbon is officially completed by all member states of the European Union

9 South Africa

[3] In the 1980s, Natal was one of the four provinces of South Africa. The others were Transvaal, Orange Free State, and the Cape Province.

[4] 94,361 square km, or 36,433 square miles

[5] Definition of terms: The Republic of South Africa and South Africa were, in popular usage, interchangeable, but in terms of South Africa's policy in the 1970s, the Republic of South Africa was considered as the geopolitical homeland of the white South Africa nation, whereas South Africa included four independent black states: Swaziland, Lesotho, Botswana, and Transkei, plus Bophuthatswana, which gained its independence in 1977. In addition, there were seven black homelands.

[6] The white rhinos are massive, have a distinctive hump on the back, and keep their heads low. Unlike the black rhinos, they are gregarious.

[7] The three main political parties were the conservative Nationalist Party, the New Republic Party (NRP), and the Progressive Federal Party (PFP).

[8] Herewith a short history of the settlement of the whites in The Cape Province:

In 1652 the Dutch settled in Cape Town, led by Jan Van Riebeeck on the instruction of the Dutch East India Company.

The French Huguenots arrived in 1688 and settled among the Dutch.

A new group of 5,000 British immigrants settled in Eastern Cape after the Napoleonic wars.

The Germans came between 1848 and 1858.

The Boers (Dutch for farmers), descendants of the early Dutch settlers, were cattle ranchers and needed lots of land for grazing.

Tensions grew with the British and led to the Anglo-Boer war, which started on October 11, 1899. The war lasted two and a half years, during which 22,000 British, 25,000 Boers, and 12,000 Africans died.

[9] The South African government, as well as the entire diplomatic corps, moved to Cape Town every year when the Parliament convened, traveling 1,600 km (994 miles) in the luxury of the "Blue Train."

Selected Bibliography

A short list of the books, both humorous and scholarly, which taught me much about the countries I described in my memoirs.

Formosa

Yutang, Lin. *The Importance of Living.* New York: Reynal & Hitchcock (A John Day Book), 1937. A witty modern Chinese writer distills for the Western readers the Chinese philosophy of three thousands years, starting with the art of loafing.
Ballantine, Joseph W. *Formosa.* Washington: Brookings Institution, 1952. Review of the major problems confronting the United States in this part of the world.

Turkey

Lloyd, Seton. *Early Anatolia.* London: Penguin Books, 1956. The grand old man of Middle East archaeology describes fifty years of excavations and exploration in Asia Minor. Lloyd was the director of the British Institute of Archaeology in Ankara from 1948 to 1961.
Kelly, Amy Ruth. *Eleanor of Aquitaine and the Four Kings.* Cambridge: Harvard University Press, 1950. Historical fiction based on scholarly research into primary sources, still today the definitive biography of Eleanor of Aquitaine.
Macaulay, Rose. *The Towers of Trebizond.* London: Williams Collins Sons, 1956. Beautifully absurd story of three English travelers to the outposts of Turkey.

Lebanon

Armstrong, Martin. *Lady Hester Stanhope.* London: Gerald Howe Ltd, 1927. The "peregrinations" of Lady Stanhope in the Near East, particularly

Lebanon, in the early nineteenth century.

Baramke, Dimitri. *Phoenicia and the Phoenicians*. Beirut: Khayats publ. ,1961. Born in Nablus, Palestine, Dr. Baramke was the head of the Archaeology Department of AUB in the 1960s and my mentor in Beirut.

Kaplan, Robert D. *The Arabists, or The Romance of an American Elite*. New York: Free Press, 1993. The role of American academics with a missionary streak and diplomats who, since the late nineteenth century, have greatly influenced the educated classes of the Near East. The expertise of the career diplomats specialized in that part of the world has too often been insufficiently tapped by the policy makers. Some vitriolic comments against the book can be found online for being anti-Israeli.

Moscati, Sabatino. *The Phoenicians*. Milan: Gruppo Editoriale Fabbri Bompiani, 1988. Enormous {765-page) compilation of scholarly research material, accompanied by numerous illustrations, of the Phoenician civilization.

Wallach, Janet. *The Desert Queen*. New York: Anchor Books, 1999. The extraordinary life of Gertrude Bell (1868–1926). Recruited by British Intelligence during World War I, Bell played a major role in the creation of Iraq. Under her influence Faysal was crowned king in 1921. She had an absolute passion for Baghdad. Her legacy was eclipsed by the more flamboyant personality of Lt. Col. Thomas Edward Lawrence, better know as Lawrence of Arabia.

Zwicker Kerr, Ann. *Come with Me from Lebanon*. Syracuse, N.Y.: Syracuse University Press, 1994. The story of a family of American "Arabists" who loved the Arab world, brutally interrupted by personal tragedy.

Russia

Massie, Robert K. *Peter the Great*. New York: Ballantine Books, 1980. On the historical background of Russia in the seventeenth and eighteenth centuries; the author describes the magnificent life of the first modern Russian tsar.

Brumfield, William Craft. *Gold in Azure*. [PLACE]: David R. Godine, 1983. A superbly illustrated scholarly history of one thousand years of monumental Russian Architecture.

Gray, Camilla. *The Great Experiment: Russian Art 1863–1922*. London: Thames and Hudson, 1962. From the "Wonderers" to the "Constructivists," the author describes the rich beginnings of Russian modern art.

Guinea

Attwood, William. *The Reds and the Blacks*. New York: Harper & Row, 1967. By profession a journalist, William Attwood spent two years (1962–63) as ambassador to Guinea with his pretty and delightful wife. Lively and candid narrative of their firsthand experience.

Nigeria

Thorpe, Ellen. *The Ladder of Bones*. UK: Collins Fontana Books, 1956. Birth of modern Nigeria from 1853 to independence. Describes the difficult life and high mortality rate of missionaries and consuls in a country devastated for centuries by tribal warfare and slave trade. A story often told with a great deal of humor.

Enahoro, Peter. *How To Be a Nigerian*. Ibadan: Caxton Press, 1966. A humorous and self-deprecating small book written by a journalist, member of the Nigerian intelligentsia, with a royal Igbo lineage. Later, in more serious books, Enahoro described how Nigeria, once the pride of Africa, met gradual failure and eventual collapse, because of ethnic strife and corruption, from the 1990s on.

De St. Jorre, John. *The Nigerian Civil War*. London: Sydney: Hodder and Stoughton, 1972. The account of a British diplomat and adventurous journalist who covered the Biafra War.

Best examples of Nigerian literature:

Soyinka, Wole. *Three Short Plays*. London: Oxford University Press, 1969.

Soyinka, Wole. *Kongi's Harvest*. Nairobi and Ibadan: London University Press 1969.

Achebe, Chinua. *A Man of the People*. London, Ibadan, and Nairobi: Heinemann, 1966.

Ekwenesi, Cyprian. *Burning Grass*. London, Ibadan, and Nairobi: Heinemann Educational Books, 1962.

Tunisia

Warmington, B.H. *Carthage*. London: Robert Hale, 1969. For both general readers with an interest in history and archaeology and students of ancient history.

Harden, Donald. *The Phoenicians*. New York: Praeger, 1962. The first English-speaking archaeologist to excavate and record artifacts in the Tophet of Carthage.

Multiple authors. "Carthage, Its Birth and Grandeur." *Archeologia Viva.* Paris: Archeologia, 1969. A comprehensive series of articles, written by specialists, about the history, religion, magic, art, literature, and political institutions of ancient Carthage.

Stager, Lawrence E., and Samuel R. Wolf. "Child Sacrifice at Carthage— Religious Rites or Population Control? " *Biblical Archaeology Review* Jan/Feb 1984.

Belgium

Dunnett, Dorothy. *Niccolo Rising.* Canada: Penguin Books, and New York: Alfred a Knopf, 1986. The first of the eight novels of Dunnett's historical series *The House of Niccolo.* The young hero rises to the heights of merchant banking and political intrigue in late fifteenth-century Antwerp.

South Africa

Morris, Donald R. *The Washing of the Spears.* London: Sphere Books (30/32 Inn Road London WCIX 8JL), 1966. The rise of the Zulus and their war against the British in 1879.

Packenham, Thomas. *The Boer War.* London: Jonathan Ball, 1979. A vivid narrative of a brutal military conflict and a thorough historical evaluation of its far-reaching consequences.

Paton, Alan. *Towards the Mountain.* Cape Town: David Philip, 1980. An autobiography Alan Paton gave us and which I treasure.

Publications by Nicole Prévost Logan

Update France. Yarmouth, Maine: Intercultural Press, 1989.

How to Live and Work in France. UK: Northcote House, 1990. A cross-cultural resource guide for English-speaking individuals relocating in France.

"La Vie à Formose." *La Tribune de Genève,* Jan. 18, 1954.

"The Career Dilettante." *Foreign Service Journal,* April 1980:7– 8.

"Week End in Beirut." *Foreign Service Journal ,* Sept. 1983:30-31.

"An Amateur Archaeologist in the Tophet of Carthage." *Archaeology* March/April 1986:88.

"No Gridlock in Ashkelon—The View from the Square." *Biblical Archaeology Review* Jan/Feb 1988:35–37.

"Back in the USSR." *Foreign Service Journal* April 1989:45-48.

"Mining Moscow's Past." *Archaeology* March–April 1992:72.

"Earthwatch Volunteers Uncover Nine Centuries of Life Near Kremlin."

Surviving Together vol. 12 issue 1, ISAR, Spring 1994:18–19.

"View from Mithridates." *Archaeology* Nov.–Dec. 1994:69–75.

"Getting to the Bottom of Moscow's Past." *National Geographic* July 1994.

"Moscow Reclaims its Past." *Archaeology* July/Aug 1997 27–35.

"Postcard from Abroad: Sailing the Volga" *Foreign Service Journal* June 1999: 84.

"Vive l'Archaeologie!" *Archaeology* May/June 2001. The Carnavalet museum renovates the *Orangerie* to house the most important archaeological collections of Paris, including several Neolithic pirogues.

Chronology

1951 Alan Logan arrives in Taipei, TAIWAN.
1952 February Alan and Nicole Prévost marry in Bangkok.
1954 Home leave: Paris, Menlo Park, Aspen.
1955 Philip is born.
1956 We move to Ankara, TURKEY.
       Sylvia is born.
1957 Alan's mother, Harriet, visits us in Turkey.
1958 We drive through the Taurus Mountains to Beirut, LEBANON.
       Diane is born.
       U.S. Marines land in Lebanon.
       Home leave.
       Civil war in Lebanon.
1959 Karen is born.
1960 WASHINGTON assignment.
1964 Moscow, SOVIET UNION.
1966 Conakry, GUINEA.
1968 WASHINGTON assignment.
1971 Lagos, NIGERIA.
1973 Tunis, TUNISIA.
1976 Brussels, BELGIUM.
1979 Durban, SOUTH AFRICA.
1982 Banjul, The GAMBIA.
1983–1997 Alan does nonprofit work as a retired executive in the USA and
       abroad; Nicole and Alan spend winters in Essex, Connecticut, and
       travel the world; Alan sails, Nicole digs.
1997 Alan dies.
1998– Nicole divides her time between Paris and Essex.

Index

CPSIA information can be obtained at www.ICGtesting.com
Printed in the USA
267703BV00002B/5/P